Feminism or Death

Feminism or Death

Françoise d'Eaubonne

Translated and edited by Ruth Hottell

with a foreword by Carolyn Merchant

and an introduction by
Myriam Bahaffou and Julie Gorecki
translated by Emma Ramadan

VERSO
London • New York

This English-language edition first published by Verso 2022
Translation of *Feminism or Death* and appendices © Ruth Hottell 2022
Foreword © Carolyn Merchant 1994, 2007, 2022
Introduction to the new French edition © Myriam Bahaffou and Julie Gorecki 2020
Translation of introduction to the new French edition © Emma Ramadan 2022

First published as *Le féminisme ou la mort* by Pierre Horay Editions
© Françoise d'Eaubonne 1974
Reissue © Le Passager Clandestin, 2020

Carolyn Merchant's foreword is drawn from her book *Ecology: Key Concepts in Critical Theory* (Humanities Press, 1994 and 2007) and is reprinted here with permission from the publisher.

An earlier version of Ruth Hottell's translation of the section "Le temps de l'éco-féminisme" (The Time for Ecofeminism) first appeared in *Ecology: Key Concepts in Critical Theory*, ed. Carolyn Merchant (Humanities Press, 1994), 174–97.

1 3 5 7 9 10 8 6 4 2

Verso
UK: 6 Meard Street, London W1F 0EG
US: 20 Jay Street, Suite 1010, Brooklyn, NY 11201
versobooks.com

Verso is the imprint of New Left Books
ISBN-13: 978-1-83976-440-0
ISBN-13: 978-1-83976-514-8 (UK EBK)
ISBN-13: 978-1-83976-515-5 (US EBK)

British Library Cataloguing in Publication Data
A catalogue record for this book is available from the British Library

Library of Congress Cataloging-in-Publication Data
Names: Eaubonne, Françoise d', 1920–2005, author. | Hottell, Ruth A.,
    1952– translator, editor. | Merchant, Carolyn, writer of foreword. |
    Bahaffou, Myriam, writer of introduction. | Gorecki, Julie, writer of
    introduction. | Ramadan, Emma, translator.
Title: Feminism or death / Françoise d'Eaubonne ; translated and edited by
    Ruth Hottell ; with a foreword by Carolyn Merchant and an introduction
    by Myriam Bahaffou and Julie Gorecki ; translated by Emma Ramadan.
Other titles: Feminisme ou la mort. English
Description: London ; Brooklyn : Verso, 2022. | "First published as Le
    féminisme ou la mort by Pierre Horay Editions © Françoise d'Eaubonne
    1974"--Title page verso. | Includes bibliographical references and
    index.
Identifiers: LCCN 2021051570 (print) | LCCN 2021051571 (ebook) | ISBN
    9781839764400 (trade paperback) | ISBN 9781839765155 (ebook)
Subjects: LCSH: Feminism.
Classification: LCC HQ1154 .E2813 2022 (print) | LCC HQ1154 (ebook) | DDC
    301.41/2--dc23/eng/20211026
LC record available at https://lccn.loc.gov/2021051570
LC ebook record available at https://lccn.loc.gov/2021051571

Typeset in Fournier by MJ & N Gavan, Truro, Cornwall
Printed and bound by CPI Group (UK) Ltd, Croydon CR0 4YY

To the "Biches Sauvages" (the Wild Does) of Brussels: to my young companion Marc Payen

Contents

Foreword
by Carolyn Merchant

In 1972, French feminist Françoise d'Eaubonne set up Ecologie-Féminisme as part of her project of "launching a new action: ecofeminism."[1] Then, in 1974, she published her landmark book *Le féminisme ou la mort*.[2] That book is translated here for the first time into English as *Feminism or Death* by French feminist scholar Ruth Hottell. D'Eaubonne states that women in the "Feminist Front" separated from the movement and founded an information center called the "Ecology-Feminism Center." Their new action was christened "ecofeminism," and it attempted a synthesis "between two struggles previously thought to be separated, feminism and ecology." The goal was to "remake the planet around a totally new model," for it was "in danger of dying, and we along with it." They called for a mutation of the world that would allow the human species to escape from death and continue to have a future. Writing as a militant feminist, d'Eaubonne placed the problem of the death of the planet squarely on the shoulders of male society. The slogan of the Ecology-Feminism Center was "to tear the planet away from the male today in order to restore it for humanity of tomorrow ... If male society persists, there will be no tomorrow for humanity."[3]

D'Eaubonne presented a litany of planetary ills, ranging from the global population explosion, to worldwide pollution and American consumption, to urban crowding and violence. Both capitalism and socialism were scenes of ecological disasters. The most immediate death threats to the planet were overpopulation (a glut of births) and the destruction of natural resources (a glut of products). Although many men attempted to label overpopulation a "Third World problem," the real cause of the sickness was patriarchal power. D'Eaubonne followed the analysis of nineteenth- and early twentieth-century proponents of ancient matriarchal societies, such as Johann Bachofen, Friedrich Engels, Robert Briffault, and August Bebel, who saw that "the worldwide defeat of the female sex" some 5,000 years ago initiated an age of patriarchal power.[4] It was the male system, not capitalism or socialism, that gave men the power to sow both the earth (fertility) and women (fecundity). The Iron Age of the second sex began—women were caged, and the earth was appropriated by males. The male society "built by males and for males" that took over running the planet did so in terms of competition, aggression, and sexual hierarchy, "allocated in such a way to be exercised by men over women." Patriarchal power produced agricultural overexploitation and industrial overexpansion. "The earth, symbol and former preserve of the great mothers, has had a harder life and has resisted longer; today, her conqueror has reduced her to agony. This is the price of phallocracy."[5]

If women had not lost the war of the sexes when phallocracy was born, d'Eaubonne maintained, "perhaps we would have never known either the jukebox or a spaceship landing on the moon, but the environment would have never known the current massacre." Pollution, environmental destruction, and runaway demography

are men's words spawned by a male culture. They would have
no place in a female culture linked to the "ancient ancestry of the
great mothers ... A culture of women would have never been this,
this extermination of nature, this systematic destruction—with
maximum profit in mind—of all the nourishing resources." If
women were returned to the power they lost, their first act would
be to limit and space out births, as they had done in the agricultural past. Demographic problems are created by men, especially
in the Catholic countries. Husbands who control women's bodies
and implant them with their seed, doctors who examine them, and
male priests who call for large families are bearers of male power
over women's wombs.[6]

D'Eaubonne saw ecofeminism as a new humanism that put forth
the goals of the "feminine masses" in an egalitarian administration
of a reborn world. A society in the feminine would not mean power
in the hands of women but no power at all. The human being would
be treated as a human being, not as a male or female. Women's
personal interests join those of the entire human community, while
individual male interests are separate from the general interests of
the community. The preservation of the earth was a question not
just of change or improvement but of life or death. The problem,
she said, paraphrasing Marx, is "to change the world ... *so that
there can still be a world*." But only the feminine, which is concerned
with all levels of society and nature, can accomplish "the ecological
revolution." She concluded her foundational essay with the telling
words: "And the planet placed in the feminine will flourish for all."[7]

In the United States, the term "ecofeminism" was used at Murray
Bookchin's Institute for Social Ecology in Vermont around 1976 to
identify courses as ecological, e.g., ecotechnology, eco-agriculture,
and ecofeminism. The course on ecofeminism was taught by
Ynestra King, who used the concept in 1980 as a major theme for

the conference "Women and Life on Earth: Ecofeminism in the '80s," held in Amherst, Massachusetts. King published "Feminism and the Revolt of Nature" in 1981 in a special issue of *Heresies* on feminism and ecology. Her article reflected the Frankfurt School's conceptual framework of the disenchantment of the world and the revolt of nature. The promise of ecological feminism lay in its liberatory potential to "pose a rational re-enchantment that brings together spiritual and material, being and knowing."[8]

King conceptualized ecological feminism as a transformative feminism drawing on the insights of both radical cultural feminism and socialist feminism. Radical cultural feminists such as Mary Daly in *Gyn-ecology* (1978) and Susan Griffin in *Woman and Nature* (1978) linked together the domination of women and nature under patriarchy. For these authors, men use both women and nature to defy death and attain immortality. Women secure their own immortality through childbearing. Nature's oppression is rooted in biological difference. For radical feminists, women and nature can be liberated only through a feminist separatist movement that fights their exploitation through the overthrow of patriarchy. Socialist feminists, however, ground their analysis not in biological difference but in the historically constructed material conditions of production and reproduction as a base for the changing superstructure of culture and consciousness. Underlying both positions, King argues, is a false separation of nature from culture. Instead, a transformative feminism offers an understanding of the dialectic between nature and culture that is the key to overcoming the domination of both women and nature. Such a position is needed if an ecological culture that reconnects nature and culture is to emerge.

Australian philosopher Val Plumwood has extended the analysis of domination initiated by d'Eaubonne and King by comparing the debates between deep ecologists, social ecologists, and ecofeminists.

Each group of eco-philosophers makes valid points but in so doing tries to reduce the others to its own critique. Thus, deep ecology is correct to challenge the human-centeredness of social ecology, but social ecology is also right in its analysis that hierarchical differences within human society affect the character of environmental problems. Therefore, an alternative, cooperative approach is needed.

Ecofeminism, with its emphasis on relations, has the potential to see connections among various forms of oppression, such as those affecting women, marginalized and colonized peoples, animals, and nature. Recognition of the weblike character of various forms of domination suggests a cooperative strategy of web repair. The ecofeminist approach focuses on relations and interconnections among the various ecology movements and leads to the possibility of a more comprehensive and cooperative theory and practice.

A major problem for ecofeminist theory is essentialism. Do women (and men) have innate, unchanging characteristics (or essences), or are all male and female qualities historically contingent? Do the biological functions (ovulation, menstruation, and the potential for pregnancy, childbearing, and lactation) associated with women that might make them different from men constitute their essence? The essentialist perception of women as closer to nature, as a result of the biological functions of reproduction, has historically been used in the service of domination to limit their social roles to childbearers, child-rearers, caretakers, and housekeepers.[9] Furthermore, do women have a special relationship to nature that men cannot share? If women declare that they are different from men and, as ecofeminists, set themselves up as caretakers of nature, they would seem to cement their own oppression and thwart their hopes for liberation and equality. However, if both women and men, as ecofeminists, care for and take care of nature, then nature can survive well into the future.

In recent years, new questions have arisen about the relationships between trans feminism and ecofeminism. Transgender and transsexual people have equal rights within the larger struggle for human rights and in actions on behalf of the environment. Transgender individuals have the same entitlements to health care, legal rights, and institutional privileges as do cisgender women and men. They may argue that nature itself is not a woman or a mother but, if personified, could be termed "they" or nongendered. One's relationship to nature could be personal, open, embracing, and caring, as well as scientific, ecological, and non-domineering. Cisgender men, cisgender women, and transgender persons would all participate equally in ecofeminist and humanist actions, policies, and philosophies to save the environment.

Freya Mathews, in an article on "Ecofeminism and Deep Ecology," sought to reconcile ecofeminism with deep ecology. The differences between the two movements were detailed by a number of scholars, including Ariel Salleh, Val Plumwood, Marti Kheel, Warwick Fox, Michael Zimmerman, and Jim Cheney.[10] Deep ecology's holistic view of the world as an extended self, writ large, contrasts with ecofeminism's emphasis on the world as a community of beings with which one has compassionate, caring relationships. For ecofeminism, each being in the community is respected as distinct rather than as part of the cosmic whole with which one should identify and into which one can merge. Mathews concluded that, through its ethic of compassion, ecofeminism can humanize deep ecology, which has become embittered toward human rapaciousness, seeing humans as a species bent on destroying other species—while deep ecology can deepen ecofeminism by asking it to see the whole as an internally connected moral order, not just a family of individuals for whom one intimately cares.

Ecofeminism, in its various forms and nuances, remains a major topic for women today. Over the years, new books and articles have appeared that elaborate on the term and the movement. Conferences have been held around the world; marches and movements continue to embrace its meaning and promote its goals. All of these manifestations have their origins in the early 1970s movements in Europe on which d'Eaubonne drew and elaborated in her book *Feminism or Death*.[11]

Introduction to the New French Edition
by Myriam Bahaffou and Julie Gorecki
Translated by Emma Ramadan

Why We Are Writing This Introduction Together[1]

The two of us composed this introduction in a very specific context: we wrote apart from each other in Bure and in Berkeley in a world largely under lockdown. While remote work, remote school, remote reading, and TV remotes set the tempo of daily life for millions of people in France and in the United States, outside, there were men and especially women, from mainly racialized and economically precarious communities, who each morning had to clean up the mess generated by the disastrous management of the virus. The COVID-19 health crisis revealed and reinforced gender, race, and class inequalities by showing how care work is at once the most vital and the most invisible form of labor. But while there should have been a resurgence of empathy, solidarity, and goodwill, the French president announced on television that we were … at war. Only a patriarchal power could choose to employ militaristic vocabulary to define a situation that is, in reality, so suited to mutual aid and humility. And so we had to do battle against a viral species on its way to extinction, against a virus that is in fact a "product of our society."[2] From an ecofeminist perspective, the bellicose imaginary evoked by Emmanuel Macron is not mere coincidence; quite the contrary, it's the most obvious form of a virilist attitude toward the living that views war, hatred, combat, and aggression as paradigmatic.[3]

This brings us to why we are writing this introduction. First of all, we believe the virus is a catalyst.[4] It allows us to clearly distinguish the oppressed from the oppressors, to understand the systemic reasons for this ecological and social crisis, its blind spots and its targets. Along with Françoise d'Eaubonne, we uphold the value of this work's title, and we reaffirm: from now on, it's *feminism or death*! In using this phrase, the author signaled the urgent need for recognizing the patriarchal nature of the widespread murder of living things. Without that understanding, and without setting in motion a radical turn toward ecofeminism, what awaits us is death.[5] So, *feminism or death*? We choose feminism, and we chose it a long time ago, for we know that gender, race, and class relations are inseparable from our attitude vis-à-vis the natural worlds around us. In our opinion, there is a clear connection between the treatment of the bodies of women, the enslaved, the disabled, and the racialized, and the treatment of lands, animals, and plants: they are all naturalized terrains of experimentation or conquest.[6] We write this introduction as a rallying cry, an act of resistance, and a response to this global emergency intensified by the recent pandemic. Finally, we write because we need a complete reinvention of existing discourses and imaginaries, and because we are tired of war, everywhere and all the time.

In many respects, this first reissue of *Feminism or Death* is indicative of the late arrival of ecofeminism in France. The rediscovery of

Françoise d'Eaubonne coincides with the resurgence of ecofeminist movements around the world in response to the climate emergency. By "climate," we are not simply referring to the scientific data that says we are experiencing global warming; this is rather a historic turning point during which, for the first time, "the exploiters at the top have chosen [profit] over their own lives."[7] As for the concept of the "anthropocene," which suggests a collective responsibility for the deterioration of Earth, we prefer to speak of the "androcene" (*andro* meaning "man"): if ecosystems are destroyed, if climate refugees abound, if the sixth mass extinction is underway, it is not the fault of a generalized humanity but that of a small group of rulers and patriarchal-capitalist societies who accelerate it.[8]

As ecofeminists, we deem that cooperative models are inherently practices that aspire to construct societies free from subordination based on gender, race, and class. Our collaboration is a response to the call of Françoise d'Eaubonne to build a bridge between theory and action, and alongside Vandana Shiva, we affirm that "ecofeminism unites them."[9] With the aim of constructing an epistemology faithful to these principles, we are committed to exploring this "we" employed here by disclosing our respective trajectories and identities in order to better situate our positions.[10]

One of the authors is a cisgender[11] racialized[12] woman who is a second-generation immigrant. Given a modest upbringing, she has, like many people, long experienced a specifically French impasse: on the one hand, the necessity of integrating the values of the Republic, hiding her dual identity, and forgetting her Maghrebi roots in order to achieve complete French citizenship; on the other hand, a perpetual reassignment to her place as an exoticized[13] Arab woman. Because of this, she soon felt isolated in milieus that were supposedly meant for her: ecology and feminism. This mestiza[14] consciousness forged a specific identity, simultaneously hemmed in and never at home, but above all awakened in her a profound interest in topics such as environmental racism, decolonial ecology, and relationships to animals, which she deems closely related to the minority groups to which she belongs. She writes from Bure, in Meuse, France, where a plan to build a colossal nuclear waste landfill site has threatened the inhabitants since 1996. Daily police surveillance and recording, the terrifying Cigeo project just a few kilometers away, and the rarely questioned whiteness of the activists she works with allows her to discern the power relations that play out in these places forgotten by democracy, both deep in the Meuse and in the low-income suburbs where she grew up.

The other is a cisgender white Western woman who is a daughter of Polish political refugees. Her family immigrated to the traditional lands of the Three Fires Confederacy: the Odawa, Potawatomi, and Ojibwe, also known as the Anishinaabeg and Lunaapeew Nations, otherwise called Chatham-Kent, Ontario, in Canada. Over the last decade, she has lived mainly in Paris, but she has also spent several years in California as a "settler"[15] on the unceded land of the Chochenyo-speaking Ohlone people at the University of California, Berkeley. The story of her family, who escaped martial law in Poland and found themselves on lands stolen from native peoples, had a profound effect on her. Consequently, she committed her work to questions of systemic oppression. Driven by the desire to understand why so many people throughout the world are endlessly displaced, and why women and racialized peoples disproportionately bear the burden of global problems, she sought answers in books and in the activist world. A common denominator soon became clear: capitalism, or, more precisely, racial and patriarchal capitalism.[16] Following this realization, she joined the transnational feminist movement for climate and social justice that fights to restore and honor the planet.

In a damaged world, we feel urgently that reinvention cannot happen except through creating microsynergies, local alliances, and piecemeal collaborations. Convinced of the necessity of disrupting the epistemological Eurocentrism that still largely prevails in our universities, our joint text seeks not only to break up the dichotomies that have served to distance humanity from itself and from nature, but also to interrogate other binaries—heterosexual/queer, white/racialized, North/South—that we consider particularly important today.

On this matter, *Feminism or Death* is ambiguous. Revolutionary and visionary in many respects, it is also problematic in certain ways. Writing this introduction was not easy. However, we maintain that this text needs to be accessible once more because it is illustrative of a moment in time and of a certain wave of French materialist feminism of the 1970s. To mask its gray areas would amount to perpetuating the discourse that, still today, continues to ignore the transnationality of ecofeminism and its necessary decolonial critique. Although we position ourselves in the lineage of Françoise d'Eaubonne, we distance ourselves from some of her analyses. That said, like her, we refuse to create a separation between our writing, our research, our actions, our emotions, and our lives. Ecofeminism is at the intersection of all of this, and if we want it to have a future, we must remember its past. *Feminism or Death* is a part of both.

This introduction is neither a biography of the author nor an umpteenth attempt to define a movement that is, in essence, elusive.[17] Here we have decided to present what in *Feminism or Death* seems pertinent today, but also that which spurred our own paths into the heart of ecofeminism.

When Feminism Meets Ecology

In the 1970s and 1980s, Françoise d'Eaubonne was known to the general French public as a prolific author of poems, biographies, science-fiction novels, and philosophical essays. However, internationally, her reputation was not that of a simple writer: in the anglophone North, she became well known for forging the term "ecofeminism,"[18] which she used for the first time in the final pages of her essay *Feminism or Death*.[19]

The colossal oeuvre of this "resolute rebel"[20] is rivaled only by her dogged revolutionary activism. When d'Eaubonne was very young, she joined the anti-Nazi resistance, then enlisted in the Communist Party. Because her involvement in these groups didn't manage to encompass the ensemble of systemic oppressions, which she sensed was fundamental, she became involved in the Women's Liberation Movement (MLF) and then in the Homosexual Front for Revolutionary Action (FHAR). Her constant engagement nourished her writing as well as the ecofeminist activism she was developing. Drawn to environmental concerns elicited by the nuclear threat of the 1970s, her ecological awareness led her to focus on what she considered two inseparable variables: ecology and feminism. The inextricable link between the two was indeed cruelly lacking from the analysis of the French left of the time, which positioned the class struggle as master of all oppressions. In addition, contrary to the majority of ecofeminist theorists who held positions in prestigious universities, Françoise d'Eaubonne was neither a professor nor an accredited researcher. Her schooling happened through her participation in activist movements. Reading *Feminism or Death*, we feel just how independent and institutionally autonomous her feminist education was. This book is also a voyage through the thoughts of an insatiable dissident living the struggle and translating it into theory without ever distancing herself from it.

Alongside her feminist comrades, d'Eaubonne would spearhead the Feminist Front, the Ecology-Feminism Movement, and the Ecology-Feminism Center—hotbeds of ecofeminist activism largely cited in international literature but whose activities are very poorly documented.[21] Although the existence of these groups was barely noticed, their denunciation of the patriarchy was completely brazen, as evidenced by the resolution written in a 1974 pamphlet from the Ecology-Feminism association: "Down with men and their flagrantly self-destructive tendencies."[22] In August of the same year, the "Mouvement Écologie-Féminisme Révolutionnaire" called for a "birth strike"[23] at the global conference on population organized by the United Nations in Bucharest. Their demands, which were certainly audacious, called for nothing less than "the total and irreversible abolition of sexism and the patriarchy"—foundational arguments in *Feminism or Death*.

A Manifesto for an Ecofeminist Society

When each of us held *Feminism or Death* in our hands, we could not deny that something significant happened. Similar to when we read d'Eaubonne's 1978 text *Écologie et féminisme: Révolution ou mutation?*,[24] we had an intoxicating and marvelous sensation: there was finally a plan! Someone had seriously analyzed the global ecological catastrophe through the lens of gender. Not only had the theoretical aspect been explored but also, above all, the book offered practical avenues, real frameworks for change, a plan for the complete deconstruction of power, an invitation to women and all gender minorities to seize a power that had been unexplored up to that point on the French political scene. The revolution was here. And we had a place in it, we who had long sensed the connection between ecology and feminism, we who detested the white, intellectual, and bourgeois appropriation of environmental discourse, we who were convinced that feminism couldn't be limited to "equality between men and women."

D'Eaubonne advocates for the transfer of power to women, embodied by what she calls "nonpower," or the destruction of all power.[25] To concretize this project of an egalitarian society—seductive notably for its resolutely anti-authoritarian framework—she insists on the necessity of a collective provision of the means of production, which differs from the socialism of her time that she criticizes from top to bottom but also largely echoes green anarchy and libertarian social ecology. She also promoted the "decentralization of energy" in favor of a soft "poly-energy" instead of the mass utilization of "mono-energy," a technique that is heavy, masculine, and capitalist. Her use of the terms "mono" and "poly" evoke the later writings of Vandana Shiva on oneness and monoculture, which, according to her, must be urgently replaced by ecofeminist approaches founded on the diversity of agricultural techniques and practices respectful of biodiversity.[26] Finally, we can only applaud her call to dismantle both the nuclear family and the nuclear industry—components of the "same fight"[27]—that we interpret as a direct invitation to destroy the patriarchal and heterosexual family model.

Françoise d'Eaubonne's ecofeminist theory is thus not a juxtaposition of feminism and ecology but an analysis of the "world-system"[28] from an angle that places the marginalized and the exploited at its center. In *Feminism or Death*, she explains that the ecological threat that weighs on all forms of life is not only a priority but indissociable from other fights. Contrary to the emerging ecological movement at the time, she maintains that the destruction of the environment is the consequence of a phallocratic[29] system that originates in masculine and pre-capitalist farming techniques. According to her, these techniques led to the appropriation of women's reproductive systems and organs, resulting in overpopulation and the destruction of natural resources.[30]

French Timidity and International Perspectives

Since the 1970s, feminism has interrogated the origins of patriarchy in order to better understand the roots of this societal structure. In France, debates were focused on "the woman question," which attempted to analyze the mechanisms at the root of the subordination of women through the lens of the connection between capitalism and the patriarchy at a global scale. Among the various waves of thought that materialized at the time, d'Eaubonne's stands out. By positing that the patriarchy led to the domination of men over women and to the devastation of nature, she not only denounces the sexist structure of society but also blames it for the destruction of the environment. Nearly a decade later, the sociologist Maria Mies[31] would locate the roots of women's oppression within a more ecological analysis of the "capitalist patriarchy"—a socioeconomic structure founded on the exploitation of not only labor but also gender.[32]

However, despite her major avant-garde contributions, d'Eaubonne's ecofeminism was met with relative indifference in France. If *Feminism or Death* seems to have aroused a certain attention in the feminist, notably Parisian,[33] milieu upon its arrival, the term "ecofeminism" was not adopted by social justice activists or really studied by researchers.[34] The merging of women and ecology was subject to controversy in a French feminist milieu that was predominantly materialist and virulently opposed to essentialism,[35] which is still the primary reproach of ecofeminism in the West. In France, ecofeminism continues to provoke mistrust among our peers, as if this concept were struggling to insert itself into the landscape of contemporary feminisms. In prefacing this book, we hope, at our level, to recognize an unjustly forgotten author and reaffirm that ecofeminism has a French history but also to legitimize our place.

It is time for this unease to disappear, for the sake of all the people impacted by ecofeminism.

In contrast, in the anglophone North and particularly universities in the United States, a privileged place of openly ecofeminist theory and political action, the link between women, gender, race, and nature was the object of numerous studies and publications in the 1980s. In many texts on ecofeminism in the United States, it is customary to note that the invention of the "ecofeminism" neologism and its theoretical expression are thanks to a French activist and writer. The cross-Atlantic exportation of the term nevertheless remains mysterious. Mary Daly, an American theologian and radical feminist, seems to be the first person to have used the word in her essay *Gyn/Ecology* in 1978.[36] Yet despite d'Eaubonne's foundational work, ecofeminism, as a school of thought, a movement, and a tool of social advocacy, developed far from France.

The Blurry Contours of Ecofeminism

Retracing the origins of ecofeminism proves to be extremely difficult, if not impossible. And perhaps this is a good thing! Although we can clearly situate the moment when a movement emerged in favor of articulating ecology and feminism by the end of the 1970s, we must also mention here a major pitfall that complicates any attempt at the historicization of ecofeminism: the word has, in fact, since the beginning of the 1980s, been primarily used by academics —a majority of them white—hoping to theorize a global wave of the mobilization of women for the planet, to describe very different experiences or movements: Love Canal, Green Belt Movement, Women's Pentagon Action, the Chipko movement... In addition, certain canonical writings in the field were "certified" as ecofeminist even though their authors had never necessarily aligned themselves with ecofeminism, such as Silvia Federici's book *Caliban and the Witch*.

The criteria for inclusion into the "ecofeminist family" seems rather simple: the integration of nature, the environment, or the earth within feminist activism and/or analysis. It is then surprising to note that many other texts in conversation with these topics are not included in the ecofeminist literary corpus. Gloria Anzaldúa, Cherríe Moraga, Winona LaDuke, Alice Walker, bell hooks, and Toni Morrison—whose writings influenced our own ecofeminist politicization[37]—are just a few authors who wrote on the oppression exerted over women, gender minorities, and lands. Without ascribing the term "ecofeminism" to any author or movement who may not identify with it, we also rightfully ask: why does the ecofeminist canon remain majority white, while literature shows us that racialized women are disproportionately affected by the destruction of the environment and climate change throughout the world? According to the sociologist Dorceta E. Taylor, that gap is one of the consequences of an ecofeminism founded in large part on the experience and the history of white women.[38] Today, as ecofeminism rises from its ashes, we strive not to repeat these past errors, and we answer Taylor's invitation to redefine ecofeminism by interrogating the whiteness of its history.

Decolonize Ecofeminism

The aim of the following lines is not to dole out criticisms of an author—who is now dead—but rather to try to illustrate a facet of her reality. We would like to reveal the paradoxes, or contradictions, of a line of thought that both attempts a radical critique of approaches of growth and development undertaken by northern countries but at the same time exerts a domination over women that

it attempts to consider analytically. In fact, we consider this introduction an opportunity to caution other ecofeminist readers against
patterns of thought that are rooted in a hegemonic feminism. In the
end, erasing that lineage would be to risk reinforcing it.

Let's state things plainly. *Feminism or Death* is problematic in that
it ignores one fundamental fact: colonization. The book completely
skips over multiple resistance movements in countries of the South[39]
that nevertheless constitute its main objects of analysis. *Object*—
that's precisely the category into which non-Western countries
are classified, asphyxiated in a radical alterity that solidifies as
the book progresses. It is strange, to say the least, that Françoise
d'Eaubonne never situated colonization at the center of her analyses as the matrix of "male power," although she does critique it
in its entirety in a number of her works. The book ends up adopting racist tropes; for example, the use of the term "towelhead"[40]
regrettably tints each evocation of African women.[41] By adopting
a decolonial critique (although it didn't exist as such and by this
name at the time), Françoise d'Eaubonne would have understood
that what she calls "backwardness" (*arriération*) had nothing to do
with an economic or cultural regression, but rather with what the
economist Samir Amin[42] conceptualized as dependency theory:
"underdeveloped" countries are those whose economy was subject
to colonizer states, which protected their internal markets and today
control policy-making structures such as the World Trade Organization (WTO), the International Monetary Fund (IMF), and the
World Bank.[43] As articulated by the economist Immanuel Wallerstein, we exist in a world-system, which is to say that all countries
exist uniquely through interlocking relations. Thus, if certain countries seem "stagnant," as d'Eaubonne wrote, this situation is neither
ahistorical nor disconnected. Consequently, reflecting on countries
in an isolated manner is absolutely sterile; the ambitious attempt of

d'Eaubonne to develop a transnational critique of the oppression of women fails, for it is not accompanied by a solid global systemic theory. So, instead of thinking from a fixed state of "economic and cultural backwardness" that exists in a vacuum, we must try to identify the results of colonial relationships and decipher how centuries of slave trafficking, slavery, invasions, economic devastation, and the expropriation of wealth could have led to new interlocking, interconnected worlds that are dependent and unequal. We cannot stress this enough: colonization is more than an episode of history; it is a long and complex process that determines the different strata of identification and disidentification of a people, whether it be based on gender, class, or race. In addition, today it continues to be a relationship of decisive and omnipresent domination in our imaginaries, in our histories, and in our daily practices—whether we are buying sugar or coffee at the supermarket or learning yoga as a simple disembodied exotic exercise. What Françoise d'Eaubonne lacks is thus colossal.

However, decolonial queer and feminist critiques have long emphasized the interconnectedness of relationships among gender, race, and class. We reaffirm the existence of these analyses at the moment when d'Eaubonne was writing. Indeed, the epistemological turning point in 1990 meant to "celebrate" the 500-year anniversary of the colonization of Abya Yala [44] began long ago on the Latin American continent. Decolonial history is thus not new: on the one hand, it critiques a modernity that relies on the discursive construction of a universal white subject, and on the other, it calls on indigenous cosmovisions and new relationships with the living. Finally, it proposes approaching research from a radically different angle, by placing coloniality at its center, whether in terms of power or gender.[45] Authors such as Lélia Gonzalez, journals like *Regeneración*—which brings to mind the "Reclaim"[46] message of ecofeminists in the United States—*La mujer en pie de lucha* or literary monuments such as *This Bridge Called My Back* show that, since the 1970s and long before, intense theoretical development has placed the Third World woman at the center of these ideas.[47] Beyond a denunciation of the colonization of land, the decolonial movement aims to show how whiteness incurs on narratives, gender, and the social sciences, with the by-product of the myth of progress and development. The blindness[48] of Françoise d'Eaubonne is thus neither an exception nor a regrettable "accident": it is a systemic ignorance characteristic of the time that refuses to position nonwhite women and gender minorities as subjects. This reticence around decolonial theories still exists today.

A decolonial ecofeminism[49] thus allows us to link the colonization of nature, peoples, women, and all marginalized bodies. Long before the white theorization of the 1970s, decolonial feminism had been at the origins of the movement because ecological catastrophes affect the South most of all, and because the colonization of these lands, even if it permanently destroyed the life and the societies that developed there, also reinforced the close links between peoples and their environments. Because women hold a central role in rural areas,[50] they are pillars of their families, working the land and assigned to a gender-based division of labor that binds them to food, soil, care, spirituality, and the maintenance of domestic and agricultural life. Today, the cultural appropriation[51] of practices such as yoga or the ecological fantasy that imagines a return to "simple" or "purer"—meaning non-Western—ways of life reveal the inability of European countries to invent practices and narratives in symbiosis with the living world. Ecologically, we have a lot to learn from the countries of the South, without mystifying or romanticizing them. Rather, we must understand the immensity of their ecological and social oppression, as well as their tools of resistance and creation. For it is marginalized peoples who have had the most painful and enduring experience of global destruction, for which we are responsible. It is also indigenous peoples who lead the movement for climate justice and spearhead solutions on a global scale.[52]

That said, we must emphasize that we do not seek by any means to present countries such as Algeria or Argentina as innocent of any relationship with domination; our solidarity with colonized countries does not go so far as to ignore the atrocities they perpetrate, from their authoritarian regimes to their sexist crimes. What we hope to do here stems rather from the complication of relationships, from the awareness of the interdependence of countries, and thus the impossibility of utilizing a "ready-made" Western analytical device. The very designation of "countries of the South" should also be questioned, for Thailand is not the Congo, which is not Brazil. Thus, inversely to d'Eaubonne, we must always strive to "decolonize our mind," as Ngũgĩ wa Thiong'o[53] teaches us, but also our language and our imaginaries, in order to try to consider the specificity and nuance that make up each people, each country, each social group. On this level, it's certainly France that is the most "stagnant."

Uterus and Universalism

Despite its faults, *Feminism or Death* is by no means a conservative text. One of the most revolutionary arguments it contains is the direct critique of maternity as a woman's destiny. The author imagines and extols a "birth strike." She considers this hypothetical collective refusal to procreate to be a radical way to obstruct the patriarchal power inscribed in the flesh and in the uterus. Through this call, she shows to what extent her ecofeminism is opposed to a "maternal" vision of life, how her theory is above all a practice. Calling for a "birth strike" in 1974 was a shocking political act, and Françoise d'Eaubonne used it to denounce the expectation of motherhood imposed on all women within the heterosexual political regime. On top of it, she delivers a chronological, collective, and feminist vision of education, going so far as to cite as an example the *Kinderläden*, anti-authoritarian nursery schools established in Germany at the end of the 1960s.

Although this notion is compelling, the argument through which d'Eaubonne justifies her call is tricky, if not dangerous. Although there are important links between demographics and the history of the patriarchy (notably concerning the reproductive rights of women), making overpopulation the main cause of ecological catastrophe is an insidious way of placing a considerable burden on women, and more specifically on women of the South. Once again, only Western feminism could imagine a refusal of maternity as a form of freedom for all women. The call for a birth strike positions the refusal to have a child as a feminist marker of liberation, which is very problematic given what we know about the colonial history of the birth control pill, the politics of mass sterilization, and the devaluation of nonwhite maternities.[54] In addition, at the time when d'Eaubonne was defending her stance at the United Nations, the representatives of countries of the South were accusing the West of hiding common racism and colonial practices behind its demographic preoccupations. The overpopulation argument, which permanently established an image of African, Argentine, or Asian women as uncontrollable "laying hens," is in fact still used in certain circles reviving a neo-Malthusian ecological analysis.

As visionary as she was, Françoise d'Eaubonne nevertheless remained formed by Western feminism as described by Chandra Talpade Mohanty;[55] we find that Eurocentric conception of the world that separates "developed" and "underdeveloped" countries into two irreconcilable "camps,"[56] with diametrically opposed values and no relationship to each other, except perhaps a possibility of the former "saving" the latter by showing them the path to liberty. Thus, the author relies on a universalist perspective that constructs one unique agent of revolutionary change (white women) and embodies a power relationship within the very definition of its feminism. In describing "the Arab woman," "the African woman," or "the Muslim woman," d'Eaubonne fixes these women into categories that render them absolutely distinct beings by *nature*. The rare mentions of Islam merely serve to corroborate an oppressive vision of Muslim women in which they are always alienated.[57] Two processes are at work here: the generalization and homogenization of the Other, as Edward Said insightfully deciphered in *Orientalism*[58] in 1978, just three years after the publication of *Feminism or Death*. Thus, the discursive construction of the "Oriental woman" that must be saved perpetuates a racist myth that is still very present today, especially in France. It constructs a monolithic image of "Third World women" as an oppressed group characterized by its immobility. Women are thus doubly submissive and the men doubly "macho"[59] in the countries of the South, and all are inarticulate, since d'Eaubonne references exclusively (with rare exceptions) Western authors to speak about them. The whiteness of the discourse thus maintains her discursive strategy, which consists of appropriating the exclusive power of naming. Gayatri Chakravorty Spivak was one of the first to identify this problem, or the impossibility of the subaltern to speak.[60] Thus, each time there is a reference to Africa, to Latin America, or to Asia, it's to express a lack, a backwardness, or a failure; once more, these countries are rarely seen as birthplaces of feminism but rather as hotbeds of tragic sexism.

Now, it's up to us to invent new languages that will allow us to leave behind those "centrisms"—Eurocentrism, anthropocentrism, logocentrism—in order to free ourselves from a binary vision that would have us choose between progress or regression. Let us make room instead within ecofeminism for non-hegemonic, liminal, mixed, and ancestral subjects.

For a Radical and Anti-capitalist Ecofeminism

The recent media coverage of the liberation of women's speech, the increasing visibility of transfeminism, the consideration of colonization as the root of power over lands and peoples, the erosion of the nature/culture binary, the popularization of the concept of the anthropocene, the reappropriation of principles of libertarian ecology, and the increasingly loud denunciation of heterosexuality as a political system might have something to do with this unprecedented time when gender, race, and ecology have become indispensable aspects of our daily life. To have a body and be able to feed it properly, live freely in it, and refuse binary categories of gender has now become a political and public concern, which in our opinion has everything to do with the ecofeminist way of life, if something of that sort exists. Theories and ideas become flesh, embodied in constructions of feminist ecovillages, lesbian lands, ecosexual workshops, subversive mobilizations, and feminist activism within *zones à defender*—protecting the land against environmentally destructive projects and simultaneously creating intentional communities (*mixité choisie*). In the conclusion of her essay *Écologie et féminisme: Révolution ou mutation?*,[61] Françoise d'Eaubonne presents us with a real plan for an ecofeminist society in which every aspect of our existence is transformed. Patriarchal capitalism is succeeded by communities founded on an "egalitarian joint management by the sexes" and a total abolition of the notion of power. In the author's projections, these societies are constructed through a combination of anarchism, utopia, feminism, and political ecology.

However, we note a dangerous absence of these radical perspectives in a significant number of contemporary French ecofeminist productions. "Productions" is the fitting word, since we are now sold festivals sponsored by large dubious organizations, events stamped "eco-friendly" that continue to offer meat for the sake of "customer satisfaction," and we are constantly one click away from any number of retreats where we can reconnect with the "sacred feminine" in nature in exchange for a few hundred euros. The entire industry proclaims itself ecofeminist, yet all it does is validate the bourgeois, white, essentialist vision that the movement is against. Sometimes, and even often, it naively reinforces a form of power for privileged women by reconnecting them to their bodies in an individual and completely depoliticized way, producing what more closely resembles personal development than any kind of fight against systemic oppression. *Feminism or Death* surpasses the simple framework of subjective reading and challenges all the supposed ecofeminisms that do not change the status quo and instead fortify capitalism by extolling a "female leadership" or an awareness of "sustainable development and of gender" within corporations. With the intensification of global finance, capitalism, and neoliberalism since the first publication of this book, liberal feminism has in fact witnessed a real rise. Ecofeminism, unfortunately, has not escaped from this phenomenon, and a commodification of ecofeminist practices is right at the heart of the resurgence of the movement taking place in France today. The domestic ecology boom (eco-friendly menstrual cups, soaps, diapers) and the commodification of spiritual or esoteric practices through the purchase of crystals and semiprecious stones extracted in horrific conditions proves that reappropriation is well underway.

This is not and was never the goal of ecofeminism. Like d'Eaubonne, we must thus reaffirm the necessity of radicality and reposition it at the heart of ecofeminist praxis. It is a difficult movement to capture, always crumbling within the definition we try to affix to it, but ecofeminism nevertheless remains profoundly, absolutely, and definitively anti-capitalist. Thus, we refuse this liberal ecofeminism, the new name of reformist environmentalism that aims solely to impose new regulations and laws that are environmentally sustainable or have gender in mind. We have always refused equality when it means having the same rights as men to assassinate living beings with impunity. We refuse to satisfy ourselves with DIY lifestyles while those who produce the raw materials are worked to death at the other end of the world. We refuse ecofeminist retreats where the goal is to create new "green" vacations among women while their racialized and underpaid nannies look after their houses. We refuse to make covers of women's magazines that cash in on "girl power" and "natural" products, which in the end only reinforce gender stereotypes in the name of a pseudo ecofeminism that is now marketed to those for whom "radicality" is a dirty word. We refuse to make corporations' eco-friendly gestures or waste sorting the new definition of ecology. And, finally, we refuse an apolitical, ahistorical ecofeminism that only re-creates a white community of cisgender women integrated into the heterosexual economy, convincing themselves otherwise through exercises in transcendental meditation learned from a Netflix documentary. We will continue to refuse all of this, and we will do everything possible to propose an alternative to ecocidal equality.

Whether they call themselves ecofeminist or not, throughout the world, women and gender minorities are rising up to demand a "feminist system change, not climate change."[62] They look like the feminist peasants of La Vía Campesina resisting the capitalist patriarchal apparatus of global agribusiness. They are the indigenous and global southern women protecting their settled lands from destructive pipelines, dams, and mines.[63] Their resistance to environmental destruction and climate change far predates any ecofeminist text.[64] They are the eco-queer bloc disrupting the oppressive hetero cistem with LGBTQI++ identities that carry a stunning emancipatory force. They are members of the African Ecofeminist Collective who employ African feminisms to fight against capitalism and multinational corporations while also pushing for the reclamation of the African commons. Honduran activists like Laura Zúñiga Cáceres (daughter of the murdered indigenous environmental leader Berta Cáceres), who use ecofeminism to denounce green capitalism and extractivism. Current-day witches who restore the power of the living through their rituals without having an Instagram presence and thousands of followers. The Radical Faeries who swarm eco-queer worlds throughout the planet. We join this constellation of ecological feminists, and, alongside d'Eaubonne, we affirm that a transnational revolutionary movement, or global "mutation,"[65] as d'Eaubonne called it, is more necessary now than ever. It is necessary to respond to the extreme emergency of the climate crisis, to its links with gender, and to the rise of liberal feminisms that call for even more institutional power and in turn solidify binary politics and the exclusion of every dissident from the One and Indivisible French Republic, ranging from neuroatypical people to queer communities, from sex workers to trans people.

With this introduction, we have tried to explore the ecofeminist analysis that d'Eaubonne's *Feminism or Death* has offered us. She would probably have disapproved of a number of these explorations, but disagreement is inscribed in the DNA of ecofeminism. It's precisely this tension that renders it so vibrant and that has allowed for the existence of its illegitimate children, its magical gatherings in the lesbian lands of the Pyrenees, with the half-goddess half-cyborg monsters that live in our now resolutely hybrid imaginaries.

—Myriam Bahaffou and Julie Gorecki, April 2020

FEMINISM OR DEATH

Introduction

For the last few years, when the question of feminism has reappeared with so much force, when it has positioned itself with an amplitude and totality never previously attained, it was not merely a question of researching the historic origins and the immediate and contemporary consequences, as I have done elsewhere.[1] Instead, it seems necessary in 1974, after the evolution of American feminism[2] and the recent appearance in France of the League of Women's Rights following the MLF (Women's Liberation Movement), to consider the question with a little more distance and, at the same time, undoubtedly, with a feeling of urgency much more searing than in 1970. It is an issue, given the recent revelation of the futurologists, to consider feminism from a much vaster plane than the one envisaged to this point, and to seek how the modern crisis of the battle of the sexes is tied to a mutation of the totality—indeed, of a new humanism, the only possible salvation.

The aspiration of equality between the sexes, as Serge Moscovici said in *La société contre nature* (*Society against Nature*), responds to a need for justice and a pledge from the heart; it is not founded on an

analytical theory, a scientific approach of the spirit. This gap must
be filled, but how?

If Pierre Choderlos de Laclos was correct in observing that we
acquire virtues we don't need with much difficulty, the same can be
said of intelligence. Up to the present time, the demands, contro-
versies, explanations, and initiatives of feminism were limited to
revealing the wrongs done to half of humanity (actually, 52 percent)
and advocating the necessity of righting this wrong. This process
could lead to the following reaction from certain extremists on the
left: "That is a lot of noise, they said, for a category of oppressed
among others. The struggle should not be fragmented. So, there
are women, true; there is also the proletariat. And the Third World.
And the mentally ill. And homosexuals, etc." This rebuke seemed to
carry some weight: why prioritize one's own issues and neglect all
the others? Was concentrating all efforts into one group not reduc-
ing the potential of the struggles for subversion?

It seems that the time has come to show that feminism is not
solely—which has already given it its fundamental dignity—the
protests of the human category that has been crushed and exploited
from the most ancient times, since "woman was a slave before
slavery existed." Feminism is entire humanity in crisis; it is the reinvention of species; it is truly the world that will change its base. And
much more still: there is no longer any choice; if the world refuses
this mutation that will surpass all revolutions just as revolutions
surpassed the spirit of reform, it is condemned to death—and to a
death extremely imminent. Not only by the destruction of the environment but also by the overpopulation directly generated through
entrusting the management of our bodies to the Male System.

It is time to demonstrate that the failure of socialism to establish
a new humanism (and thus to avoid this destruction of the environment and this demographic inflation) stems directly from the refusal

to place the fundamental blame on the sexism maintained, under different forms, by both the socialist camp and the capitalist bloc.

And it is not the liberation of women as approved by the auspices of socialism, but rather the emergence of a socialism of an entirely new type, mutational, characterized by women taking control both of their own destiny and of the irreversible destruction of the patriarchy.

Finally, in conclusion, it is urgent to emphasize the death sentence of convulsive agony that has been dealt to the entire planet and its human species by this system if feminism, by liberating women, does not liberate humanity in its entirety—that is to say, wrest the world away from the man of today to transmit it to the humanity of tomorrow.

FEMINITUDE, OR RADICAL SUBJECTIVITY

Are there not any happy Jews?
In spite of their Jewishness, perhaps.
Because of it, in relation with it, no.
One cannot do otherwise than find at the
same time the trace of tragedy. As it is a tragedy to be colonized,
AS IT IS A TRAGEDY TO BE A WOMAN, a Black, or the
    proletariat.

—Albert Memmi, *Portrait of a Jew*

The Tragedy of Being a Woman

The Hydra of a Thousand Heads

I am a woman. You are a woman. She is a woman. What does this mean?

This:

The day always comes for us when we know, we discover, that we are a woman. Not by an abstract and collective condemnation like that of death; but by the ploy of a *natural* effect, this individual and inevitable misfortune erupts in front of our incredulous eyes. We ask ourselves. We ascertain: Is that me? Is that me? (*Au fond de l'homme, cela*[1] is the title of a work by a man. Deep down inside man: the feminitude.) This flesh for rape, this object that resembles a being, this zombie, this negativity, this hole: that's me. We are not born as such; we become it.

Each woman responds in her own personal way to this collective evil. And, in so doing, sharpens and particularizes the condemnation that cannot be avoided, that can only be lived, in tragic drama or in resignation. Woman-guy or lesbian (honorary goy), hetero-masochist or rebel; forgetful, evasive, or provocative beauty; whether she responds by defiance, refusal, total abandon, it is by a jolt that her condition began; the face of the oppression has varied, but the oppression remains the same.

How many hours spent, in my youth, with the girls of my generation, seeking to classify the thousand heads of the Hydra, talking until we were out of breath, spending hours that, according to psychologists and fine connoisseurs of that time, we would have better spent dreaming and flirting, getting ready for the dance, contemplating the pictures of a handsome boy, or changing our hairstyle! We sought to penetrate the mystery. This evil of being a woman—what was the origin of it? Was it religious? Socioeconomic? Biological? Metaphysical? Each of us had her own solution and mocked the others'; the most courageous talked about an "inextricable mixture of a bit of all that." How much "lost" time spent sorting these idiocies, trying to understand them, to defend ourselves—indeed, consoling ourselves![2] Our sole point of agreement remained on this fact: it was not a case of "anatomy," it was a tragedy; it was a promise, perhaps, but certainly a punishment. Our condition as woman ("feminitude" was not yet used) could be glorious, sought-after, persecuted, or flat-out denounced (old maids and nuns); it was never *comfortable*, it did not resemble anything *natural*; it was, above all, lack, deficiency, and strangeness. We lived it with the anguish of vague indignation, like the certainty of a curse due to which the least damage was paralysis, amputation, limitation; anguish and afflictions transmitted from mother to daughter, either in silence or in whispered secrets but equally discernible in all that surrounded and sustained us, the stories, the texts, the spectacle of the world, religion or secularity, experiences, folklore, and the male gaze. This look, this gaze that, in such frequent derision or in uncertain admiration, froze us in the same dehumanization as the look of non-Jews (insulting or in solidarity) who soon thereafter were supposed to spit on the yellow star or remove their hats in its presence.

After so many years and with the development of things, the difficulties of analyzing feminitude have been reduced; they are no less present. Still today, we discuss the Hydra's thousand heads until we are out of breath, instead of raising our children, decorating our home, meeting with our children's teachers, and being an activist in men's political parties. And we start throwing out words again, concerning the origins of the oppression: religious, economic, metaphysical, political. The only difference, perhaps, is that we reject more radically today the biological or essentialist explanation. We can't believe any longer in sexual or substantial essentiality: the metaphysical has become a phantom. We know that an "essential" women does not exist, any more than that the proletariat is predisposed to being such or that criminals are "born such," other than in Cesare Lombroso's fascinating fantasies. Subbreeds are fables, like the prelogical mentality. So we have at least one point settled. One less head of the Hydra.

Consequently, it is not my "nature as woman" that secretes this "spirit of contraction"; it is not my "feminine vanity" or my "feminine futility" that pushes me to adopt, due to "style or fashion," to "look good," an inauthentic attitude of revolt that the first invitation to dance would crumble. To the contrary, it is this fear, always nourished by history, that contributes to this anxious and illogical behavior—on the one hand, the anguish of the oppressed, on the other, the frivolous conduct that tends to desperately mask the anguish; it is the male society, the place that I occupy in it, the idea that it forms of me and sometimes incites me to accept, that provokes a masochistic attitude where previously there was none. Make any guy live like a woman, and he will become a masochist; just see how many homosexuals and Jews have to defend themselves against it. Suddenly appears the day of discovery about which I spoke earlier, when I discover the tragedy of being a woman, and its menacing weight and the misfortune of living in a world of men, where this menace is maintained for each generation and every age of the individual. For the hangman never tires of executions, and with no sadism in his mind, in general, solely with the awareness of his own worth and the unconscious of the Other that a perfect lack of imagination supplies, he will pursue, *prudent, wise, and calm enemy, never exaggerating his half victory,*[3] his work of destruction up to our very last days; well beyond all alibis of desire, of procreating and their horrors, well beyond even the look. Do you see, then, next to the sad fate of old men, the total abjection of old women?

Because I am woman: and, finally, I cannot afford the luxury of evading through words the realities that crush me. Deflowering, rape (criminal or legal, physical or spiritual), pregnancy, abortion, childbirth, menopause (or rather: the end of male desire, which is so profoundly equivocal that it is a menace to me but also possibility of defense and of security)—all these things can be softened, endured, even forgotten; they are not any less condemnation and limitation, and their terror will oppress me up to my death.

They cry exaggeration; they angrily accuse me of generalizing, of slander, even of awakening paper tigers. They reply, indignant: "But I ... I love women! But I am a feminist!" Calmly, with lucidity, I repeat it (and I cry it, and I shout it out loud, and I pronounce it, and I will express it, through spoken words and through the pen, forever and always); I believe in generalities, in depth, in the universality of the misogynist deeds: yes, always and everywhere, among capitalists, among the proletariat, in the Euro-American camp and in the socialist camp, in the Third World and in subcultures, in the Vatican as well as in Cuba; I see it in the young man with the hard-on and in the old impotent one; I believe in the phallocratism of every second, of each one, in each class and each country. Men of goodwill, liberals, egalitarian champions of universalism, I do not accept their advice. Discretion, silence when faced with the urgent problems of the proletarian world, graceful memory lapse in this bourgeois world, cultivated, sentimental, and chivalrous, or eternal hope of Red Father Christmas. I politely return all these theater tickets to you.

The Misogynist Fact

"I have never treated any Jew with contempt!" cries the philo-semite. Very well; so the history of genocide, of degradation, of discrimination has been modified?

The misogynistic reality, like all repressive relations, couldn't care less about the goodwill of Piotr, Jim, or Jacques. It cruelly overruns individuals. It is a part of our institutions; it underpins mental structures. We can only understand the female malediction if we keep in mind what it is first of all: a worldwide, general, historic, community phenomenon, a fundamental relation between the woman and the *nonwoman* (the best definition of the male). It affects all cultures and takes form more strongly yet in the uncultured. It guides all the rapport between the sexes, and those of individuals from the same sexual group among themselves. It is at once the most intimate of our specific being and the most common of our collective spirit. It is the air we breathe.

Of course, I don't consider all guys as the menacing oppressor! And when in the company of the one I love, or among homosexuals, activists in the same movement as I am, writers on the same side, I can forget my feminitude. But my ever-present misfortune risks springing up in front of me at any moment; in a flash, everything can fall apart, like at the end of the film *Malpertuis*, when the main character leaves the psychiatric hospital on the arm of his beloved, drunk with happiness at the thought of becoming *like everybody*, and as he was opening freedom's door, it closed around the familiar world of his nightmare. Just as he finds the interminable hallways again, the walls illuminated by torches, the doors in ominous succession, I can recognize in the bat of an eye a word, a gesture, a silence from a friendly colleague, a warm comrade, a companion who gives me my dose of happiness, this little thing that I am not permitted to abolish: the conditioned reflex of the *nonwoman*. With the homosexual, in particular, the most important of my comrades in arms, there is a greater ambiguity of rapport; crushed as I am by the patriarchal structure, he both benefits from the privileges of his status as male and is rejected, scorned by his kind as traitor to this status; if he revolts against the sexism that oppresses us, it is as an erotic minority, not as a male—as I do, myself, as a female—even if I am in the erotic majority, a heterosexual. In addition, he stops being a threat to me as a male—unless he is bisexual—and, at the same time, can become a new danger if he decides to see a rival in me; worse yet, he will contribute to perpetrating my misfortune, often by dedicating a resolute passion to a stereotype, envied for itself, of a fake woman for publicity pictures; and that is an object of worship I despise and fight against as one of the direct causes of the dumbing down of the world and of my own calamity.

A Word Too Strong?

I have drawn here the portrait of the "guy traitor to the guy culture because he likes guys." What to say of the others? They all participate in a society that renders life intolerable to women *as women*. Yes, I feel that, and I know that. Let's think about it: What is a fantasy? Am I neurotic, embittered, a shrew? Numerous are we who respond to this sad cliché. There were more than 5,000 of us doing that at the meetings on May 13 and 14, 1972. I am truly sorry if "these words are too harsh," as the apostles said. What can I do about it? I was born into this male culture, like everybody; I have assimilated it, I have respected it, I have sometimes loved it; revolting against it tears me up more than one can believe, because it means revolting against a large part of myself. That those who composed this culture and taught it to me are my enemies as oppressors, that all of them, including the realistic ones, the friends, the allies, participated in the malediction that crushes each woman as a woman. It is not a truth that I cry triumphantly; it is an observation that I formulate in pain and consternation. These words that are "too harsh," they are not less true, but brutally true, up to the dramatic end. I refuse to give in to what Sigmund Freud denounced as a temptation of the human spirit: to hold as false all that which is disagreeable to us. Because, finally, I owe my life to a man, and I have a son who owes it to me; the poets to whom I owe a rebirth were men; most of the characters of literature that I have admired also; the masterpieces and the delights of my destiny almost all carry the masculine mark; why would one want me to unleash my fury gratuitously against approximately half of humanity? By what strange perversity? Why refuse a priori to admit that my reasons are "good," if not out of fear of discovering your own shadowy image in the response that we are forwarding? Is your irresponsibility worse yet than your responsibility? Yes, every nonwoman, whoever he may be, whether he means to or not, participates in the disasters for all women, even if he strives to represent happiness for one lone woman. Better yet: without these disasters, he would be limited, diminished, less capable of a direct hold on the world as it exists today; it is in the same fashion that I, as a Western woman, benefit from the disasters of the Third World, even if I detest the idea.

Let me explain; there are many degrees of brutality in the same source. Even death camps had privileged people; but the marks of hate and disdain, gynophobia, distracted or virulent scorn, derision even, they are all always there, all the themes of misogynistic discourse. He is always there, the male ready to ridicule, to snicker, to strike, to rape, and to spit on all that he rapes. And, at the end of this sexual racism, as at the end of all racism, we find the final Hitlerian solution; the gradual degradation leads to death, as in the *Story of O*; in the most liberal of men sleeps a master of Roissy if he loves woman's flesh. Don't people cry out to him from all sides that without "a little sadism," he is not a true lover?

This Oh-So-Banal Sadism

Without a doubt, I only recognize the misogynist discourse as trembling from old age, whistling with viper-like hatē, bathed in shameful homosexuality (declared homosexuals are, in general, women's ally) or wrapped in the gift paper of Latin chivalry, of papal paternalism; I constantly have to complete it, correct it, surmise it, ignore it sometimes—excellent conditions for the galloping paranoia that shrews create for the weekly comic pages! But it comes at me from all sides: from school, from the family, from the streets, from professions, from the book that teaches me, from the mouth that I love, from the voice that I listen to with respect or cut off by flipping a switch.

And it is from this asphyxiating gas that is born, that is "fulfilled," that is engendered, that withers and dies, the human being that constitutes 52 percent of humanity: lungs eroded by this fog of words without ever having completely breathed the world's masculine oxygen. And by admitting that I reject this poison so subtle that I no longer even feel it, that I become yoga-like, that I affirm by respiratory exercises (social success, for example) a serenity in the face of all hardships, I won't live any less separated from it, like all the others, different, marked among the race of nonwoman that comes out of the woman. Such is feminitude.

I am not deaf to your protests. I still hear that I am exaggerating and that I am generalizing by accusing all men of the sins of some. Yet I do not believe for one instant that the professional misogynist, such as Jean Cau the Chameleon or the late, evil Stephen Hecquet ("Must we reduce all women to slavery? Yes!"), or the subtle and nuanced phallocrat, such as Maurice Clavel, are simply the monsters of aberration. It is out of the question for the liberals to use these scapegoats; on the contrary, they and so many others are only the paradigms of the cultivated male mentality, liberal and of goodwill. They are the living models of the erotic fantasies, the master of Roissy from *Story of O*, this marvelous handbook that every young virgin should read; this admirable unveiling of the love of the woman for the man (and of the man for the woman). The traits of these "sickos," of these "pathological exceptions," turn up in the most ordinary men: the CEO, the corner grocer, the pimps of Pigalle or Chicago. Psychiatrists can gloss over the harmful effects of those who go to the extremes of sadism; the age-old refusal of Marquis de Sade is the striking proof of the terror that leads the male society to deny the evidence, the sadism as the fundamental structure of its mentality and its system. Cases on the fringes have always been treated as pathology, but why does male pathology turn into misogyny? Is it because his own society offers him this sexual racism before all the others, as the most convenient, the most common outlet of schizophrenia, of bourgeois sclerosis, or of the paranoia of the repressed agitator? The gynophobe is undoubtedly sick; but every society produces the malady that is most specific to it. To make these striking sadists or these disdainful fools the sole purveyors of misogynist discourse seems too simple a solution for the cowardice of nonwomen.

The Separation

However, I (and when I say "I," I mean that you are listening to any and all women) became conscious of myself only through this misogyny, the primal matter of the world where I had to live, and that separated me from it. That this is the lot of other minorities, American blacks, Western Jews, etc., serves only to underscore the inexorable scandal of the destiny of the biological majority of the species: women, the only majority to be placed between parentheses and separated in the way oppressed minorities are. So it was that facing my condition as woman, placed in this position between parentheses in my youth already, I (as well as any woman) discovered the crucial aspect of womanhood: that of *separation* (like the Jew in Albert Memmi's work). And it is perhaps the knowledge of this rift, of this rupture, that made me search with such a burning thirst for the totality of an absolute, the absolute of the sexes as well as the absolute of the world; and I can only tolerate the idea of a struggle if it throws itself, like the river into the sea, into the fight for the totality.

Majority or Minority?

Separation or Difference?

Yes, every woman is *separated*, just as Eugénie de Saxancour by the old man Restif.[1] A lot are *destroyed*, such as Simone de Beauvoir's main character. Broken, separated: these are the realities of everyday observation that we can, in all good conscience, oppose to the electoral formula "equality in difference."

Difference? That is a problem. Separation? That is a fact. "Let's start from the concept of a fact rather than a problem." Since it is *my* culture that taught it to me. Yours. The male culture. To be specific: Judeo-Christian and bourgeois. Would there be such a great difference on this point with that of Peking, Cuba, Moscow? I don't believe so.

Despite the protests, so numerous and so loud, by those who, being women, passionately proclaim both their feminitude and their success—that is to say, their integration and their expression—in spite of these women who reject all barriers, all placement in parentheses, so strangely. I know this dialectic far too well and in far too much detail: every separation reinforces the difference that it underscores and creates it even if it doesn't exist. (The salary gap between the sexes leads to a decrease in the quality of work and absenteeism among women, the same as lack of promotion provokes a disinterest in the work.) Ten times, we crushed the false problem of "innate difference," of the "essential" woman, of the "Feminine Eternal"; the separation continues all the same, imposed by those who don't even believe in it any longer, accepted by those who never believed in it. Do we need to say the following, along with Albert Einstein? "It makes no sense to want to convince others, through all kinds of deductions, of our equality; because their way of acting *does not come from the brain.*"

Indeed, it takes root in the sense of profit for some, in the fanaticism of intellectual comfort for others. To give up one's profit is almost as difficult as giving up the prejudices that allow one to live without the affliction of having to think. I have already written about this;[2] the arguments don't change the situations; at the most, they provoke a crisis of awareness. Likewise, in psychoanalytic treatment, if a reorganization of life conditions does not follow, the "recovery" serves no purpose; why have a driver's license, if I can't afford to buy a car? In the past, people believed that devotion to virginity was necessary to solidify marriage, that homeland as religion was indispensable to the joyful sacrifice of soldiers; today, girls get deflowered at parties at fifteen or sixteen years old and become good bourgeois mothers, and the boys disguised as heroes go off to get killed, without a word, for the industrials that they know full well are called fatherland. So, why argue otherwise? Why write and speak? Well, as Memmi says, "if words proved that the way out was not verbal," they have already served a certain purpose.

Equality in difference! My God, my God, that old dinghy taking on water from all sides is still floating! It would be ideal if *human* relations could be egalitarian. "*And, of course, I could not want for any other paradise.*" But who is ignorant of the fact that they are not egalitarian *anywhere?* Oppression reigns everywhere; and oppression is none other than an interiorized repression. How could it be otherwise in a male world, that is to say, competitive? From this perspective, *difference* (meaning otherness) is always at the expense of the one who is different. The nonwomen want the woman to be different from them, which means obviously that they are different from her; but the woman suffers all the consequences. If she wants to create, to command, to invent, to change, she parrots man, shame on her, but the honor will be doubly great for those, the women-guys, the "Queen's pirates," who will be all the more valued for having crossed that barrier. Additionally, if the man proves to be intuitive, ingenious, full of good taste and sensitivity, he does not decrease the glory of his sex: the philanthrope, the grand designer, great chefs, nobody accuses them of "mimicking women"; he doesn't need any "Queen's pirates." To the contrary, it is a triumphal argument against us: "Even all the great chefs are men." That which is *great*, thus embodying the universal, is necessarily the deed accomplished by the nonwoman. *There is no longer an issue of difference if the male is involved.* Except on one sole point: erotic behavior. The homosexual is a "bastard," in the traitorous sense of the word. Such was the critique of the Abbé de Choisy by a grand lord: "he pretends to be a woman, whereas he has the good fortune of not being one." The scourge of being a woman has never been so clearly admitted.

What Man's Great Voices Say

At the time when we were debating so intensively, young girls whose memories fill the shadows of my walls, we were being nourished by the very culture that we were denying; we listened with respect to the great voices of humanity that had built the world where we lived; and here is what those voices told us:

"Woman is the natural, hence abominable. The young girl is a little imbecile and a little bitch" (Baudelaire, *our* Baudelaire of *Les fleurs du mal*!). Saint Augustine: "Women can neither teach, bear witness, compromise, nor judge." (Unfortunately, they can still educate. An example: Saint Monica, the philosopher's mother.) Hesiod: "To trust women is to trust thieves." Saint Jean Chrysostome: "Woman is a sovereign plague." (Remember, it is our church that calls her "Golden Mouth.") Saint Antonius: "Whenever you see a woman, keep in mind that it is neither a human being nor a ferocious beast, but the devil himself." Tertullian: "You should always wear mourning and rags for having caused the downfall of the human species." Saint John of Damascus: "Frightful parasite that has attached itself to the heart of man, daughter of the lie, sentinel sent from hell." Saint Paul, the leader of our church: "I want the woman to remain silent; women, submit to your husbands, etc. etc." Let's leave these bigots behind, shall we? I agree. So here their enemy is named, the good giant of Western humanism, the Jupiterian, the skeptic, the first champion of equality among men and of sexual freedom, François Rabelais: "When I speak of woman, I speak of a sex so fragile, so changeable, so fickle and imperfect ..." Let's turn to classicism. Jean Racine: "She floats, she hesitates, in a word, she is a woman." Pierre Corneille: "Father, I am a woman and am familiar with my weakness." Pierre Beaumarchais: "O Woman, weak and deceiving creature!" Alfred de Vigny: "Woman, a sick child, twelve times over impure." Pierre-Joseph Proudhon, in keeping with Molière and his famous *chrysalism*, that a woman knows she is always "a Housewife or a Courtesan." And elsewhere: "To us you are ugly, venomous beasts, what do you have to say to that?" This socialist, this revolutionary, this author of the saying "to own property is to steal," spells out the consequences: "Man will be the master, and the woman will obey." Before Freud, he decrees "that she is missing an organ if she wants to be anything other than an ephebe." And Auguste Comte, in the letter announcing his marriage to his friend: "At the end of the day, the wittiest, the most refined of women is equal only to a rather lesser man, just with a lot of added pretense."

All this has been just about French culture. Let's move on to Islam, where the Quran gives the woman to the man as "a field to plow." Unless you prefer the Bushido, the honor code of the samurais, striking parallel with Greek homosexual culture, where the young noble Japanese man learns that it is shameful to love a woman, whereas there are so many young men. Do you have a preference for Germany? For Arthur Schopenhauer, I am an animal with long hair and short on ideas; for Friedrich Nietzsche, "the sub-man is superior to the super-woman"; for Freud, the great, we are all failed men, envious from birth of our little brother's penis. All that exists only in books; we know that; culture is the opposite of life. Fine! Let's study the wisdom of nations; let's look at how those who don't know from point A to point B express themselves in proverbs. Scandinavia: "Woman's heart is like the turning wheel, so don't trust her promises." Hungary: "Woman, your name is silence." "Money is good for counting and the woman for beating." Poland: "Horses pull the wagon easier after the woman gets off." "If the husband doesn't beat his wife, her liver will decay." France: "Beat your wife as you beat your wheat; you'll have good flour; you'll have beautiful children" (from the Dauphiné).[3] North Africa: "Beat your wife. If you don't know why, she does." Do I need to add to the list? Do we need to include the most faraway religions: Buddhism, Zen, the Vedas, pre-Columbian cosmogony, the devil and his followers?

I ask you: What man, faced with such litany, would not be terrified? Who would judge himself a complete human without doubt?

Who would not feel separated, different? Condemned? Perhaps only Jews can comprehend it. For those of us who were searching to justify being women, it was in these texts that we learned at school and in the voices that we revered as messengers of our religious faith that we received this venom; it was distilled in us at the same time as cultural and spiritual nourishment. One young woman who bears my name—in the days when Michèle wasn't yet camping all over France with parachute material, with no heat or food, and when Lina, before she lost her sanity, was still a brilliant student—the young girl that I was wrote at the end of a collection of these quotes: "Women, how much muck has to be thrown in our faces before we open our eyes! It is only in the gospel that mud cures blindness." Yet I, too, learned to forget, faced with the violence; I repressed, I buried it, I closed my eyes; and I refused to see the depths of "colonized" in my destiny. It was either that or die. But I can't get over this cowardice.

The Court Recused

Needless to say, today I reject with no difficulty the legitimacy of this *universal* tribunal. Universal in time, in space, yes: not in the human, since it represents only the males: a little less than half of humanity. Jews, homosexuals, they are affected by the majority judgment; but we are the majority in the legal trial. Michel de Montaigne, more enlightened than Freud and his famous "women's indifference to justice" (and Nietzsche has already affirmed that we had little sense of honor) wrote: "Women are not wrong at all to refuse the rules in place, especially since men made them without them."

"Without them" is not precise enough; he should have said "against them."

Let's clarify. With the tribunal rejected, it is not at all our intention to deny the differences between the woman and the nonwoman; we could, to the contrary (in this world where all minorities are oppressed in the name of the majority), prove proudly, to begin with, that this numeric difference is *in our favor*, if we use the standard discourse of the outraged proletariat: "We are the people of the earth: we are a force moving forward."

We, the Majority

Will the oppressor dare to respond that the scarcity of something determines its price? In the name of what would you substitute the word "thing" with the word "beings"? That is what we are, both beings and things; beings by nature of our human condition, things by our status. Things that *are being had*. In all the meanings of the term. The infinitive "to be had" equals "to be fucked": a popular expression. To be "had": a masculine noun, the synonym of things possessed. Didn't early communism want to put together, on common ground, possessions and women? And what about this hippie that *Women's Lib* quotes: "I don't have any sense of ownership, I lend everything to others, *even my wife*." We, the majority, are the "had" of the male society—the minority. Women, humanity comes out of us, comes from us; it belongs to the *nonwomen*; it is against us. The oppressor never integrates with the things; never will he be able to respond to us; "the scarcity of *beings* determines their price." The male, the nonwoman, considers himself both as the positive and the neutral of humanity; he is the white one, that is, both color and the absence of color. And this mentality predominates also in the man of color: with regard to his wife, he is the white man. "We are your Negroes," protest the wives of the Black Panthers. A song from the days of the Front Populaire, singing to a woman:

It is the massacre of the innocent puppets!
Ah, aim well at your poor mouths
Since you are all too cowardly
To strike at the powerful …

We have come to this: the oppressed ones are obliged to present certain advantages with fervor if they want to put up with the oppression, to make their nests there, to survive there. The woman must be beautiful, just as the Jew must be rich. A woman without beauty is promised social massacre, just as the penniless Jew is promised a physical massacre. The first has to make a defender out of one of the oppressors; the second has to constantly prepare his escape or his "recycled self," as the comic character in the film *Oliver Twist* says. But even this reformist solution risks fomenting a new catastrophe; the Jew's wealth, this "Jew gold," is "stolen from the world"; and it is the motivating force behind the Inquisition, the pious pogrom. Woman's beauty is the devil's trap, in the Middle Ages she is a siren destined for drowning, a witch for burning, and in our gentler times a whore, a bitch that you have to tame with your raised hand, to slit her throat even, *to teach her* like in noir fiction series, the eminent culture from this "matriarchy," from this "feminine paradise," America. Even black men have to gain great strength to defend themselves physically; indeed, to become a show animal, a prestigious gladiator in the ring. But then there are so many rants about the "beastiality" of this brute, of this wild animal! His muscles of steel, his superb member—what great pretexts for a lynching!

The Permanent Court

Even if the final catastrophe is avoided, the advantageous feature, the obligatory privilege in order to answer to the persecution becomes another argument for her and confirms it theoretically. Jews are a problem, with their greed, their profit; women are peril, the peril of losing his soul before, today, that of compromising his freedom or of squandering his money. Thus it is with mutual consent to the institutional smut of the Male Society that the woman will be beautiful and the Jew rich: on the victim's part, it is a defense on the personal level; and on the part of the oppressor, a theoretical necessity to justify the oppression on the collective level. And if so many suffragettes of the past, of feminists today, reject the values of elegance and aesthetic criteria so resolutely, it is useless to argue; it is the spectacular lyric epic of the Gauls heading to combat bare-chested. It is not only heaven that weighs on their shoulders.

We have decided not to deny a priori all the famous "differ-ences." Of course, a lot of "feminine traits" are imaginary; most of them are even fabricated entirely by the male culture. Others are exaggerated with deference, for the purpose of their survival, like the famous maternal instinct that does exist, however.[4] But does our difference limit itself to this? I don't think so. After much hesi-tation and questioning, I hold the feminine today to be a value and not solely a cultural variation on the universal theme. This is what comes the closest to universalism; what the man-male pretended to be when he was presenting himself as neutral; it is at the base even of the most immediate values of life, and it is in this way that the feminist combat joins the ecological combat.

The most naive woman interiorizes and lives in her unconscious, as early as puberty, sometimes even earlier, all the judgments that males have leveled at her through the centuries. That is what molds her behavior, her mentality as the accused. She is accused by man just as he was accused in the past by God. And the most naive woman looks around herself with fear, looks for excuses, lives as a lifelong defendant. She doesn't need to have read Tertullian or

Nietzsche. A woman has to justify herself at every instant of her life. That is what makes her seek beauty, love, mystery, children so desperately—not as values as naturally desirable as power or possessions for man, but as so many alibis, good points, witnesses in support of the defense. Because, as Virginia's Woolf's Orlando says, at the outset, she is not at all "chaste, perfumed, covered in delicious finery." She can undoubtedly justify her existence through this man whom she fascinated enough to choose her, through these children that she fashioned by violating their freedom; she can justify herself in her role as intermediary; thus never as herself, like her partner and master in the minority, the nonwoman. As a pretty, refined, supremely elegant woman, as Albert Cohen says: "the pathetic need to attain a state of grace" (*Belle du Seigneur*). Her lover is moved: what state of grace would he merit? He is the man. The woman in love has to seek pardon. Among all the oppressors' gazes, the beloved's gaze is chosen as the symbol of the universal tribunal. It is at the moment when she discovers her feminitude in love that the woman is the most painfully at odds with her femininity: the eternal defendant confronts her masked judges, like a character in Franz Kafka's works. (There is always this parallel between two kinds of pariahs, to be a Jew or a woman.) Because this constant summons is an integral part of feminitude, of the calamity, of the condemnation of being a woman. Being, in addition to this true difference to which we will return, part of an invented difference. The anathema leveled at Eve.

That old story again?

But that old story also concerns the nonwoman! He, too, has to define himself in light of this trial and its relation to him. He, too, has to accept or refuse the constitutional misogyny of his status as man; in a general way, he will both accept and refuse the status, in infinitively variable doses. (The same as I, as a goy, have to define

myself in relation to antisemitism, and as a Western woman in relation to the Third World.)

This is why the attitude of the nonwoman, this false majority, this
nonmajority, is significative also concerning his attitude toward all
minorities (blacks, Jews, the Third World). His brutality, his paternalism, his guilty conscience, or his efforts at solidarity express his
other positions regarding the Others whose exploitation or invis-
ibleness (to him) assures his material well-being—better yet: his
mental health! Just think of the accusations regularly leveled at
revolutionaries, the dissenters, the subversives, the neurotic; it's
not just about one sort of denigration. (Karl Marx was right; man's
treatment of the woman determines his treatment of man.) What
good is mental health that dissimulates the real and that I owe only
to a lack of imagination?

So, through her reduced, limited, restrained, disturbed, or literally tortured condition, her condition as *accountable to the law*,
the woman, always free only under limitations, not only endures
outrageous situations: she provokes, she guides, she excites these
aggressions. She is the historic lack. But history is nothing without
her. "The man makes History, the woman is History," writes
Oswald Spengler—with such interesting brutality!

People will object that I am joining in with sexism here. I would
have said they were right on the points where they could see clearly;
but this opposite of love is much blinder than they are. The sexist,
the phallocrat, I am not joining in with it; I am explaining it, I am
encompassing it, I am absorbing it. The sexist does not even see
the depth of this difference that he invokes indiscriminately, for the
sake of profit or laziness. He is so far from the point that Valerie
Solanas's great delirium would be more rational on this matter: it
concludes purely and simply in an inversion of the values. Because
the unfortunate sexist ignores the fact that femininity goes far

beyond feminitude; being a woman goes far beyond woman-male relations—oh, and how far beyond! Feminitude is an incantation of phallocratic culture. Femininity itself is this look—and this exchange of looks. It is exactly this trial—and the judgment of this trial, never rendered by the society of nonwoman, and for a reason! Femininity determines the woman as much as the nonwoman to whom she returns the accusation of having betrayed the human in mystifying the universal; and by identifying her as a simple variation on this universal—when it is not a simple projection of his own negative aspect: his passivity, his masochism, his ambiguity. Feminitude is merely the interiorization of this accusation, a nest for the Hydra of a thousand heads; femininity is the radical rejection of it, of both the gaze and the situation. Put simply, in a few words; feminitude is a myth; but femininity, that exists, since *women* exist.

Some Examples

I have said it: male culture in the beginning was not an indignity for us; to the contrary, we revered it, just as French Jews can revere French literature, or American blacks the sagas of the pioneers of yesteryear. Look at how our great works rescued the travelers from the lead-sealed wagons from 1940–1945, and what solidarity tied Buffalo Bill's descendants with Missouri's lynch mobs. Who did not feel more or less a citizen of the community at the beginning of his or her life? You can't talk about naivety; without that naivety, the baby would commit suicide by jumping from the crib. Yet, very early, the men who gave us the fruits of the spirit spoke to us across the centuries. I repeated earlier that they taught us who we were: resolute sinners, backward ones, devious ones, imbeciles and bitches, whores or little housewives; we lost the world, killed Christ, brought death to the earth, we corrupted souls, we spent all the money, we talked instead of listening, we were at times the fatal destiny of the bleeding sphinx, at other times the mediocrity of the little housewife; in a word, we infested the planet. They burned us often in the Middle Ages, like the Jews, but we were always still there. What to do about it? Make little of us! Make us forget; by allowing us to work twelve hours a day, typing on a machine what the male voice dictated, changing diapers, ironing, sewing, cooking, peeling, mending, cleaning, raising and deforming our children; preparing the girls for the same thing and the boys for war. Except for the privileged few who would have nothing to do but play bridge, show their butts, mix a cocktail, parade around in a car, change dresses, and spread their legs. Such were the messages of the wise men of this world.

> I hear their steps, I hear their voices
> What are these ordinary things saying
> Like what you read in the paper
> Like what you say at home in the evening[5]

Will I admit it? These horrible things I was being told about women seemed less oppressive than the praises sung of the models proposed to us. Their virtues reinforced the accusations; the white doves were nothing more than deterrents. To start with, they were always laudable only in relation to someone. Marie agreed to have a child, and under what conditions? Something like this: "Do that for me!" The Gracchi brothers' mother cut her sons from a pattern (here are my jewels). Andromeda was merely the memory of a shadow. Even Joan of Arc only agreed to step out of her *role as woman*, apparently, for a nice king. When it came to an authentic female creator, they had to emphasize her rapport with the masculine right away. George Sand didn't write anything of great value:

above all, she had been Frédéric Chopin's and Alfred de Musset's mistress. Even the minor authors, Madame de Ségur and Madame d'Aulnoye, wrote only for their grandchildren. You'll find only a few lines about Madame de La Fayette; not a word about Louise Labé or Marceline Desbordes-Valmore. Honors were bestowed on the Marquise de Sévigné because she was a great woman of the epistolary genre, for the Précieuses and the "philosophers" because they were the affluent classes of the salons; so it is that, from the beginning, and even for those whom one couldn't ignore and about whom one spoke with esteem, it was always a question of tying them to one or more men, to worldly and cultural institutions; arbiters of language, not its creators; male honor was safe. Not much more brilliance found in the sciences. Not a word about Sophie Germain's mathematics; not any more about Hypatia, the astronomer and physicist who invented the aerometer; not about Anna Morandi, a professor in Bologna in the seventeenth century, who discovered the exact insertion of the ocular muscle; nothing about Marguerite Winckelmann's comet; nothing about Catherine Scarpellini's catalogue of shooting stars, even though it was the first. Joseph de Maistre claims that we have neither discovered nor invented anything: this little bit of knowledge was on my final high school exam. And Marie Curie? That's easy: she had "helped her husband in his work." These are the consolations offered to my generation for the gynophobic discourse I discussed earlier. While I was stuffing my memory with these examples, the cardinal Eugène Tisserant was taxing the states to stop preparing women for a profession and to concentrate rather on preparing them for domesticity. And while Michele was traveling the roads of France with her dangerous suitcases, Vichy was programming both man's return to the land and "woman's return to the home."

The True "Feminine Mystery"

Thus it is that, as far as I could go in searching the past, I kept asking myself why I was different, and how. A question that always brought another: why this difference that I didn't know where to situate? Because why would an orifice in the place of a protrusion carry more importance than a blue eye as opposed to a black one, than blond hair as opposed to dark? Would that guarantee me a destiny obligatorily secondary and subordinated? Why was I to be somebody with not much personal importance, who would always feel, at best, only half of the other? (And yet, still half! Without me, he would have felt entirely whole, no? Funny math.) Why should it be me, this object that makes people laugh with derision, with indulgence, with tenderness even, but about whom they laugh like an accident of nature, not a fact of nature herself? Why did the wise ones hold this deforming mirror up to me? Why was I super-fluous, an excess? Why was the entire world spitting in my face? Undoubtedly, I had weapons. This "mystery," for example ... But we mustn't delude ourselves. Caliban is mysterious to Prospero, too, and the towelhead to the colonist. As soon as oppression exists, mystery arrives to help it. Woman's mystery remains damaging; at the center of this venomous flower is Eve's apple, the bestial refusal of the divine male spirit, the hole, the abyss. I was merely a hollow mold, and I had to be punished ... Why? Because the Bible itself, that condemned me, called humanity *the masses of woman*. Statistics have confirmed it: 52 percent. Those were the nonwomen, in this case, the accident of nature. So? I felt the little boy's surprise in *Macbeth* in myself: the riffraff was crazy to get caught in the snare of decent people, since they outnumbered them!

That's what the true "woman's mystery" was all about!

Work and Prostitution

Nature Says: "Please"

When you see a little boy in a Soviet cartoon tell a little girl: "We are leaving for the North Pole; but you can't go because you're just a girl!," we understand that the USSR has not yet attained as much equality between the sexes as the socialists would have us believe.

When you see American students respond to a survey conducted by Betty Friedan:

"What we need is to take things as they come and assert ourselves physically ...We mustn't show enthusiasm for work *or for anything else* ... that makes people feel uncomfortable."

"When your husband is a manual laborer, you mustn't be too cultured."

"I don't want to get interested in the world's problems; I don't want to be anything else other than a fantastic mother and a model spouse."

"My psychological profiles for professional orientation show that I am destined for success in advanced studies and should have a brilliant career, but all those things don't help attract men; attracting men is what counts for a woman."

It makes you wonder how the United States managed to pass as a "gynocracy" or "matriarchy" for so long!

Moral Codes Condemn You

I spoke earlier about the obligation for the woman to please men and the parallel reproach made for doing it. One of my friends told me a story one day about how she lived that personally. She was a strong person, athletic and intellectual. She was admonished for her lack of "femininity" (confused with "feminitude," as always). One day, she dressed up for a party: a dress, hairdo, makeup. On the way to the party, she walked in front of a construction site. The workers stopped what they were doing and started making catcalls, saying: "Oh la la, look at that!"

"I can't win, no matter what I do," said my friend. "So, too bad, I'll put my pants back on and leave my hair as is."

When people criticized her again, she replied:

"Guilty as charged, at least I am happy with myself as I am."

Fanny Deschamps took a survey of males in the France of the Fifth Republic[1]:

"I can't stay with a woman whom I don't find attractive," declares "Nicolas." "I can't stand her, she has to leave. I am very strict about that, I am very picky." (Nicolas is a manager.)

"The intellectual side and her personality interest me only if the physical side interested me first."

"A woman is first of all a body, a figure."

"A woman must be beautiful. Otherwise, I wouldn't want to talk to her. *To do what?*" [sic]. (Alain)

And the same man:

"And if she's not beautiful? In that case, I understand that a woman … would want to do a lot of things since she doesn't have what it takes to be a real woman."[2]

And it goes on for pages and pages and pages. In 1968, the year of all the protests.

A woman has to please and feel justified in pleasing, like the Jew who has to be rich in order to have a minimum of peace and security and count his fortune incessantly, like a black man who has to be strong, with much sexual prowess constantly in order to ward off the accusations of bestiality.

Between pleasing and going to the North Pole, pleasing and "being interested in world issues," "being too cultured," "showing enthusiasm for work or anything at all," the choice is supposed to be natural, instinctive, spontaneous.

"It is natural for a woman to please, woman is made to please."

Hostile Work

That is why participation in work and worldly affairs would "kill her femininity." Just as advanced studies would lead her to conduct herself badly. "Free thought for a woman makes us think of free morals," says Stendhal. And we also remember Madame de Beauvoir's scruples and fears, forced by the "misfortune of the times," to let her daughters pursue their studies. And Pierrette Sartin:

"I remember a good mother struck with horror when, upon returning from Mass, she found her daughter, who was preparing for the high school exit exam, in the midst of reading *Le traité des passions* by Descartes!"[3]

We'll admit that prejudice against studies has been lessened among the bourgeois class. These studies only lead to several sectors, of which the most important is secretarial work in all its forms and two or three liberal professions: teaching, first of all, then law, then medicine. In all the other areas, the presence of women falls to unbelievably low proportions. But it is above all *work* as such, that vague and multiform specter, that is condemned as the great rival of the *necessity of pleasing*. To talk of work is to talk of anguish and difficulty, and it is the idea of the most uncouth, the most repulsive, the dirtiest, and the most difficult work that runs through the minds of the paternalist misogynists as soon as they hear a woman talking about liberating work. "Go to the USSR and watch women carrying rails on their shoulders."[4] What feminist hasn't heard this kind of cliché? In an argument with me through letters, a doctor of sexology predicted, ironically, that one day women would be "cleaning the gutters."

"It is truly an idea condemned to failure to want to throw women into the struggle for life," preaches Freud in a letter to his fiancée.

All these defenders of compromised femininity forget very easily that, in the past, fifteen-year-old girls worked as miners in the depths; that in some parts of the countryside, as still today in underdeveloped countries, women pulled the plow instead of horses or bulls, as related by the author of *Jacquou le Croquant*;[5] that finally, a fact entirely *hidden* today, as late as the nineteenth century, you found women in the gallows.[6] So what about their fragile, exquisite beauty then? What became of the natural, the biological, their destiny to please?

Honoré de Balzac was much more coherent in his division of women into two groups: On the one hand, female workers who have no right to aim toward femininity—they are beings neutered by work just as bees in the hive. And, on the other hand, the ladies of the bourgeois and noble classes of the Faubourg Saint-Germain, who are true women themselves. We can join this mighty cynicism with the definition of "beast of labor or animal of luxury" by Jean Fréville in his preface to *La femme et le communisme* (Women and communism).

Let's look closer at the question. Will they claim that the deplorable cases of discrimination we have been discussing here belong to the past of the society of castes and the exploitation of workers in the crudest state? And that, in our modern, evolved society, so aptly called "of consumerism," everything moves toward the disappearance of such shocking exceptions and that every woman, even among the working class, has the right to enough leisure time to maintain her femininity, her beauty, *to please*, finally, as it is her *natural* destiny.

The Sociologist's Confession

Let's look at the thoughts of a contemporary sociologist, who certainly cannot be accused of tenderness toward revolutionary ideas and who defends "morals" in the name of their normalizing benefits, even to the point of classifying masturbation still among *anomalies*:

> The true biological differences that exist between the two sexes are not of great importance relatively and serve as a pretext more than a reason for the social differentiation attributed to man and to woman in the life of the community ... The substance that constitutes the difference in roles, masculine or feminine, is extremely variable ... The biological inferiority of the woman is particularly overrated in our modern civilization ... When considering activities recognized as essentially masculine such as the hunt or war ... we find a large number of exceptions approved by the community. In Tasmania, for example, the hunt for seals, very dangerous, is reserved for women. Ethnology

studies show us also the famous case of the bodyguards, very cruel and warlike, of the King of Dahomey, exclusively made up of women. In opposition, we find Atheneum, a Greek writer from the third century who exclaimed: "Who ever heard of a woman in charge of cooking!"[7]

Whether she hunts seals or goes down in the mine, she still must please Alain and Nicolas; the feminitude of the Tasmanian woman, the female character in *Germinal* or the French women of 1968 have nothing in common with a biological diktat, with a subtle pile of hair or this uterus that Norman Mailer (*The Prisoner of Sex*) wants to make an "interior space" tied to the destiny of a woman to such an extent that contraception would be an offense [*sic*]; all these attitudes, variable according to the sexism of the society, always originate from the law of the dominant caste, the male group.

The affirmation of the natural does not correspond in any way to a biological given, to the contrary, it constitutes an irrefutable proof of the norm. That which is "natural" is not biological nature, it stands for the mores once they are adopted by the collectivity.[8]

We must emphasize that man is the only animal that creates his own nature[9] and that feminitude does not have anything at all in common with femininity, the latter being constituted only by the ensemble of biological traits preexisting before all cultures, but susceptible to being profoundly modified by them, as is proven by the disappearance of breastfeeding in modern times.

Prostitution as Law

The supposed law of pleasing formulated by nature and the supposed moral condemnation that nature exacts are only the expressions of the same legislator, who has nothing to do with the entity called nature: the male, the nonwoman. All the satires against the loathsome feminine, from Hesiod to Henry de Montherlant, including Boileau and the Fathers of the Church, are merely tirades by the same actor who changes his voice: man, who orders women to seduce him in order to punish her later, as the medieval Church confiscating the Jew's goods after having confined him to attrition.

> The first man that she meets
> Will demand her virtue;
> She gives it to him, "Aren't you ashamed?"
> He asks after having had her.[10]

"Hide your face, woman, I see your husband's kisses on it," declared Saint Ambroise, the representative of the Church that made *marriage* a sacrament.

How would she not feel her condition of feminitude as deficiency and incongruity, this transmitter of life, this "receptivity," this "passivity," at once human and rejected by the human, this bizarre being closed up in a contradiction pieced together, presented to her as natural, deemed by biology or heaven? How could she not find nature the opposite of comfort, of the natural, of the instinctive, which moves always toward ease and harmony? How could she not feel in constant false bearing, relegated to this "oblique" and "equivocal" character trait that furnishes one more accusation against her? To summarize in one point: to the mystified woman who takes feminitude for her femininity, nature appears as counter-nature.

Once again, they will cry that the ancient prejudices have disappeared; they will protest against the still vibrant, stubborn belief in such constraints. They will remind us that women were emancipated by two world wars and the necessity for men (by the development of their own civilization) to call their household slaves to participate more and more massively in work to produce, thus removing them from their servitude, including the requirement to please at all costs or be condemned to social death and economic misery.

"To have the woman participate in productive social work, to tear her from domestic slavery, to liberate her from the mind-numbing, humiliating, eternal and exclusive yoke of cooking, cleaning the children's room, that is the principal objective," declared Vladimir Lenin at the beginning of this century. And the United Nations commissions that are preparing for "1975, the year of women," take up, what a surprise, the same language!

Nevertheless, how did the rest of history justify this program?

"Guilty or at least blamed if she chose a career, the married woman and the mother remain guilty; but they are blamed also, now, if they stay at home, where their work is unjustly devalued," says Pierrette Sartin.[11] It is very interesting to see that the first commentary on this subject of evolution concerns yet again the shaming of feminitude. Like my friend, mocked for her onetime elegant appearance after having been mocked so many times for her lack of elegance, it follows that a woman would be brought to this fatalist conclusion: "Guilty as charged, may it be at least for what I prefer."

We will see later that it is highly insufficient to speak of household work as "unjustly devalued" and that work for married women belongs, on the contrary, to invisible, free work that is absolutely indispensable to the edification of paid, visible work call "productive."

Be that as it may, if you compare the situation of working women at the end of the twentieth century to that of the beginning of the same century, progress must seem enormous at first glance. Opportunities are becoming more and more numerous, and no independent career is forbidden, *theoretically*, to women. The victory must seem striking. But has "productive" work reversed the alienation of women in the way that Lenin proposed?

"But work is punishment! Why do you want us to impose that on women?" protested the Spanish men surveyed by Pierrette Sartin.

This folkloric Catholicism (the curse of Adam and Eve) could make us smile. It still contains a naive denunciation of a truth that you only have to open your eyes to see.

Is work, could work be, a liberation when the positions are menial, with no required qualifications and no hope for the future? Could it be liberation when it doubles up with a day of house-work, even if softened by modern machines, and in large cities and urban centers, accompanied by a long haul on public transporta-tion requiring an inhumanly early wake-up time and combined with crippling fatigue even before starting the workday? Is it, could it be, liberating when the mere word "promotion" appears an incongru-ity to the employer when he hears it from a woman?

Discrimination in Work at All Levels

I have said earlier that few sectors open up *in practice* to work for women, even if, *theoretically*, they are all open to her, even if large areas among them have become almost exclusively feminine, such as secretarial positions that today have almost replaced the old fem-inine work of the needle.

In France, one-third of workers are women. Yet in 1968 only 8 percent of executives were women.

Among 303,800 supervisors, there were only 18,000 women. Among 139,000 engineers, only 3 percent were women (rarely admitted in the sector of production, says Sartin).

Out of 371,000 top executives, there are 45,200 women, who earn only around 68–70 percent of what men are paid.

Among lawyers: 19 percent are women. Among physicians: 7 percent. In architecture ... 1 percent. There is one woman in the Court of Audit[12] and one woman in the government as undersecretary. Women do not have access to positions as prefects, inspectors of finance, or diplomatic careers. And this, in spite of the law of October 10, 1946, stating: "No discrimination between the sexes will be allowed in recruiting for positions in the state."

Moreover, it is interesting to note the obscuring of the false promotion of women in countries other than our own: for example, in the USSR, where 75 percent of doctors are women because it is one of the most underappreciated and poorly paid professions since its nationalization. And, concerning medical research, we see how, in the famous novel *Cancer Ward*,[13] a woman who is one of the greatest of her profession is brought down by the most humbling household work. In Québec (as in France) the invasion of the judicial and teaching sectors by women (except in higher education!) signals the drop in prestige of these positions and the fact that men no longer want them.

When you discover how work in a male society treats those privileged with higher-level degrees, there is no reason to be surprised by the continuing scandalous abuses afflicted on others: here, just as in the times of protests by Marx and Lenin, their feminitude reinforced the exploitation of their proletarian condition; their alienation can be measured, in mathematical terms, as "power squared."

The same reactionaries, indignant at seeing Soviet women (who, however, have strong physical bearing) carrying rails on their shoulders, or Chinese women steering locomotives, hardly bat an eye about the fate of data processors who punch 15,000 holes an hour on a machine (and for what salary!) or the electronic fitters who, not knowing how else to use their technical school diplomas, do fine-tuned, close-up work keeping up with required high standards, suffer spectacular nervous fatigue and the rapid degradation of eyesight, as much as the lacemakers of the past; aren't these the "light jobs"? So light that no man wanted them. They do not feel capable of this "high-precision labor" that is so feminine that it generally comes back to women still naive enough to have been trained for embroidery! But these are the worst-paid, often below minimum wage, whereas they demand a visual acuity, a steady hand, a rhythm that only an exceptional man would be capable of. Here is where we come back to a comment by Marx: "The most delicate qualities of her nature are used to exploit her and make her suffer!" It is rather rare to find a man pronouncing the word "nature" in reference to a woman without illustrating the stereotype from the dominant class so that one takes pleasure in quoting, as an aside, that remark.

All this does not prevent women being given the most difficult, the most demanding, the dirtiest jobs in times of labor shortages. There is no mention now of the feminitude so dear to Alain and Nicolas quoted by Fanny Deschamps. Pierrette Sartin tells how, during a visit to a factory in the East, she saw young women who were neither Soviet nor Chinese cutting iron bars and lifting them afterward in packets of several kilos to put them on wagons where men were waiting with idle arms to roll them forward after the women loaded them. The head of the company explained that "no man wanted to do that work" and proclaimed his admiration for the women loudly; but he paid them at the level of unskilled worker, which is the lowest. One of the managers visiting the factory hardly shared the admiration, albeit token, of his colleague; he ended with: "Well, if they weren't doing that, they'd be on the streets."[14]

The government work inspection program either ignores completely these kinds of anecdotes or closes its eyes to them.

Not only are these jobs the most tedious or sometimes the most grueling, very often the most demanding, and detrimental to their health—because data processors can't keep working after ten or twelve years and can't find ways to retrain themselves, and those with fine-tuned, close-up verification work with magnifying glasses see their eyesight weaken so quickly that they have to stop working around thirty years old—but also the salaries everywhere are of such inequality that no number of protest days can have an effect on them. It is true that worker protest days are the actions taken by movements led by men and masculine unions.

However, the Treaty of Rome (which created the common market) decreed an equality of salaries that was ignored everywhere, even in countries with "bourgeois socialism" such as in Scandinavia. But this treaty also planned (article 119), at the same time as protection for feminine salaries, a discrimination unfavorable to women: "That the remuneration accorded for work paid by the hour be the same for the same position" is a principal destined for men to avoid competition from women; their productivity is less than that of men in certain areas, either by an occasional lesser physical strength that automation has not replaced everywhere, or by all the other reasons that they come up with (like the social barrier raised between the sexes according to the differentiation between positions).

Évelyne Sullerot compared hourly wages[15] and discovered that everywhere, except in chemistry, men's salaries were higher by 10 percent. In the United States, while women are paid less than black men, "sexism is greater than racism." In France, during the period of salary adjustments that followed the May '68 movements, they discovered with horror that substantial numbers of workers were paid less than minimum wage; but what they did not publicize, says Sullerot, is that 75 percent of these exploited workers were women! As recently as the end of the last century, in England, women disguised themselves as men in order to be paid twice as much. In what sector? Hard labor? In book binding ...

I don't know the salaries of female workers in Japan today, but in Tokyo in 1946, a female worker in machine precision work was paid three times less than the fourteen-year-old boy who poured water on the machine to keep the gears moistened.

One of the most revealing details of the iniquity that continues to bolster the ideas so convenient to phallocratism is: "A woman's salary, the right salary," the implicit belief so perfectly integrated into the whole of our cultures, that a woman possesses a capital: her body; and that if it is not sold wholesale into the institution of marriage, it should be sold individually into that of prostitution.

Near the beginning of this century, a store owner in Lyon refused an increase in salary sought by the "outdoor saleswomen" (those selling the store's products in stands outside the store), saying: "But you have three feet of pavement at your disposal!"

I'll be accused once again of dredging up the past and trying to apply it today. But in 1966, the manager of a major chain store said to the young saleswomen there: "But you can easily earn more money with customers to make ends meet" (quoted by Sartin, according to an interministerial commission).

These answers maintain, with perfect logic, the male mentality of misogynistic disdain expressed in the responses to the interviews conducted by Fanny Deschamps. Afterward, women can be accused of hysteria and of frigidity, of being eternal crazies, bitches or fanatics, whores or pitiful outcasts, depending on whether they submit to or reject this "morality." If, stepping forward in revolt, they defy their condemnation by provoking this male desire that people from all sides teach them to revere, people will say: "Ah, the bitches, not an ounce of modesty!" If, on the contrary, they are so traumatized as to write to a lonely hearts columnist, the author will respond: "Oh, come now, you'll see that the time when men don't pay any attention to you anymore will come too fast." (Marcelle Ségolène, 1955, and other years.)

Here is how work can "disalienate" the woman. Lenin wanted it to liberate her from housework; it doesn't even free her from prostitution and, perhaps worse yet, from the belief that prostitution is the inevitable structure of her condition, of her feminitude.

What is more, the tension between familial duties and work outside the home continues to be carefully maintained more or less all over where women participate in this famous "productive" work that is considered the sole one, where the other is invisible—and thus free of charge.

In the cases where measures are taken to "lighten women's double burden," so dear to the discourse of legislation of work, they are always only at the level of the profession, and never at the domestic level, because it is, once again, "natural," and the level of work is superfluous and an add-on. Instead of increasing the number of childcare facilities or improving facilities in the home, they prefer to extend maternity leaves, allowing the young woman to leave her job for a year without losing it, moving up retirement to fifty-five years old. All these reforms, just like the false one of "part-time work," treated so enthusiastically by the paternalists, the government representatives, the liberal phallocrats, have no other actual goal than to discourage employers from hiring women and push the women to return home. Let's talk about the compromise solution, given like a miraculous cure, the one-income household; all you have to do is know a little about the realities of the work world to understand that it is just as insufficient to compensate and increase a salary as to remunerate for work in the home; it is to the actual salary what a student's "pocket money" is to a scholarship.

(And, what is more, keep in mind that around 3.5 million days of maternity leave are not taken by those eligible. Why? Because the famous daily amount allowed by the Social Security system and that, it says, "massively strains its budget," is totally insufficient.)

Part-time work, this famous employer trickery, was presented to be in popular demand by a survey conducted by l'INSEE, showing that 900,000 women were ready to accept it. Was that because of the harassing servitude suffered by the proletarian family mother or the civil servant, ready to renounce half of her professional life? Not even! They took care to distribute this survey to women *who had never worked outside the home*, and the published results of the survey made it a point not to share this detail. Instead of being used to alleviate the labor shortage in "periods of high demand," feminine part-time work, on the contrary, has a tendency more and more to be used in zones of underemployment; what's more, it allows the employers a happy substitute for any increase in salary or possibility of promotions, and an escape from other demands by women in the workplace.

As Andrée Michel and Geneviève Texier predicted in 1964:

> Unions as well as women's organizations truly concerned with promoting female workers have denounced the pseudo-advantage of part-time work and warned against its harmful effects. From an economic point of view, admitted even by its supporters, the measure was recommended to remedy a temporary need for labor. As a result, from a professional point of view, part-time work is destined to turn rapidly against the women who benefit from it ... With the planned system, technical school opportunities for women will be even less available. Discrimination by gender in the workplace will increase.[16]

Who would not realize, in recognizing the truth of what I have written here, that these supposed improvements for the lot of the married female worker and the mother are merely aiming at eliminating her as much as possible from the working world in favor of family life, and not at lightening her load of work in the home in order to improve her productivity and chance of promotions at work? These hypocritically humanitarian measures are above all designed to favor the bosses by sparing them from one part of the demands of the working world and employees, their nightmare.

Keeping such a picture in mind, the motive of this body of accusations leveled at women in the workplace becomes completely comprehensible: they are unstable, they miss work a lot, they don't care as much about their profession as men do. You will notice that women, so frequently accused of the faults just mentioned, barely even show emotion when faced with these rebukes and are averse to defending themselves against them. They know only too well what, in reality, this "work" is that they are accused of neglecting by their access or by the period. They don't lose interest in it at all, we must note, in the independent, rural sector, or in the part of the commercial sector where the woman is a supervisor or the manager; there is never a question of absenteeism here. Not only do these sectors inspire a personal interest that hourly paid work cannot supply, but on top of it, it does not pose any unsolvable problems for childcare in the absence of childcare centers or day nurseries. In the other areas, we note as well that the woman has to change her job often, even if this position interests her, when her husband changes his. When does the inverse occur?

It goes without saying that, faced with such a somber picture, one can challenge the participation of women in paid, productive work outside the home. Even more, we can see feminine demands, including in developing countries, aiming at what could appear to be additional slavery, like in Sweden, where women are demanding the right to work at night! Here, we are in complete contradiction with the tendencies of less economically developed countries, tendencies that place an accent more and more on the concepts of Latin culture and Catholicism, and according to which the progress of conditions for the female worker can only be attained through lightening the professional load, never of her family life.

In reality, the most difficult servitude of professional life is, for the majority of women and more and more, considered a line of fire to fight against family, conjugal servitude. It is astounding that this thinking appears in the areas where the work is the most difficult and the worst paid—that is to say, in the world of hard labor.

"Women who work raise their children better because they are more broad-minded," says Madame I, forty-four years old, printing-press worker, to Madeleine Guilbert.[17] "Working women are not as happy, but they are more broad-minded, they understand things better." Madame J., a welder.[18]

Pierrette Sartin cites these two workers:

"When I am arguing with my husband, I can always tell him that I earn as much as he does."

"One day, my husband, banging his fist on the table, told me that he was the boss, that he gave the orders. I responded calmly, without getting angry, that I had a good job, a good salary, and that I didn't need him to support me. That made him think twice."

That is what the outrageous Noël Lamare, an intern with the Paris hospitals, denounces as one of the causes of male impotence and of the end of conjugal harmony: a woman who earns a living—*even at less pay than her husband's*—traumatizes him so severely that he can no longer fulfill his conjugal duties, "virility being an enduring all-important element."[19]

It is invigorating to see that women are dreaming less and less of returning to the home and are starting even to feel guilty if they devote themselves entirely to the household. But we must note something very significant. The remarks quoted above came precisely from the world of the proletariat and would be practically unthinkable in the upper-level domains of work; how many female executives or executive secretaries could tell their husband that they earn as much as he does? The higher up you go on the professional pyramid, the fewer women you find, and proportionately, the more the difference in salary grows. In spite of the inequality of salaries, it is possible, depending on the sector of the industry, that a woman could earn as much as a man; it is less common as soon as the level of the position rises. When people demand salary equality, they often forget that this equality is denied all the more at the upper levels of salaries, honorariums, and professional perks.

"To earn as much as a man, even though I had ten years of experience behind the camera, Ortrud H. confided in me, I had to threaten to take the head technician to court."

When necessary, when the inequality of the work has to justify that of the salary, they invent something:

"In 1967, I learned to film directly on location, out of the studio. 'At any rate, girls can't film on location, a camera is too heavy for them.' General agreement among the men. He said that to me although I am 5'4" and weigh 198 pounds!"[20]

To social and economic discrimination in the professional sphere is added cultural discrimination, that is to say, the reflex of inferiorization, perfectly assimilated by the victim as much as the oppressor, and this at the highest level. In the world of film: one of the rare female filmmakers of our times lived with another filmmaker who was famous; after a few respected but secondary films, she found greater success with a unique film on an audacious subject. Her partner left her after ten years of life together. (Had he read Noël Lamare, and feared for his "virility"?) Now, this woman felt so guilty that she kept the true cause of their breakup a secret until the day when, attending a feminist meeting where they were discussing masculine jealousy when faced with women's success, she finally decided, with extreme emotions, to reveal her secret.

You can't deny it: if economic oppression weighs heavier in the worker and employee sectors, if familial loads constitute one of the most debilitating and abominable servitudes of modern times, in late capitalism as in nascent socialism, guilt imposed by the culture and unconditional ubiquity mars the superior sector much more openly, the sector of advanced studies and independent professions, such that the number of women reaching that point is diminishing, and the economic advantages obtained there are still inferior to the amount or the quality of the corresponding work.

"I had demonstrated talent in the sciences, I was very gifted in math ... On the first exam of the year, I aced it ... When the prof (a woman) handed back the exam, she said: 'What a scandal that a girl got the best grade. And I hope it won't happen again.' And, of course, it never happened again. (There were six girls and fifty-four guys in the class)."[21]

"My sister ... did not succeed on the competitive exam for an elite school that year and asked the prep school permission to repeat the year. The director refused. She said: 'And this other guy [her boyfriend], will he be allowed to repeat?' 'Yes, he will.' My sister: 'Why? I have better grades than he does.' The director: 'Listen, it's an arbitrary decision, that's true, but you two are a couple, and we don't like that. We are going to separate you.' She said: 'But my average is 15/20 and his is only 11/20. If you are just taking the arbitrary stance, go with the law of numbers.' He replied: 'Hum, *you are a girl*. In this case, we are sacrificing the girl. *It is not in our best interest to have girls pass the entrance exam.*'"[22]

"My brother was set back a year in school. For my parents, it was never a question of whether or not he would quit school and work. He continued his studies because he had to have a diploma ... I passed the entrance exam, but I didn't make the cut to continue after the first year. For me, it didn't go over well at all. For my parents, it was obvious that, for me, as a girl, it was different, no need for a diploma; and they found a job for me in the Social Security office."[23]

The famous "collaboration" of women masks a very simple pimping from most of the men in a high position who married a cultivated woman—in spite of Auguste Comte's predictions describing the "intellectual mediocrity" of the female companion. How many illustrious examples of "muses" that are followed today by the spouses, mistresses, or inspirations for the well-known names! They still praise the gentle, discreet, and efficient shadows of our great men. They gladly bring to mind that Madame Berthelot became the scientist's secretary, sacrificing her career as a painter; and that Madame Alain transcribed the philosopher's manuscripts. As for Marie Curie, in my childhood, I heard her dismissed summarily: "She didn't discover anything at all, she just helped Pierre Curie." We still remember Georgette Leblanc writing nearly half of Maurice Maeterlinck's work, under the auspices of "secretary."

Under such conditions, what becomes of the "disalienation" of women through work? It exists as a model, a tendency, of hope, but very little in reality. According to a survey by the National Council of Women of Great Britain, in 1968, only 10 percent of women find economic independence in their work, and only 10 percent find an intellectual and social interest. (It would be interesting to see if there was any overlap between these two groups of 10 percent.)

People will object to my arguments, saying that man himself is most often more alienated than liberated by his work. But we can all observe, after this enumeration of the facts known to all, that the upper sectors where he can disalienate himself are only rarely accessible to women, that they afford to them more limited economic possibilities without any rational justification for this

discrimination—and that, what is more, the load of work in the
home continues to overburden women, even though less so than in
the lower levels. At the base, social oppression grows; at the higher
levels, there is progressive elimination and decreased advantages;
this is how work for women is composed at all levels. And, however,
the disalienation is so relative that all it takes is a slight appearance
for women of today to choose more and more massively this hardship that increases their daily difficulties but gives a new dimension
to their sexual condition.

The law of pleasing is not less imperious in male society of late
capitalism, even if the moralist reproaches aimed at this obligation purported as a choice are more and more restrained, because
they are difficult to support in a society laicized and known for
"consumption." The absurdities found in the works of Henry de
Montherlant, Gioacchino Toesca, Stephen Hecquet, are visibly
"dated." The diatribes against the immoral "kept women" so dear
to our forefathers, including in some socialist texts where they
joined in with the worst antisemitic manifestations (because moralist misogyny, like antisemitism, is "the socialism of imbeciles"),
can only make us burst out in laughter today.[24] However, the contradiction is not entirely suppressed, especially among the working
masses, as is proven by the story in which my friend was an involuntary participant; elegance, refinement, stylishness are immediately
suspected of "whoring around" to the good prole; how could a
woman "afford that on her salary"? Style, "class," the original sin,
signals a woman "born higher up" and exposes the middle-class
working woman to all sorts of insults from her fellow sufferers,
born as they are into misery.

"It just so happens that the friends who were telling me, 'You
need to wear makeup,' were leftists and my buddies; conversely,
my parents said the opposite," says a young girl from the working

class, in *The Book of Women's Oppression.* Why didn't these parents want her to wear makeup? "You have to be *natural.*" They believed in biological nature, like all less-informed people; the leftists, better informed, believed in cultural nature; the young girl alone remained uncertain regarding her own nature! Where was femininity, and where was feminitude? They told her that she needed to seduce boys, that the law said to please; when she was sixteen, her parents wouldn't let her go to the movies with a boy, explaining the dangers to her. "I was completely terrorized." The result: to make yourself ugly to avoid attracting boys. "I began by no longer bathing." This poem follows:

> The woman moves forward, the presentation starts
> On the mirror hurry the spiders
> I can no longer see myself
> I can no longer see if I am a woman or if I am not.

Such is the punishment for the woman who gets caught up in the contradiction between femininity and feminitude, the law of pleasing and the repression of sexual attraction. You can't please everybody and your father ... To be sure, but there are so many fathers. The male society is the father that dominates all others.

"I felt inferior but lived in the guilt of the discovery ... I was always false. I was always preventing myself from being myself out of fear of displeasing, of fear that I wouldn't be liked," said another young girl in this same collective work. "So, I took sides with men, to be men's buddy. I wanted to be a man, I felt like I was sitting across from girls with a guy's brain. I wanted to remain a woman, all the while benefiting from the status of man. I had to become a man in order to exist. But when you fight among the men, it is against women!"

The law of pleasing reinforces the difference that work tends to erase. That was one of the reasons that the moralists from the past brandished to prove that work was the enemy of *femininity*. (Of course, there was no question of feminitude.) But it is hard to speak in verse and prose at the same time. Too bad for the women who are obliged both to seduce and to dedicate themselves to work that will kill their seduction. It is understandable that, with so many contractions, she ends up reacting with a certain amount of fatalism, translated, notably, by the absenteeism so often cited against her in the working world.

The Difference between Work as Prostitution and Prostitution as Work

Work, they still say, is already a prostitution in itself; man sells his body, too. So be it. But he sells it under a form of *activity* and not *function*; according to the criteria of our society, activity is honored as a "natural" expression for the man; a just formula, for once, since man's nature is to transform himself by transforming the outside world. The *function*, on the other hand—that is, what the woman exchanges for money by prostituting herself—was scorned long before Christianity, although in certain cultures, in certain rare cases, she was a religious representative, expressing well the ancient dialectic between the sacred and the profane. The disdain for the feminine function (that only procreation justified) was denounced by more than one author from the Greco-Latin world: "You will come to believe, you women, that you have everything if your loves are going well" (Euripides), joins the insult addressed to one of the young female editors of *Women's Oppression*: "So, everything centers around your ass for you?"[25] But, it is in Hesiod's writings that the accusation is the most modern; the woman doesn't do anything, has nothing to offer but her body, doesn't participate in man's dominance of the world but, to the contrary, shackles him by her vile maneuvers of seduction. (Here, we come back again to the gynophobic Proudhon in his *De la justice dans la révolution et dans l'église*: "Unproductive *by nature, passive, no constructive ambition*, no reason, no justice, and no modesty.") From this very ancient accusation, Herbert Marcuse formulated the most accurate explanation, at the base even of his opposition between the principal of pleasure and the principal of productivity: woman's beauty and the pleasure she promises seem fatal to productivity—that is to say, to work destined to accumulate goods for consumption.[26] We know how much the birth of the Industrial Age, with the Protestantism that expresses it, develops this accusation. However, obligatory seduction remains the law of the most puritan of cultures, and none of them has been able to eliminate entirely the logical consequence of what horrifies them the most: prostitution.

"Prostitution thus acquires this trait that makes of it, first of all, in contrast with a form of marriage that pretends to monopolize all sexual relations," wrote Helmut Schelsky. But this is not contradictory with the fact that many societies both disapprove and sanctify prostitution:

"The American judicial system expresses the condemnation of public opinion without changing the fact that prostitution exists and that it has been adopted as a convention."[27]

Kate Millett, in *The Prostitution Papers: A Candid Dialogue*, minutely dissects the routine, unconscious nature (and with as little significance as a faithless ritual dance), of the American repression against this feminine world of the street; arrests, hearings, prison sentence, or fines, all take place in the indifference of a ceremony of automatons, an indifference in which even the victims participate to a certain extent. Getting picked up, punished, then continuing until the next time are all a part for American prostitutes of these inevitable inconveniences, inconveniences like sleet or ice in agricultural work. And Millett draws the obvious conclusion: "Prostitutes are our political prisoners. They are chastised for having a cunt."

In fact, how do you add "and for selling it" when a study, even superficial, of the so-called condition of feminitude teaches us that the entire male society considers woman's body as an object forming part of its capital? The law of pleasing, even more crushing in a society of consumerism; the very simple and very natural concretization of woman reduced to her appearance that comes up in the responses given to Fanny Deschamps or in the suggestions made by management to the striking saleswomen; the persistent refusal to give consideration to the right to work or to study, for the woman, as a given like that for men; all the examples that I cited earlier show that the idea of the woman sold, either to one man (marriage) or to the male community (the street) *is one of the most resistant mental structures of our society*.

So it is that every woman lives at the edges of this possibility, knows to the depths of her being that the question could come up for her one day—that all her life, prostitution will be an invisible presence, like the paradigm of her condition. The devalorization of the moralist taboos from the past will be one less barrier between this ignominy and her personal destiny; much easier than in the past, the little housewives from the projects will see a solution "to make ends meet" in what the males hypocritically call *the world's oldest profession*; young mothers who are abandoned or with an insufficient monthly allocation, belonging sometimes to upper society or the intellectual elite, won't hesitate to participate in a network of call girls, at the risk of falling prey to blackmail or arrest, of being marked or beaten. (This is not at all in our imagination or an exaggeration; one day, the silence will be broken, and the scandal will erupt.)

Everything in feminitude points toward, if not leads to, this abyss, one of the blackest of the human condition. The crime of receptiveness, the price for being malleable, for being this hollow mold for the nonwoman, that is what the system of consumerism-production chastises immediately by the tacit incentive of creating a way of escaping work from such a handicap; and even when the worst kinds of work are preferred to it, its possibility will always be present as a form of mockery and an anathema: *"Well, if they didn't do that, they'd be working the streets!"*

Thus, it is not only the ploy of underpaid work that makes the social fact of prostitution present in the heart of feminitude; it is found everywhere, including for those of the privileged bour-geoisie, of the most esteemed intellectual, of the most respected mother, nuns, lesbians; the curse of this possibility that so many factors render probable raises its head to each woman as a second original sin. Even old age won't save her; those taking part in a medical visit for prostitutes observed, to their great astonishment, an enormous proportion of elderly, very elderly, women came to the visits. ("How do you expect me to live with what the state gives me: 90,000 old francs every three months?"[28] That is what one of them asked me.) So we know that neither status at birth, nor principles, nor work, nor merit, nor intellectual qualities, nor even erotic differences can save a woman from this sine qua non condi-tion; suicide—or murder, as in the recent crime of young female hitchhikers—can be the last shield against this menace that is never completely removed from a woman's life.

If the great majority of women die without having known this degradation, every one of them has been reminded all throughout her life or at certain moments that she could fall prey to it. "Whore!" is the first insult that comes to a man's mind when fighting with a woman; afterward, that justifies the punches. Those most concerned are obviously those who already know, as salaried employees, what it is to sell themselves at work; forced to sell to a manager as demanding as Alain or Nicolas the sight of their smile, their hairdo, their skirt brushing against him, or their sparkling nails and discreet perfume to the store's clients (whether or not they have "three feet of the street"). There are very few professions open to women where they don't have to sell themselves in effigy, even if they resist the call to sell themselves directly in the flesh. Will this refusal even be possible tomorrow? What stroke of luck might divest her of this lesser evil, "imaginary prostitution"? At any rate, there is no talent, no flattering distinction that shelters her definitively; in Emily Brontë, in Marie Curie, in Simone de Beauvoir existed an eventual prostitute. All the more so for every "ordinary" woman, that is to say, less irreverent than those who dared to be somebody, although being a woman; if torture begins with familiarity, it is in respect for the system that the whore begins. Sartre expressed strongly, by the title of his play *La putain respectueuse* (*The Respectful Prostitute*), the link between prostitution and deference.

These women are chastised to denounce the contradiction of the male society that models more or less all women in their image but, however, forbids them to be so without an alibi, without justification, without ambivalence. That is why they can only be condemned in order to be freed, and freed in order to be condemned. No absenteeism in this profession! Kate Millett was right: whores, our death masks, are also our political prisoners.

Rape

A Crowd Movement

On May 13, 1972, when the working group dedicated to the question declared, from the stage of the convention "Denouncing Crimes against Women," to the general assembly:

"What woman here does not live in fear of rape?"

There were some objections, protests.

It is rather remarkable that feminism began with lofty demands to come, so late, to the most humbly primordial questions.

The female theorists of the French Revolution claimed the right to be considered as free and equal beings, worthy of participating directly in the working of the state; before them, at a time when the word "feminism" did not exist yet, the privileged classes demanded access to studies and creative arts; in the nineteenth century came petitions and struggles for legal rights, family issues, universal suffrage, then the basic and insignificant question of salary equity. We had to wait until near the end of the twentieth century for this fully fledged human being, after having called for education, citizenship, work, and paid wages, to decide to call for the right not to become pregnant against her wishes, then to no longer be raped.[1]

The emotional reaction from this feminine public showed how unpleasant it is to be brought back to the beginning of the struggle after such a long journey.

Our manner of thinking, our indoctrination into common culture by the mass media, makes us react to the word "rape" just as to the word "prostitution" with the remarks: "That doesn't concern me, cannot concern me, it's other women's problem." Undoubtedly, it's the same tropism that protects us from all disasters: only others die. But in our case, for us, there is something else going on. This reaction is more one of class. Aren't prostitutes only the poor, rootless, classless, those fallen into extreme poverty, with little intelligence, "infantile, immature" (psychotherapy's words for the problem)? Only girls in the slums are raped, children of alcoholic farm workers, occasional victims of a sadist, kids in the projects filled with gangs. At any rate, laws are there to punish, to quash. Few women know this very simple legal distinction that contains the most cruelly camouflaged implicit menace:

It is only a question of *rape* if she is a virgin; a woman can only lodge a complaint for having suffered *aggression*.

Even in the case of rape, when the habit was ongoing "for a certain time" and not a onetime, horrible accident, it is significative to see what the law takes into consideration and its expectations. We remember that, in the case of Violette Nozières, the bourgeois justice preferred to blame the victim. That was in 1934, when women did not even have the right to vote.

The Rape of Chantal

Here is a more recent example:

Excerpts from the information logs of the police in Champagne:

Chantal, raped by her father from nine to fifteen years old. Now twenty years old, she is in a supervised home. It was she who lodged the complaint against her father.

Apart from these accusations made against the father, he is

—an excellent husband,

—a brave soldier,

—an honest man,

—a good worker,

—a true member of the working class,

—an upstanding man with good morals,

he is honest, courageous, loyal, faithful, so very generous, and a handsome man on top of it all.

The loss of parental rights does not seem applicable as the father admitted to his acts.

Excerpts from the psychological exams for the young girl: "She presents traces of inhibition and withdrawal, tendencies of depression poorly compensated for by instances of oppositional, emotionally disturbed behavior."[2]

"Political" Rape

Rape can be used as a weapon, like an instrument of torture, for political ends. Recently, an issue of *Charlie Hebdo* proposed having new female soldiers raped by conscientious objectors. No longer a fantasy but, rather, put into practice, was the rape in Issy-les-Moulineaux on July 14, 1972:

About fifty fascists wearing helmets and armed with iron bars invaded the weekend dance of thirty families, most of them Yugoslavian and Algerian, squatters in the abandoned, run-down buildings of the area. A huge brawl followed. The attackers dragged two women into their car: one, a very young girl; the other, around thirty, a teacher. They took them to woods near Versailles and undressed them; they stopped at feeling up the minor, and they taught the other three times "what power there is at the end of a phallus."

Abandoned, then picked up by a hitchhiker, the two victims lodged a complaint immediately. The teacher reported her wounds, her head that had to be bandaged because she had been knocked out, her clothes in shreds, and the quantity of sperm with which she was filled. The report was completed grudgingly by the attending physician. He even declared:

"Sperm doesn't prove anything. How do we know that it wasn't your own little buddy who did that to you?"

And the cop who took her complaint:

"You had no business *hanging out* in such a place."

About ten years ago, I was a witness to a case of assault and battery in which the victim was a young Algerian secretary who had already been stalked for some time by an Algerian; she entered a café where he was at around 3 a.m. after attending a play with friends. I heard the presiding judge ask the thirty-two-year-old "girl," who had just been on leave from work for three days due to her wounds:

"Don't you think, my child, that you should have been in bed at that time of night?"

Such examples make us not find too excessive the theory that women are raped with the complicity of *all* men.

"They say that:

at any rate, we asked for it

we were reckless

we shouldn't go out with men we don't know

we provoked them

we were complicit

we didn't deserve any better

let this serve as a lesson.

we shouldn't go out without a protector."[3]

This last remark makes me think of the passage from a novel by Panait Istrati, *Domnitza de Snagov* (1926), in which a passerby is surprised to see a couple of Romani alone on the side of the road; the same surprise as for horses or cows unleashed in the open. In the former Romania, the Romani were slaves. So, what is thus expressed on the level of the species, at some time in history, is formulated or afflicted on the individual woman.

"When two girls are walking together: 'So, you're alone?'"

"Three girls out together: 'So, you're alone?'"

"Four, five, etc. girls out together: 'So, you're alone?'"

"How many of us does it take not to be called alone?"[4]

From the courtly proposition to accompany us, up to rape, the same process of the male society raises its head: to make woman comply with the law, gently or forcefully. The law that is: the woman without a man (and not *this* woman, or three, four, ten others) is ALONE.

(Man without a woman, he is *free*. Who would rape him?)

"It goes without saying that every little girl has to be raped, actually or symbolically, to be in compliance with the law."[5]

It is through the explanation of this condition, "actually or symbolically," that the response to the reaction of disbelief on May 13, 1972, roots its answer.

Few women, in fact, are literally, physically, raped in the strict sense of the word, and as reported in the news. This relative safety prevents them from fathoming the symbolic rape that they all undergo throughout their lives, except for very rare exceptions, and rape in the form of presence and menace (fantasies, ritual precautions, the always open possibility) that constitutes, at the heart of her condition, the very idea of rape.

A Subtle Distinction of Justice

It goes without saying that we reject the hypocritical distinction of French law: whether the hymen has been broken or not, a woman is always raped when she is taken by force, without her permission, and suffers the same outrage to her dignity as a human being as a political prisoner forced under torture to give information or to act against his will.[6]

Apart from this tragic extreme, the only one recognized as permissible by the law, with all the ill will that accompanies it, shown by the many examples I have cited, we still remind women of the countless symbolic "mini rapes" that they suffer day after day. The guy who follows you, the guy with the insults whom you can't get rid of, the guy next to you in the cinema who makes you change your seat, because few women choose to provoke a public showdown of which the results are uncertain, and most of the time unpleasant for her; the sex maniac on the phone, in the hallway, in the street; and, like in the case of the secretary I know, the pimp, the customer in the same café who harasses and threatens; the supervisor or the manager with the rights to sexual harassment; all these examples belong to the daily feminine condition. They are complicated further by a certain "leftist solution," when the rejected man shouts xenophobia or racism against Arabs or blacks.[7] In the time

following May '68, a group of female students answered fellow pro-
testers who asked them to stop their sexual racism regarding their
Arab comrades in the following way: "There is no reason why we
should be objects of consumption for them, not any more than for
you or for anybody else."[8]

These direct affronts, this harassment, these constant attacks
resembling a war between the sexes justify the mental state of "fear
of rape" and contribute to inciting the woman alone, the unmarried
woman, the free woman, to return to the ranks and submit to the
law. For the average woman, a guy is first of all somebody who
helps you live (who "makes you live" seems too ambitious, already,
for our times) and keeps you from being "bothered in the street";
for the average man, a wife is first of all somebody "who cleans the
house and all that stuff" (typical expression).[9] For the man, marriage is a simplification; for the woman, a wall of protection. All of
society constructs, by its complicity, the fatal mechanism that leads
them to this pitiful concept. The woman: she who saves the man
from chores and masturbation. The man: he who saves the woman
from being raped by all the others.

Virtual Rape and Threat

Rape as a threat or actual act pushed enraged women, in different
countries, to organize defense commandos. Members of the color-
ful Dolle Mina group in Holland follow girls alone in the streets
and beat up attackers. British women in feminist movements organized judo and karate lessons. The MLF[10] in France is considering
similar measures.

But these means of struggle remain at the level of reform. It isn't
even conceivable to demand stricter laws against the abuses of male
power, because the issue is to destroy male power itself. "Rape is

merely acting out a daily ideological reality."[11] Countries that, like the United States, tried to react on the judicial level only brought down greater sexual misery and thus an increased incitement for sexual violence against women. These last few years, in the streets of Paris and public places, there was a male vagrant, particularly unkempt and repulsive, acting like he was going to throw an enormous puppet marionette in the form of a rat on women, bringing about screams, fainting sometimes, always a huge stir and sensations that ended inevitably in great bursts of laughter. Watching the man as he was doing this was instructive: he was foaming at the mouth and squinting, cross-eyed, giving all the signs of intense sexual pleasure. After his "little joke show," he passed the hat around. Some outraged people talked about locking him up, having him committed. "Only in Paris are such things tolerated!" Another person responded: "But don't you think that it is precisely because of such tolerance that Paris is the capital city with the lowest number of sexual crimes?" He was certainly right. It was certainly much better for the rat thrower to continue his exploits than to turn into Jack the Ripper. It seems appropriate to judge a society by that even, a society that has the choice only between these two ways out of sexual misery and misogynistic discourse.

"How can you know if the rape is real?" asked several opponents to a proposed law, in 1971, legalizing abortion for raped women. That is truly the extreme height of feminitude: guilt by suspicion. Many women, the majority perhaps, refuse to report a rape out of fear of this suspicion. To hear remarks like those leveled at the young teacher, still trembling, her head bandaged and her clothes ripped, next to a young girl in tears—that is an ordeal that seems too much like a second rape to the victims of the first.

Nature or Law?

"Rape doesn't exist.

"They say that it's nature.

"We say that it's the law.

"Rape exists in reality. By the father, by the brother, rape of young girls who don't dare to speak. (Brigitte, fifteen and a half years old, attempted suicide. She couldn't endure being raped by her brother.) Rape, in any case, exists in women's heads as fear, as dread. It exists in men's heads as a right."[12]

Now we arrive at the heart of the problem:

Rape, as virtual reality at the heart of feminitude. Just like prostitution.

The man proposes a roll in the hay to a woman. The law implies that a woman is always consenting "in principle." If, *in fact*, she is not, it is because it's not the right time or because the man is pathetic. The result is that the rejected man takes this refusal as an affront, just as he refuses the idea that the affront is actually for the woman having to suffer hearing this kind of offer (on the contrary: it is a tribute). An affront makes him furious. The insolent woman is, one more time, accountable. Why not, seeing forced on her what was offered so graciously?

"A man is a being who commands and, if need be, who imposes his command," stated Noël Lamare, the doctor quoted earlier, on the subject of man's virility and its manifestation, when questioned.[13]

Perfectly conscious of this belief that man holds of rape: a right, woman is already warned of this idea, before having the least experience of its reality. Rape exists in her as a state of anguish, like an invisible Sword of Damocles hanging over her head. The structure of the male society repeats to her that she is complicit, provocative, that she *should* provoke; sometimes she gives in and actively reproduces the seduction that she is supposed to endure passively, with the hope of escaping it; it's the famous "forging ahead," "running out to meet the enemy," by the soldier dying of fear, frequent behavior in adolescence; but most often, she seeks to avoid, to shield herself; prudent, worried, fearful, suspicious (the "gotta watch out, gotta watch out," espoused by Zazie), she would rather deprive herself of meaning and freeze in her steps than run to her downfall; she mutilates herself from the joy of her sexual organs and protects the amputated body fiercely, this body that in the end is no longer hers. Apparently submissive, these numerous women confront the male order with a long and hard and wretched resistance; they could repeat the poem given by the authors to the feminist meeting of May 13 as the summary of the work group:

> *Frigid ones*, we are saying that the void is not made to be filled,
> *Deaf ones*, we are saying that the word is not made to seduce and
>   order around,
> *Paralyzed ones*, we are saying that the march is not meant for
>   shuffling about,
> To move today from silent resistance, solitary and painful for our
>   bodies
> To united struggle, speaking out loud and joyful for all of us.[14]

If it is true that, as these women said in their text (and in the publication of their text, these words were written in capital letters), "There is always an unavoidable moment in women's lives when they are taken by force,"[15] it is because their lives are inevitably at a disadvantage when "anatomy is destiny": not a "natural" law but a concerted effort—thus law, in a human society where the male dominates.

With Each Woman, It Is Humanity as a Whole That He Is Raping

The effects of these efforts are the most serious and long-lasting; they seem sometimes to have no rapport with rape, potential or real, as the effects move away in time. Because any human male who rapes a woman, his own kind and his sister in the species, demeans the entire species; finally, he rapes humanity, of which he bears the image himself and which he defiles by his own hand, as in murder.

Man rapes the woman. But he rapes man: the one that he debases today, the one whose arrival he delays. It is himself, in the end, that he rapes: his work, the society coming from his own hands. Exactly the same as in murder-assassination or war, he destroys it.

The most complete rape, in the condition of feminitude, is not in reported current events or sexual harassment; it is found in the obligation commanded to the woman to live sexually against her will, to be a mother against her will—or to not be one when she is dying of desire to be one; the most encrusted, the most serious, the most accepted because the most rooted in time, is the appropriation by the male of human procreation, of his dominating power over contraception and his ban on abortion.

This aspect that is part of feminitude will be studied in the second part, intended to show the necessity of moving beyond the idea of revolution and coming to that of mutation.

FROM REVOLUTION
TO MUTATION

Ah! Race of Abel, your carcass
Will fertilize the steaming soil!
　　　　　—Charles Baudelaire

No woman is required to build
the world by destroying herself.
　　　　　—Rabbi Moses Sofer

The Stress of the Rat

Exponential Demographic Growth

One of the two most serious dangers weighing on our humanity is the current rate of population growth. The other, which is parallel to the first, is the destruction of the environment. I will come back to this point in my conclusions regarding the necessity to create an "ecofeminism."

In *Birth Control in the Modern World*,[1] Elizabeth Draper traces the historic curve of demography. According to a rate completely demonic since 1650 (in spite of the extermination of wars), the earth will have doubled its population in thirty-five years. "A population of six billion expected by the year 2000 constitutes a modest forecast."[2]

Some have dared to postulate, in spite of the Vatican's commands, that to maintain the sacralization of the obligatory function of motherhood was becoming a very bad and very dangerous joke.

But this increase in birth rate is not the same, obviously, all over the world; far from it. Whereas India is overpopulated, East Germany is reduced to pardoning Nazis and establishing a zone of surveillance to protect against the escape of the "most precious capital," man. But above all, while the countryside is deserted and entire villages collapse around their polluted rivers, full of dead fish, urban concentration produced in the metropoles, after the "inconveniences" of the beginning of the century, constitutes such a worsening of life conditions that we can talk about catastrophe with no hesitation at all.

The rise in the number of physical and psychological illnesses is one of the first consequences. In France, cases of cancer, more abundant in cities, increased from 3,316 cases in 1943 to 9,144 in 1963, and the numbers continue to grow. In England, there are two times more deaths from lung cancer in the city than in the country-side. And the acceleration of other respiratory illnesses is soaring. The number of deaths from emphysema *doubles every five years*. The Western world seems more privileged than other regions: in the summer, in 1972, in New York, people are dying in the street and begging for rain just like the most "primitive" sons of the Ubangi; we know that in Tokyo, "in 1980 every inhabitant will have to wear a gas mask."

Next to these alarming observations, we are watching an equally high rate of growth in the most serious mental illnesses, particularly in paranoia, and the most aggressive and dangerous psychopathologies. It was the Marquis de Sade who said, among many other extraordinary scientific predictions, that the murders and predilections toward torture of his sinister characters would grow exponentially in future ages with the growth of urban con-centrations (he said "with the number of inhabitants in the large cities"). A simple look at the current status in New York, where every subway car, after a certain hour, carries an armed cop, is enough to believe Sade; and the American film *Little Murders* that deals with this situation would certainly not be renounced by Sade, author of *Juliette, or Vice Amply Rewarded*.

A scientist named John Calhoun in Maryland in 1958 piled white Norwegian rats into a barn. They observed that the rats' behavior differed greatly as a direct result of the growth in numbers. All the traits combined of this new behavior reminded the observers of the defensive behavior in high concentrations of inhabitants in urban centers. A particularly significant fact for us: the females, in growing numbers, destroyed their nests and refused to mate.[3]

Paul Leyhausen, a German ethnologist, drew sociological conclusions from the Calhoun experiment. He reminds us that among the ten most frequent causes of death following urban crowding is suicide. And he added that madness surrounds man divorcing his surroundings, under all forms and characteristics, ranging from depression to psychosis, juvenile delinquency, and alcoholism (this last plague currently growing in the USSR). *Actuel* in October 1971 declared, after having noted the studies by Calhoun and Leyhausen: "You know enough to realize that the Apocalypse is not necessarily a figment of our imagination."

In Number 12 of *Tout*, already quoted here, an article referred to the same studies on the white rat and made the following comment on their significance: "And is it possible that women, in their current campaigns for free access to contraception and the right to abortion, are translating the quest for the human race for survival that only a decrease in birth rate can assure?"

This apparent paradox represents a profound truth. The ones that backward Catholics blame for "selfishness" prove, on the contrary, to be the best and most supreme defenders of procreation with a tendency to suffocate itself, like the beached whale asphyxiated by its own weight. But this demand that jeopardizes the oldest right of the patriarchy, the possession of procreation by the male, butts up against a phallocratic barricade: religious in the bourgeois camp, ideological in the socialist camp.

Race of Abel, love, pullulate
Even your gold has progeny.
Race of Cain, with the burning heart
Beware of these intense desires.
—Charles Baudelaire

There is a way to stop these devastations without allowing the freedom of abortion or increasing access to contraception, the 1957 Stalinists declared for a long time, Jeannette Vermeersch first among them; we need to give all women "the possibility of being a mother"—that is to say, give them a place to live, to attend to their well-being, and a job, and all that comes with it. In this case, they say, abortion will remain only a bad remedy to a catastrophic situation; *women would no longer have any reason to refuse motherhood!* But the birth rate? Here, the communists (who agree to abortions to a certain extent but distrust contraception) mark a prudent silence; through this silence, we hear the tacit agreement with the left: easily accessible contraception will suffice to put an end to rampant population growth. But isn't contraception women's right, to control their own bodies? Oh, but if it becomes widespread and free enough to become a true danger! ...

Contradiction upon contradiction.

Contraception: 63 percent of women having had abortions admit that they didn't know it existed. Only 10 percent of French women use it.
—Editorial in *Guérir*, November 1971

Currently, 5 percent of French women have access to contraception.
—Dr. Peyret, quoted by Noël Bayon, *Guérir*, same issue

Six percent of French women have access to contraception.
>   —*The White Book on Abortion*, *Nouvel Observateur*, 1971

>   Race of Cain, cross and pullulate,
>   Your gold no longer procreates.

Let's pick the communists' torch back up, like those before us, along with Jeannette Vermeersch, held theirs up, the Catholics Paul Chauchard and Jérôme Lejeune, pioneers of Nestlé and the "right to life" movement (and let's end with "so that they can kill us") who declared this most pious wish: "to practice a *large* family political policy." Namely: abolish injustice, slums, malnutrition, the staggering slave labor of the mother overloaded with childcare ... Ah! There you have it, the perfect solution. The only way of refusing freedom of abortion!

The sad thing is that this solution would require, precisely, the revolution that those currently in power know would be their downfall, since they still refuse the right to abortion and liberal distribution of contraception, *that they need more and more urgently*, out of the sole fear of this hideous specter, a specter of which abortion itself, along with the liberation of sex, would be merely a precursory firestorm. Hence the immense mess in which we are all struggling in unison, oppressors and oppressed.

Besides, even given a kind of capitalism that is "bourgeois socialism," like in Scandinavia, that would establish an equilibrium between the well-being and the sexual freedom of workers, on the one hand—a solution absolutely impossible in our regions with a totally different, traditional capitalism—the number one question would not be resolved, because the birth rate would not lower at all with such a system. We observed this in the case of the white rats, blessed with all the "well-being." What's more, this touching and idealist solution to which the Stalinist communists and backward Catholics clung at different times does not take into consideration, like all the solutions proposed by these kinds of politicians, the multiple reasons that would push a woman to refuse motherhood, beyond the ones that are always put out first: lack of housing, poor health, material difficulties. More or less as if all women were livestock for which the only valid right, the only demand granted, would be to have a good pasture; a clean, ventilated stable; a shining coat; and an attentive veterinarian. Given all that, what perversion would make them refuse to give the farmer as many calves as their generous flanks and their constantly hot vulva could produce?

Meanwhile, we are verging on a worldwide catastrophe, thanks to the exclusive propriety and use of human fertility by the male society.

What would the birth rate have become in the hands of a female power—or, quite simply, shared by the two sexes? The very serious current danger would not exist.

Solely One Responsible: Male Power

Even under male reign, the woman has always had fewer children than man wanted to inflict upon her. Contraception, far from being a recent discovery, has always been used by women, sometimes imaginatively, sometimes dangerously: Soranus of Ephesus and Saint Jerome were the first to warn of the dangers of the recipes used. Male history only mentions amulets for "fertilization"; women, however, knew others: French women secretly carried salamanders; German women, a weasel's testicle; English women, rosemary and myrtle; and they did this up to the nineteenth century. Stones were also very popular; once again, in the male version of history, they only speak of potions and love charms, but the secret chronicles of women speak of "the stone to keep your husband away from your bed." Jasper was considered contraception in Japan; the emerald very prized in medieval Europe. Still other rituals: Albert the Great, for whom the Place Maubert in Paris is named, tells of a legend saying that if a woman spits three times into the mouth of a toad, she won't become pregnant throughout the year. In Japan: eat dead bees; walk over a cadaver. In North Africa, the Muslim woman must wrap a verse of the Koran around her waist.

Medical methods joined these purely superstitious methods. Drinking very hot tea made from the bark of the willow tree was as popular in ancient times, before "the pill," as was drinking quinine. Other ingredients were recommended, and among the most respected were the following: the slobber of a camel in Asia Minor; an egg yolk, plantains, a leaf from a walnut tree in Northern Europe; cannon powder in Russia, a pill of oil and mercury.

In 1856, in Cincinnati, Ohio, an American, Soule, discovered the means for preventing ovulation, using an empirical Indian contraception. *We had to wait until 1950* for the sociologist Norman Himes from this same America to take up the question where it had been left: a striking proof that the problem of overpopulation is obviously due to the will of the male society.

At the beginnings of civilization, the science of the Hebrews had already discovered the days of the fertility cycle of women; this knowledge only served to guarantee and increase fertility. It was not until 1955 that doctors in Massachusetts started their research on developing the contraceptive pill.

Up until the most recent times, methods of contraception were limited to the practice of coitus interruptus and the use of male condoms, which appeared in the eighteenth century. Even though the first condom mentioned in history was the type for women, according to the legend of Minos and Pasiphaë in the text by

Antoninus Liberalis, and that we find a brief mention of a "rubber skin sack" in the works of Madame de Sévigné, the creation and the commercialization of condoms could only be made according to a masculine type. For a long time, there was no issue of avoiding procreation but only of contamination; and the eighteenth-century Englishman Daniel Turner found "this armor against love" so distasteful that he preferred to run the risk of catching syphilis. It goes without saying that husbands would never have dreamed of using them with their wives. In the case of condoms and of coitus interruptus, at any rate, the woman had to trust her partner and to believe implicitly in his self-control, his good faith, his sobriety even.

When the first biochemical contraceptives appeared, as unreliable as they were, they were not for sale in Roman Catholic countries, except for Gynamide, which had a success rate of only one woman out of two; yet, in 1955, I had to make a scene in order to get it in a particular pharmacy in the country (that liberally sold male condoms as soon as they opened in the morning). The social structures made themselves obvious: fertility was *a man's business*; free for him to impose or to refuse. The French elected officials, warned to take measures to control the alarming increase in birth rates, could have answered in all good faith that male citizens only had as many children as they wanted; for the others, the females, what did their opinion matter? To what use on this subject would they put their ballot, the right to vote granted in 1945 (only then, finally)? There was no proposed law, no changes in laws; no member of parliament, male or female, included it in their platform. Even better: Charles de Gaulle, like Philippe Pétain before him, like Michel Debré today, implored France to have more children!

The Church, great enemy of contraception and abortion, didn't always show such a rigid attitude; just as people believe that birth control is a modern problem, even though we see that traditional methods, oral and mechanical, existed since the most ancient antiquity; just as people think that the Church has always applied the fanatical precept of procreation, by virtue of Judaic morals that Christianity follows. Just as we had to wait for the Council of Trent to make marriage a sacrament (all the while repeating the ban on anybody who judged it superior to celibacy, even secular); just as the date when abortion became a crime is 1588, twenty-eight years after this very Council of Trent, by the virtue of Pope Sixtus V. Up to that time, the Church couldn't logically forbid the practice before the third month of life of the embryo, since that was the moment it became gifted with a soul (with the difference according to the sex in obvious favor of the male fetus, according to Saint Augustine). That was, besides, in direct relation with the teachings of Hippocrates, who granted life to the same fetus from the third month. That a precept aiming to increase the numbers of the faithful in a century when the total population of the earth did not attain that of present-day China is still in force today when the planet is overflowing, that's the absurdity that the current pope expects to maintain among the hundreds of millions of followers.

Make babies,
  don't make love.
  —Pope Paul VI
  (American humor column)

"Ah, two are not enough for you, I'll give you a third one, bitch!"
  —Remark shouted by a man from Auvergne beating
  his pregnant wife, who had just talked to her lesbian
  friend. The third child has been born today.

Strange thing when we examine the behavior of the two sexes in relation to procreation: to a great majority, women love children, significantly more than men do. Frequently, even, the child becomes an accomplice for the woman against the man, in the community of the same oppression. The man wants to prolong himself, but instinctually, he doesn't like what prolongs him; on the contrary, he distrusts it and is jealous of it. The Oedipal complex should be called the Laertes complex: it is the man-king who sees a rival in his son (he takes the love of the woman) and a future assassin (he represents, through his youth, old age and the death of the father).[4] The most certain indication of a feminine importance in any society, as ethnologists know well, is the favorable status of the child. The more a society is phallocratic, the more the child and youth are treated badly, in the declared goal of making "men" of them. (In the case of a girl, it is often the mother who avidly seizes the motives of repressing her daughter as much as she was oppressed herself.) "To raise a child," said Sartre, "is to make an adult through violence. There is no such thing as a good father, it is the link of paternity that is decayed."

> The opposition against women is the first rule that helps men of God assuage their conscience for being the army of the Father.
>
> —Carla Lonzi, *Let's Spit on Hegel* (Italian feminist manifesto)[5]

Now, of the two sexes, *it is the one who loves the child the least that imposes it on the other*. Women's bodies, more infinite than nature, grew and multiplied while those of the earth withered slowly under the phallus-plow, the compression rolling pin, and the poison of chemical coating. The male has triumphed, but from the principle of *death*.

There are many reasons for man to want to procreate. To prolong his lineage through sons is the first of the most ancient male dreams; there is also the need to reign over those who are younger and weaker and depend on you, a doubling up of the satisfaction that the phallocrat draws from the woman-spouse; but in the cultures of the past and up to this day still, among the working classes, in the countryside above all, it is a question of chaining the woman to her own species, of "preventing her from running," to make her feel concretely her weight as an animal, an inferior. "To seize her by the heel, she who walked so lightly on the water," says Virginia Woolf about one of her female protagonists (*Jacob's Room*).

> Humanity has reproduced itself enough, now it must unite.
>
> —Leo Tolstoy

The hateful declaration of the man from Auvergne ("I'll give you a third!") is not an extreme case. They *inflict* a child on a woman; that'll teach her to be a woman. The author of this text heard the same words of triumphant phallocratism, in the harshest terms, from the father to his son. Such is the attitude of supremacy. Reproduction, in so many cases of this male culture, is the opposite of uniting.

The man in the patriarchal system is thus, first and foremost, responsible for the insane birth rate, just as he is for the destruction of the environment and for accelerated pollution that coincides with this insanity to render a planet unlivable for what prolongs it.

"The feminist movement is not international, it is planetary," says *Let's Spit on Hegel* by Carla Lonzi.[6]

Thus, it is urgent to transfer power, then, as quickly as possible, to destroy power.

The transfer must be made from phallocratic man, responsible for this sexist civilization, to women, awakened to the disasters.

Because, as we have seen, without hesitation, we can determine that man is responsible for the current lamentable demographic situation, and not only male power: man at all levels. For each woman from a Christian family who persists in using the Ogino method,[7] we find ten other women who, as reactionary as they may be on the sexual level, demand, at a minimum, greater access to therapeutic abortions and to methods of contraception. We read in *Elle*, which is not a wildly progressive weekly, the following statement after the announcement of papal positions: "I am a Catholic and I don't agree with him." As persistent as is the resistance of the Catholic Church that, in France, counts a significant feminine clientele, even the least courageous women have a tendency to seek information, and even to revolt on occasion, if they benefit from a minimum of social standing when it is a question of their bodies and their command of the future.

We are talking about French women here. The picture would vary in addressing other countries. American and British women are much more determined in their demands for total sexual freedom; but, in addition, Americans are exploding with rage regarding their access to hiring and their position in the workplace. Spanish and South American women keep silent in the countries where abortion is often impossible even to save the life of the mother; we don't know the number of clandestine abortions, undoubtedly impressively high if we can judge even just from Italy. But, in a general manner, feminine opinion, in Europe or in America, is sensitized in the extreme on the subject of contraception and abortion. The idea of limiting the number of births has *always* been an obsession for women. Whatever the weight represented by the excessive birth rate for a father or for a nation, it is never, by far, felt as it is for the feminine Atlas, this weak body that carries the entire weight of the world.

That the Catholic Church, where women are excluded from the priesthood, is the principal obstacle to the reevaluation of abortion shows well that it is a problem for men. That those who officially have neither a sexual life nor children are put in charge of controlling and directing not only sexual relations but even the fertilization of ordinary people isn't even a scandal in our modern millenary culture; it suffices that these persons are men. The pope decides *ex cathedra*; the priests apply his will; except for this part of religious humanity, the rest of the world will refer to people who are often the faithful followers, or who are not, and who lead a sexual life, have children. But, legislators, judges, doctors—always men.[8] Men didn't start to take an interest in the problem of birth rates, just like for the destruction of the planet, until the moment when the situation became catastrophic, virtually desperate.

Perhaps people will disagree with me when I say that, in this case, all the ills of our society are of masculine origin, since masculinity is the very essence of this society: why put the blame on one rather than on the other? Basically, that's true; but it merits some nuances, and important ones. On the one hand, the worst negative actions by women are due to men who formed and molded them according to their customs and desires, without a doubt. On the other hand, some of these negative tendencies can be maintained in them—just as in oppressed categories, when the culture evolves, the worst reactionaries, the oppressor's accomplices—even against the evolution of the male attitude. Let's look at an example: in modern attempts to emancipate sex, as modest as they may be, since total emancipation can only happen with the revolution, the most determined adversaries to this change are feminine masses. (Just as, in the past, the strongest protests against state family allowances came from the elderly underclass, those who had raised their families without the help of the government.) The slowing of the progress of sex education and information sharing, of prescribing the pill to minors, the greatest endorsement for the continuing repression of homosexuals—these negative tendencies came from a feminine majority. They continue to defend the oppressor's morals even at the moment when he starts to doubt them. On the other hand, once a woman becomes aware, just one time in her life, nothing can stop her.

The Mutants: Marginal People and Women

At the current time, women are the only category who can lead the oppositional minorities, since they are the only majority to be treated as a minority.

> The reappearance of woman has introduced a possibility for youth to live marginally and to show its will to begin again from scratch, in all possible ways, destructive, but pacifist.
>
> —*Let's Spit on Hegel*[9]

It is necessary, today, that the spirit of the revolution to come surpass what was called up to now the "revolutionary spirit," as much as it surpassed reformism. In fact, it is no longer a revolution that we need but a mutation, in order to resolve a global problem of which the demographic menace is only one of the extreme aspects, although undoubtedly the most urgent.

Regarding Abortion

A Question

The Manifesto of the 343[1] was the ballistic missile that propelled the new feminism to the forefront, that of the Women's Liberation Movement (MLF). Since this campaign started, we have been able to ask this question:

Multiple demands are being forwarded today, thanks to women's awakening of consciousness; there are so many choices: on the professional, wage, social, and political levels, they are treated as subordinates, relegated to the lowest zones, blocked for promotions —in a word, disadvantaged everywhere. Why then has the emphasis on awareness been placed on these "hot spots" that nobody expected: contraception and abortion?

The true sexual revolution (and not the caricature that they try to sell us) centers around this combat. It is here that the most vital interest, the most intimate, the most individual for women intersects with the safety, endangered and compromised, of the entire human species; and, remarkable fact, it is here that it is met forcibly by a resistance so desperate that it brings to mind the death drive analyzed by Freud.

Nothing could be more edifying than the incredible texts published as documentaries by the *Livre blanc de l'avortement* (The white book on abortion), edited after the day dedicated to this debate at the club of the *Nouvel Observateur*, in the Pleyel auditorium.[2]

These texts led the philosophical *Nouvel Observateur* to conclude: "Even if the MLF is right on the content, what difference does it make? It's not true that we are trying to make people happy against their will ... [*sic*.]." Let's cite some of these texts here:

> For a geneticist, there is technically no difference between an abortion and an infanticide: in both cases, a human being is at issue.
>
> —Jérôme Lejeune, professor

> What rage makes them kill their babies?
>
> —Lejeune, published in *Le Monde*

> For pity's sake, a little fresh air in your columns, *Nouvel Observateur*!
>
> These 343 leftist asses, bloodied and carefully aligned under your nose, are a little nauseating, and they are spewing out the odor of a mortuary.
>
> Whatever the political regimes, beliefs, social milieu, abortion remains a degrading adventure.
>
> —Dr. P. M. Hellemmes

> It's hysteria, pure and simple, in the proper sense of the word drawn from the Greek hustera, that is to say, "matrix" (raving mad).
>
> —C. W. Wasquehal

> The problem is to bring back her dignity to woman, to open childcare centers, daycare centers. We have to awaken women's social and civic

sense, to find work for her and her children[3] ... dignity by proclaiming her right to kill and announcing five murders as so many victories.

—The self-proclaimed papal representative
(dim-witted, fascist, reactionary)
de la G. (Rodez)

The "Manifesto" that you have published is a four-pronged shameful challenge to morals that respectable people must denounce.

—*It is a challenge to modesty*, this virtue that was exalted and respected by civilizations when they were at the height of their greatness and renounced in their periods of decadence.

—*It is a challenge to morals*, whatever the philosophy or the religion to which one belongs, each person carries within themselves, like a primordial principle, the notion of good and evil.

—*It is a challenge to the family*, which is, in spite of what some of the signers of the Manifesto believe, the primary living cell of any society.

—*Finally, it is a challenge to the law*: there is, in fact, a law known to all—it dates from 1920—all those who perform abortive measures on themselves or others and all those who helped them are sentenced to prison and fined. So, when somebody proclaims it publicly (etc.)

The highest State authorities must be informed of these crimes.

—Dr. M.-T. G.-D., gynecologist, mother
of five children, Aix-les-Bains

The list of the 252 "family names" of the doctors supporting free and accessible abortion plunged me into perplexed thoughts. Barely more than half seem to be "really from here"; 40 percent of the others have a totally different ring to their names.

... They are coming into our midst,

To abort our daughters, our companions![4]

—J. A., Paris

The MLF is anti-feminist. It has shown that giving voice to women has ended in a true catastrophe, that their strength still resides in tearing each other's hair out, and that their arguments turn into songs, graffiti, and hysterical howling.

It's pathetic. I am truly hurt and humiliated as a woman. I am hurt also to see that the majority of these militants are very young, and to observe with what glibness they are dealing with our problems.

Why do young people always want to monopolize the most serious of questions?

—S. O., Paris

POLLUTION WILL KILL OUR CHILDREN.
                    —A slogan written and carried on signs during the
                    International March for Abortion and Contraception
                    organized by the MLF, November 20, 1971

To the undeniable phallocracy of the so-called bourgeois society, built in the nineteenth century, we can fear that a hysterocracy will follow that will only reverse the problem. Given my age and my vow of celibacy, I am not directly—if I dare say so—involved, but I am in solidarity with the brothers of my sex, young or old, who are directly endangered, no longer with castration, but with annihilation.

… A world of women alone whose "bellies," as they say, are no longer only a means of production seems rather worrisome to me.

                    —Father Marc Oraison, author of numerous texts
                        on the social integration of homosexuality

Controversy and Testimonials

Let's stop talking about these negative texts and move on to those that are mixed: approvals with nuances and reservations, discussions, presentations, discursive or polemical testimony, "objective" view-points. The representatives of a union in Bordeaux think that prevention is better than healing. Professor Paul Milliez sees the remedy in sex education—don't be mistaken! "not erotic" [*sic*]—and not in abortion; because to allow abortion is also to normalize homosexuality, "which is a pathological deviation."[5] On the other hand, Évelyne Sullerot believes it to be necessary still "in *many* medical and social cases." Madame B., from Paris, believes that the law against abortion must be softened "in certain precise cases," but was "sickened by the list of the 343." C. B., from Villemontais, gets the impression that "our militants fighting for abortion don't want to be bothered in their cozy little lives." For J. P., from Caen, "there are grave or rather serious cases where abortion is a necessary evil." But, also, that "those 343 bourgeois women shouting out their self-ishness sickens me."

Madame F. T. from Alès thinks that unwanted births are a false problem: just give the child to a hippie community. An editor for *Claire Foyer* finds that "to give birth is to give the Light" and that those who refuse it haven't "gone past the level of their guts, have renounced satisfying all their instincts." Madame J. C., from Neuilly-sur-Marne, declares that free access to abortions risks making the woman "an object, a machine," that you send to the shop for service; "that's where the woman is a slave to man since she is submitted to his pleasure." A male student in Toulouse proposes giving up the child as the preferred option: there are six applications for adoption for each child given up by the mother. Finally, the Protestant Federation proposes criteria for making abortion legitimate: "serious danger for the physical and mental state of the mother," "a serious danger that the child would suffer malformations and deformities," "rape and incest," and cases where the mother is "a minor under the age of sixteen."

As I read and reread this second contingency, I wonder if I don't prefer the first.

> To look for reasons not to walk on a man's face is to accept that people do walk on his face.
> —Simone de Beauvoir, *La force des choses* (*Force of Circumstance*)[6]

Another story. The last one. This one comes from the country of Maria Chapdelaine and quintuplets, Catholicism in power, and the trappers of our children's literature.

"I was a member of the Movement for the Liberation of Women in Toronto when the Toronto contingency decided to take part in the campaign in favor of abortion.

"... We brought a coffin. It symbolizes all the Canadian women who die each year from clandestine abortions.

"... Instruments used in these clandestine abortions are on top of the coffin. I can't look at them ... Elsa is going to read a description of the usual use of the instruments. Women move forward, holding the coffin high, but the police push them around.

"Finally, they let us by. Elsa starts reading:

> There are plastic sacks on the coffin; they are used to fill up the uterus and force it to start labor. Since they are not sterilized, they can cause serious infections that, when not fatal, provoke sterility. There are knitting needles on the coffin. They are introduced into the vagina to pierce the uterus. That ends up producing waves of blood. There is a bottle of Lysol on the coffin. It's used to clean floors. Those who want to abort inject it into the vagina. The vaginal tissue is seriously burned and hemorrhages. Death follows in a few minutes. The pain that precedes it is intense, burning, unbearable. There is a piece of a vacuum cleaner on the coffin. The tube is placed at the entrance of the vagina

to extract the fetus, and the entire uterus is aspirated and pulled out of the pelvic cavity.

"I feel sick, like vomiting. I'm dizzy; everything is swimming around me. I can't hear Elsa's voice anymore; all I hear are Mary's sobs next to me and the horrified silence all around me. All that is happening to women at this very moment, all over Canada, while we are sitting on this lovely lawn, in front of this pretty house ..."

That's an example of how the "bourgeois women" refuse to move beyond the "level of their own guts" and to "be bothered in their comfortable little lives," ready to spread "a funereal odor," that makes those writing to the newspapers clamor for "a little fresh air." Good grief! Their belly, "as they say," what a symbol of self-ishness and of rejection of the "Light" ...

I know some of these bourgeois women who didn't want to be bothered in their comfortable little lives. I heard some of their stories. One of them who is "lightly nearing menopause" (sweet little expression by Father Oraison) had an abortion in secret, on a kitchen table, with a flashlight and a camping knife. She came out of it sterile. Another, who lived in poverty until she became famous later in life, nearly died, bleeding to death, in a clinic in the poor suburbs where she ended up and where she was treated like a mangy sheep. Another, a teacher, married, mother of three children whom she adores and raises in unbelievable conditions, aborted a fourth when her husband, tired of the financial difficulties of poor teachers, left her for a woman with more money. She, too, almost died. That's what they look like, these bourgeois women who shout out their selfishness!

When you have spent nights at the bedside of a woman whose lips have turned blue, when you have emptied tubs of blood, made phone calls, yelled at the guys with the stretchers, emptied your pockets to pay the house call of a medical student scared to death, when you have wished ardently and in vain for the police summons "as an accomplice" to be able to pour out your heart and copiously insult the male order's guard dogs, the hetero and patriarchal order, ah! Virtuous censors, signers of the garbage (not even household) cited earlier, little ignoramuses who haven't read a word from the Cassandras, known by the names of U Thant or the Commission of the European Technical Council, who announce an expected population of 7 billion by the year 2000, as we have trouble resisting the desire to believe finally Mr. Chauchard and Mr. Lejeune, these pure and ardent advertisers for that good Nestlé milk, becoming, for real, "murderers." Theirs. (Or, should we say, their executioners?)

Response to a Priest's Quips

Even though Father Oraison's position has evolved since then, we can't help but recall his declaration regarding the incriminating demands: "These militants are expelling the delicate question of love!" Recently, the professor of French law René Garraud, whose classes serve as gospel for generations of judges, had formed the spirit that reigns in our country over legislation concerning sex:

"Every individual is master of his own body, just like his own mind, and can make decisions concerning it even if those decisions corrupt it."

This principle, drawn from the Declaration of the Rights of Man, must have been used to guarantee the practice of prostitution considered as the "free" exploitation of its capital: the body. (The woman's, of course.)

Nobody has yet taught the judges, doctors, and priests, who decide how to manage women's bodies, how to use them and govern procreation (even at the present time, with the population level gone wild), that they were blithely avoiding the delicate question of liberty guaranteed by the French Revolution and by the multiple international agreements signed since the war.

What has become of the "serious violation of physical and mental integrity" defined by the accord of the Big Four countries, December 10, 1948, as a "crime against humanity"?[7]

For a Planetary Feminist Manifesto

Why This Battle?

Before considering in depth the first two of all the problems—the destruction of the environment and the birth rate gone crazy—we must draw conclusions from what came before.

The feminist combat, today, can no longer limit itself to the abstract "equality of the sexes" (that phallocratism has always been careful to mix with "identity") or to the more modern "liberty of eroticism." At present, it is an issue of LIFE OR DEATH.

The phrase "free disposition of one's body" takes on new meaning.

It's no longer a question of "demanding an equitable right to pleasure," like in our mama's feminism; the question becomes finally, according to Fourier, "a scandal that could overwhelm the very roots of this society." It goes well beyond these limits, "women having the right to reign over their own bodies," so dear to the Utopian socialists; it is the possibility of salvation, of the *stress* finally capable of correcting the inflation of birth rates, and the only one doing it today, to save the planetary ship that will sink bodies and goods after having exhausted its food supplies and its oxygen.

Does that mean that answering the urgent needs for contraception alone would solve the feminist problem?

Certainly not: "The feminism of the past died from having centered its struggle around universal suffrage; limiting ourselves to contraception and abortion would mean emptying out our struggles of their content; when these demands are met—and they will be, out of necessity—we will have forgotten that the goal of our movement, the very reason for its existence, is to defeat phallocratism," say the militants of today.

Phallocratism, Sexism, Hetero-cop Structure

"What is phallocratism?" ask some revolutionaries, skeptical. "When we read your articles and your leaflets, we get the impression that you're limiting yourselves to one simple detail, a character trait of this Judeo-Christian civilization; it is only a secondary phenomenon, an aspect, and you are confusing it with the base." And Marxists continue: "Capitalism is the infrastructure. You are succumbing to philosophical idealism; you are replacing political analysis with subjectivity."

So we have to define phallocratism here.

Having begun in a faraway time, after what Bebel has called "the great defeat of the feminine sex," phallocratism corresponds both to a mental structure and a political and social fact dated historically, necessitated most probably by man's takeover of agriculture, which was up until then woman's domain.[1]

(a) As a mental structure, it's a question of the justification of *power*, a social and political fact, by a fact of nature, quite simply put, of the possession of a certain member called a phallus, that determines more or less the secondary anatomy and presupposes that all beings born thus *endowed* (we remember the word "plow," for the cart!) are, by divine right, superior to those who, in that same world, are deprived of it: the eunuch, the woman. (Woman assimilated to the eunuch, by all morals, by all religions.)

(b) Secondary beliefs come to join this assumption: the one with the longest, the strongest, the most easily erectile, etc., should command over all the other men who are less endowed.

(c) The third stage of secondary assumptions comes with the development of civilization. The one who should command all the others is the one who possesses the most representative *"phallic symbol"* of the culture; for example, in the Middle Ages, courage, aggression, physical force (and the story of the Great Ferré shows that even a peasant could, thanks to these qualities, take a place alongside the noble class); later, after feudalism, money becomes the subtle marker of power, thus of phallic force (which they justify later by referring to the necessary *virile* qualities to accumulate a fortune and keep it growing: intelligence, temperance, persistence, work, wisdom, etc.).

(d) From all this, at each stage of civilization, appears a prohibition concerning woman; she must be "a woman above all," "natural," "genuinely a woman," etc., that is, everything that is expected of her; I have emphasized elsewhere that for the beginning of Christianity and Saint Thomas Aquinas, the woman, according to nature, was the one who was submissive to man, her boss, just as Christ is the Church's boss; and in the United States in the 1950s, the qualifier of "natural" applies to the woman who gives up the idea of a career to obediently buy her floor wax and vacuum cleaner. (Cf. the texts quoted by Betty Friedan.) Thus, always defined by man, the bearer of the phallus, the woman sees above all that her condition begins by a prohibition: she is *not* a man; she must *not* act like a man; let's add that she cannot *do without* a man, except if she submits herself directly to God, in the Christian Era. When the world moved away from Christianity, she even lost that escape route; living with a man and giving him children remains the sole justification of this existence of hers, in excess, mutilated, human being without a phallus, and "female by virtue of a certain lack" (Thomas Aquinas).

The phallus, in the third stage indicated, having become symbolic, the woman must be lacking, stripped, if necessary, of this symbol: physical force, aggressiveness, activity, money, leadership positions, possession of the sources of production in that later stage. (And this is what brings us back to the problem of capitalism; few people know that access, through inheritance or other legal means, to the possession of a source of production in the form of private property has only been possible for a woman since ... 1969.) Some will argue that there have always been rich women; it is a profoundly political question that Virginia Woolf poses in *A Room of Her Own*: "Why have women always been poor?" In fact, legislation, in all the countries of the world, Christian and others (the others even more, undoubtedly), was striving to help the cultural mores so that any feminine fortune was in fact usufruct (lent to her) and thus not property. The masculine right of ownership over all riches or sources of wealth, whatever they may be, is one of the most strongly anchored principles in all human mental structures.

The historic problem is undoubtedly not so simple. It possesses very interesting internal contradictions, on which women could have played throughout the centuries. For example, the second stage sometimes confronts the third stage: phallocratism has anchored pride of the phallus as such so well in the man that a man from the oppressed caste could take revenge on a man from a superior rank, by humiliating him through a possible personal superiority, that of an actual phallus, organ of procreation; he can diminish the other's power and even take his wife with a certain general masculine complicity: see *Lady Chatterley's Lover*. The issue could even border on seeming satisfying on the moral plane, like the democratic pleasure of seeing a commoner become a governmental minister or a general in the height of feudalism. But the proof that it is only a question of modalities and details is that, when we are dealing with a man-woman situation, the superiority of caste becomes the most fragile of defenses for the female; that's the proof that sexism is greater than the class struggle. Nothing is more normal for the system than a rich and powerful man playing Don Juan with little maids, secretaries, or employees; but up to the present time, a great lady who chose a gamekeeper exposed herself to perils that never endangered her masculine homologue. The Swedish film *Miss Julie* confronts *Lady Chatterley's Lover*.

This observation has always delighted phallocratic moralists, like the character in the *Kreutzer Sonata*, who snickers that "men's indiscretions, at least, don't increase the family's size!" (A remark that ignores the number of men who impose a bastard on their wife, making her raise it.) But if science hadn't remained, like everything else, in men's power, efficient methods of contraception and freedom of abortion would have entered into moral spheres a long time ago. We have seen that, throughout time, rituals and superstitions to limit women's fertility existed, and history has *never* mentioned them before now, even though we have an abundant amount of folklore on the rituals of fertilization! We have seen that it took a more-than-alarming demographic situation for research to decide to orient itself in that direction. In this area, as everywhere, masculine lies and their *systematic* participation in oppression (oppression baptized: "naturing nature") is exposed in a bright flash of light.

Here is, then, phallocratism as it exists; the structure at the base of all societies—whatever they may be—but tied also to one of the most ancient mental structures that corresponds to Pascal's formula:

"Rather than putting Force into the hands of Justice, we preferred putting Justice in the hands of Force."

All civilizations bear this mark that is much more ancient than capitalism, than feudalism, predating the Greco-Romans, and still present today, in spite of multiple concessions that erode the very principle of authority here as elsewhere. Phallocratism, as universal behavior of the male society, created sexism. It is this concept that holds the place of the son in this trinity that will complete, starting with Judeo-Christianity, the structure of the *hetero-cop*.

Sexism is the division along gender lines of work and participation in life, in the progress of human affairs. What the Germans call *mitsein*. It is sexism that tells man: "You will do A and you won't do B, because you are a man." It's the fixing of sexual roles—to the benefit of male power, of course.

What is the place of the hetero-cop structure in this system?

There is nothing surprising in the fact that, in such a context, homosexual behavior is the most subversive and the most charged with transgression. Is there a behavior more rigorously imposed, in each one of the two cases—the masculine and the feminine—than heterosexual behavior? That's why, ever since the onset of Judeo-Christian sexism, homosexuality became evil in its purest state, Lucifer's revolt. And that is why the revolt of the erotic minority, that modern psychology considers more and more as a second norm, joins, "strangely," women's revolt.

Arriving at this point, perhaps we should caution briefly against a certain botany that was useful in the past, but now, maintaining it today would risk prolonging judgments that would maintain the injustice. Any being who commits sexual acts with someone from his own sex should be considered both as a homosexual and as susceptible to committing these acts in turn with *any individual, no matter whom*, who is not oppressed by an upbringing that is too repressive; in the end, everybody is homosexual, even if very few people are. Also, he who bears the phallus yet believes himself to be a woman and carries himself like a woman, other than simply as a game, is extremely rare and represents a case of exceptional mental inversion. ("Divine would have been sorry to be confused with one of these horrible females," said Jean Genet.) We must be careful to avoid taking for "inverted" the man that claims the part of femininity that exists also in him, since every human being is bisexual, or for "inverted" the woman who claims her symmetrical part of masculinity, quite often beyond any homosexual behavior. In many cases, it is simply an issue of anti-phallocratic lucidity.

A lot of people believe, in good faith, given their lack of information, that a homosexual man or woman belongs necessarily to one of these two types: either adapting to the sexual stereotype of his culture, sometimes even in excess, like in the case of the "fags" who play the part of the bearded *super male*, decked out in leather, a biker, cop, or warrior; and these "dykes" who mimic the odalisque, the creature of dreams—or, to the contrary, the absolute revolt aiming to adopt the traits exactly inverted: the virile lesbian, the effeminate or transvestite gay, the only kinds recognized by the public. In reality, between these two extreme couples, infinite series of nuances exist, to such an extent even that the hetero-cop structure is contested. And what must be retained above all is that in no case does an exterior behavior, dress, or lifestyle correspond to a fixed psychological reality or to a defined erotic conduct. So many homosexual "supermales," enamored by leather and boots, are gentle souls and die-hard romantics, or passive monogamous ones; so many Sapphos in feathers and pearls are hardened little beings with an intelligence as sharp as a ball of steel and much more preoccupied by their independence than by their partner. What incited homosexuals up to the present to act like they were in a musical comedy was the presence in our cultures of the hetero-cop structure that completes the trinity mentioned earlier.

This trinity is born with Judeo-Christianity, for the reasons analyzed elsewhere.[2] To summarize briefly: the Judaic tradition, the first to bring adolescence to the Occident that was lagging behind in infancy with polytheistic paganism, is entirely based on the value of one Unity: *God Is One and He Is the Only One Who Is One.* Hence the origin of the deep consciousness of a divine punishment in the *cleavage* comprising *sex*, the anathema against homosexuality considered the sacrilegious refusal to submit, refusal to accept the punishment, the blasphemous imitation of the Unity.

This is how, as Wilhelm Stekel explains, monosexuality—thus, exclusive heterosexuality—appears with the rise of monotheism. On this metaphysical and philosophical base built with Christianity is a completely different value, the superstructure corresponding to the fall of the Roman Empire. The repression of homosexuality, all the while claiming to be religious, serves above all as a guarantee to Occidental sexism, with its fanatic exaltation of marriage and the family unit; that is, as the systemic oppression, methodical, rigorously organized, and skillfully led, of the reduction of the second sex to slavery. The home has become a fortress for the woman; it is the only place where a man can save her from all the others; it is also a ghetto, the closed space where she is removed from the world, cut off from the *mitsein*, reduced to procreation and "raising" children, obliged to replace *activity* (the sole human value, that transforms the world by transforming the human) with the *functions* that humanity has in common with the animal world. The man, solely, will transform himself by transforming the world; the woman doesn't transform anything at all: she grows, she embellishes, she maintains. Spengler summarized the situation thus: "Man makes History; Woman *is* History."

This is why purely patriarchal civilizations have always hunted down homosexuality more rigorously than those where patriarchy is softened by women's influence; it is a question of male power to repress the traitors to phallocratism that homosexuals constitute.[3]

> The abnormal, the scapegoat, becomes the absolute enemy; history is full of examples in this sense ... Jews, homosexuals, blacks; these last three categories reap a good portion of the irrational hate and organized disgust from humanity.
>
> —Massimo Consoli, *Appunti per una rivoluzione morale* (Notes for a moral revolution)[4]

But the hetero-cop structure doesn't have the sole goal of maintaining, for better or worse—and today, for worse or for better, with the evolution of civilization and the general challenge to the principle of authority, above all in sexual matters—the repression of homosexual treachery; it contributes to connecting to a precise anatomy; here, the presence of the phallus, elsewhere its absence, not for social behavior any longer but for qualities and aptitudes; it reinforces sexist stereotypes; it is a question of *being* before *doing*: the man is A and not B, the woman is B and not A. Hence, intellectual faculties are attached to the phallus: critical intelligence, analysis, speculation, the gift of abstraction, and even creative genius and moral qualities—force, courage, endurance, energy and audacity, loyalty, the sense of responsibility; and the admitted faults: egotism and sensuality. To the vagina, or rather the absence of the phallus, is attached the almost absolute absence of all the intellectual faculties enumerated above, and will be granted *intuition*, this recourse to a sort of magic prescience for anything in a feminine intelligence that could vex masculine pride; then the moral qualities: self-denial, the sense of sacrifice, the gift of love, the thirst for devotion; and the admitted faults: weakness, lying, absence of moral sense, conservatism, disaffection for matters of great interest.

As a quick look proves, the qualities and faults that correspond to the "masculine-feminine" stereotype were rigorously chosen and selected by virtue of the dominance of one sex over the other: qualities and faults that are, in the masculine model, those of the leaders, the masters; and in the feminine model, the qualities and faults are those of the servers, the directed. In order to repaint this old building's façade a little, the last shield for modern sexism—namely, the system's schools—tried to place the masculine stereotype under the rubric of "instrumental" and the feminine as "expressive." The magician's trick! That's how they teach us, with scholarly knowledge, that the instrumental is "tenacious, ambitious, original, sure of oneself," and the expressive is "gay, nice, obedient," with a tendency toward being, alas, "negative, chatty, quarrelsome." And then, what a surprise, we discover that the instrumental is above all masculine and the expressive feminine! (This is what Kate Millett calls the "intermediary terminology.") All that is only desperate resistance by the hetero-cop structure against the general challenge to the principle of authority.

Socialism neither Suppresses nor Resolves This Problem

"In the beginning was the Word"; in the beginning was Phallocratism. Those who protest that it is the capital, number-one enemy of women because it is for men of the oppressed class are only going back to the antiquated schemas of the old revolutionaries: socialism will resolve everything, and the oppression of women is only one among so many others. (That is why, during the entire Stalinist period of the French Communist Party, you could see the words "mother" and "wife" immediately attached to that of "woman" the minute there was mention of women or of the Union of French Women in *L'Humanité*.) Not one of these militants hanging on to the forms of the past and to the "great parties of the masses" (from which, so often, the minor leftist groups pick up sad archetypes) can respond to this, the simplest of remarks: But why were women *still more* oppressed before capitalism? And why does sexism continue to reign in socialist countries?

In the World: USSR, Africa, Algeria, Cuba, Latin America

Because, in the end, no reform of the status of women in the USSR, no acceleration of the massive "culturization" for the gender that previously included the highest percentage of illiterate people, no opening of masculine positions and careers, and even the most important innovation, the legalization of abortion—none of these evolutive elements diminished the issue of sexism in the USSR, not any more than in any other country in the world.[5]

> Unions and the German Social Democratic Party have understood the emancipation of women uniquely at the level of social and legal assimilation to the current rights of men.
>
> —Reimut Reiche, *Sexuality and Class Struggle*[6]

As we know, African women remain among the most alienated women of this world, including in the recent decolonized countries where the goals are oriented more and more toward socialist regimes. Guy-André Smal, a specialist in physical therapy, and Joseph Mbuyi, from (then) Zaire, remind us in the book *Femme africaine, réveille-toi* ("Wake up, African woman"):

The African woman, the Zairean woman … still undergoes the terrible male laws imposed by the ancestors in many cities, and especially in the villages. Confirmation of virginity is required; girls can still serve as merchandise, of exchange; married, she is often a slave to her husband, to his clan; married without children, she is repudiated … widowed, her life crumbles, she renounces her personality, loses her children and all acquired goods … Dead, she is forgotten rapidly.[7]

Excision of the clitoris continues to be practiced, including in the regions, like Ethiopia, where women have the right to vote; and recently, a *leftist* African intellectual was heard delivering an impassioned defense of this despicable practice; because, as he said with conviction, to stop it would be to ruin "tribal solidity."

As a reminder, we only need to cite the more than anti-feminist, the misogynistic, declarations of Muammar Gaddafi explaining male superiority with "biological science" and forbidding, in the most bizarre way of total exclusion, certain industrial zones to women: cement and chemical products![8]

Examples abound everywhere in the regions of the Third World that move from obscurantism to socialism, from maintaining to sometimes reinforcing sexism through their boring declamations that are enough to make you snore about equality and liberty, without counting the hypocritical homage given to the "admirable partners in our struggle." The situation for Muslim women is particularly tragic in this regard. The militant struggle, the unveiling, had built the base for a certain amount of emancipation in Algeria; however, the interior attitude of the heroines, *perverted* from infancy (in the true sense of the term), their submission to the male remained very ambiguous; Frantz Fanon cites the case of an Arab women whose silence had protected her husband and the entire organization; she had been raped:

"And yet, recounts the man, she didn't tell me: 'Look what I have undergone for you!' No, to the contrary, she said: 'Try to forget me, start your life over, I have been dishonored.'"

And Fanon adds that the man himself approves this point of view: "In his eyes, his wife and his children were stained, unclean."[9]

Sheila Rowbotham, who cites this trait in *Women, Resistance and Revolution*, emphasizes the custom of "separate cells" that reinforced sexual segregation after the liberation, men and women ignoring their reciprocal problems, and also the fact that women never saw the Algerian government take up a reform of marriage and the family; the proverb remained: "Let the women take care of the couscous; we'll take care of politics." In 1964, they heard a political orator, El-Hachemi Tidjani, proclaim the decisive inferiority of women using this argument: "There are no female prophets!" After the fall of Ahmed Ben Bella and the ensuing swing to the right, says Rowbotham, "the oppression of women, far from ending, continued instead in an open and insolent manner." In 1967, an Algerian peasant suspecting his wife of adultery could still kill her with a clean conscience. Concerning Houari Boumédiène, he said officially in 1969 in Algiers, while handing out scholastic awards, that he "reserved different futures for girls and for boys of the country": for women, he reserved the care of the children and the vigilance of religion; for men, he reserved political responsibilities. It's the Hitlerian principle "Kitchen, Church, Children" with an Algerian sauce. Nazi or "socialist," the male leader practices the same treatment concerning yesterday's ally: German women of the Third Reich had contributed to bringing Adolf Hitler to power by a massive vote, Algerian women had fought in the underground and suffered rape and torture so that their country could gain its independence.

The Cuban situation is more complex and more nuanced. A "Federation of Cuban Women" was founded in 1960 to fight against illiteracy; it launched anti-sexist campaigns with some success. Since the liberation, we find female technicians, engineers, mechanics, tractor operators, urban planners, and editors: most of the cities have nursery schools and childcare centers; the Youth Organization created study communities that made adolescents independent of their families; faced with sexist resistance from their employers, women don't hesitate to talk about "counterrevolution" and to herald their heroines such as Lydia and Clodmira, Che Guevara's partners.

However, true equality between the sexes meets with harsh resistance, above all as soon as there is a question of "morals," this weak point of the Roman Catholic mental structure, and of sharing household tasks.

Fidel Castro, the author of the text "Women must be doubly revolutionary," also wrote a speech to this same Federation of Women, that *New Left Notes* published in 1967 and that Germaine Greer commented about with indignation:

> Who will make lunch for the children when they come home to eat?
> Who will take care of the babies and the children under school age?
> Who will prepare the man's meal when he gets home from work? Who
> will do the dishes and take care of the house?

In *The Youngest Revolution* by Elizabeth Sutherland Martínez, a Cuban painter, Thomas, affirms that men are traumatized in Cuba by the evolution of the status of women, and that "the most interesting question today is the new relationship of men and women."[10] At all levels, as Sheila Rowbotham states, "there is machismo which continually sets the limits for female sexual liberation." A puritanism that is common to all budding socialisms, where Catholic prejudices easily join the fear of Eros unchained, has provoked monstrous persecution of homosexuals (note: of the "passive ones," the active ones are subject only to ridicule) and calls for help in front of the communist schools accused of being the settings where "girls' virginity was to be sacrificed in an orgy of red free love": Allen Ginsberg, furious, asked if the regime proposed masturbation as the sole alternative for youth.[11] Cuban women said to Sutherland: "The idea that sex is for the woman's pleasure as well as the man's ... that is the taboo of all taboos."[12] And Rowbotham concludes—rather justly, it appears—"In Cuba, women face the particular subjection of a group colonized within a colony. The forms of possession vary but in essence they remain the same."[13]

After seeing the persistent machismo of Cuba, what about the rest of Latin America?

To get some idea, we need to read the book by Marie-Thérèse Guinchard: *Le macho et les Sud-Américaines*, with its subtitle: "the myth of virility."[14]

Brazilian women number 55 million in a country of 90 million. In that country, "the mother takes her daughters outside the home only to attend church or work in the fields. For women, it is the *farm* that they fear: an entire life at the service of the same master, just like in the times of slavery." In the Amazon jungle, the male is polygamous, and he has all the rights; if he kills a jaguar, he can choose any woman, even if she belongs to another. The female director of the newspaper *Jornal do Brasil* declares openly that, for men in this country, "the problem concerning women exists less, if that's possible, than the problem for Blacks or Indians." Young middle-class women do pursue studies, but 60 percent of them never use their diplomas. Women have had the vote since 1936; 60 percent of them are still illiterate. There are only two women elected to parliament. An internationally important lawyer, Madame Anina de Carvalho, describes abominations of torture.[15]

In Argentina, the man has a reputation of being more lethargic than his wife; a diplomat who has been living in Buenos Aires for eighteen years declared for Guinchard's study:

"Without his wife, the Argentinian man would die of starvation!"

In that country, men never miss the chance, at all parties for social or work reasons, to practice "sexual segregation." On Saturdays, the worker goes to his club, like an English gentleman, and the women left behind meet on their own in "centers" where, under the guise of entertainment, women from the upper classes teach them how to cook pasta and to sew pearls on bags. Intellectual women, up until this most recent generation, preferred to remain single; it was impossible to combine ambition, even a modest one, with the husband's machismo. In the country, a woman has a hard life; she gazes at the gaucho's lands from her kitchen window; she gives birth among the cows and washes her children in the stream; she gives herself, without complaining a lot, to the steward or the boss. The feudal custom of the woman about to be married taken by the lord on her wedding night.

In Uruguay, legislation is very feminist; but there are three to seven women to one man. The president, José Batlle y Ordóñez, like a character in a romantic novel, proclaimed the woman "master before God, and for good reason, before men." But the disproportion of sexual categories leads the woman to dreaming of the "macho" instead of judiciously using the legal advantages that she never learned to use due to no deep change in customs: the Spanish and Catholic tradition continues to maintain a need for support and protection, not of independence. A young girl has no other choice than to live with her parents while she waits for marriage; if she is an orphan, she must seek refuge in a convent. "They show," says the author, "that *macho society* lives on above all because they are consenting, more even: complicit."

Paraguay fought a war for independence in 1870 in which women distinguished themselves through their heroism: the Joan of Arc in this war was an Irish woman who was the inspiration—far from the actual woman—of the superficial creation played by Brigitte Bardot in *Viva Maria!* This country lives under a dictatorship and is one of the poorest in Latin America. A woman earns 10 to 20 percent less than a man for the same work. Women and intellectuals form the most radical elements of the opposition to Alfredo Stroessner, nicknamed "the blond dictator" due to his Germanic origins. The activity, energy, and endurance of women substituted the machismo with a strange system called maternalism (40 percent of mothers are single mothers ...)

> The girls from the old society have only one desire: to live their lives as women and mothers alongside a husband, even if he is unfaithful and tyrannical; they give up all professional ambition to dedicate themselves to their home life that they begin as early as fifteen or sixteen years old.

However, a new generation is arising in which women seem to distinguish themselves not for the struggle for their rights, which theoretically are acquired already, but for a radical change in customs.

In Bolivia, Indian blood is mixed in strong proportions with the blood of the whites who colonized the country; the inhabitants are the most mixed in Latin America, along with Peru and Ecuador. This is why Olga Bruzzone de Bloch, "the poet with the spirit of revolt," wrote bitter and lyrical poems dedicated to the women she calls "living stones, souls of the earth ... Pain, love, rebellion," that is, to the Indian women reduced to slavery by the Spanish occupiers.

The standard of living here is the lowest of all the South American continent. The brother of Jean-Luc Godard, the filmmaker, directs a children's hospital there; he said to Guinchard: "It's not hospitals that they need to build here but childcare centers and public food kitchens." Beds: there are none; the ground: dirt, beaten earth; modern comfort: no water, no toilets; such are the conditions in this hospital that "is filled to the brim with young girls picked up from the streets, raped by their fathers."

In Cochabamba, a town of 100,000 inhabitants, there are up to twenty-five female associations that range from the society of theosophy to the league of female workers, to the "civil and social" feminine union. It is undoubtedly the draft of a feminism "à la Portuguese" that must be beginning.

In Santa Cruz, where women, although ruled by their husband according to Catholic tradition, have more of a tendency to maintain a private life and to work outside the home, a woman who lived for a long time in Europe and saw her feminism mature there declared bluntly to the same researcher that "the man in Santa Cruz is not only unfaithful, he is also brutal, cruel, lazy, and jealous." As concerns the wife, "she is his 'thing' as early as fifteen or sixteen years old," and when she is twenty, she finds herself abandoned at home six days out of seven; the man spends only Sunday with his family.

Chile is an underdeveloped country, but it had a liberal regime up until recently. Men there say with bitterness: "The date of the elections is that of women's independence!" The women's vote, in fact, does exert a strong influence: it was women who elected President Eduardo Frei Montalva and prevented the election of Salvador Allende as president in 1958, then elected him in 1970. One of the most remarkable leading figures in politics is Carmen Lazo, one of the nine female representatives in the former chamber. She analyzed the situation for women thus:

"The infidelity, the heedless lack of concern from the males have made the Chilean woman an emotionally revolutionary conservative."

Today, 700,000 Chilean women work, whereas this country of 9.6 million inhabitants counts only one-third of its population as workers. However, as the same researcher, Guinchard, states: the exceptional fertility of the Chilean woman "makes her a victim of the macho system more than all the other South American women." The birth rate is the highest in the world.

In Peru, the language heard by the researcher is significant: "We are against the equality of the sexes; the man must protect us, provide for us, spoil us. He must be the master. Otherwise, what would our femininity become?" Young women, eighteen years old, talk like this. Up until 1936, there had only been one female senator; the first, Madame Irene Silva de Santolalla, sat alone among fifty-three men up until the dissolution of the chambers in 1968. Out of 60,000 students, 30 percent are girls; 60 percent of them give up all professional occupations or ambition upon marriage. As concerns women among the lower classes, they work ten times harder than the men and are submitted to trial marriages, they sleep on the floor and have only frozen potatoes and boiled corn to eat. They give birth alone and often cut the umbilical cord with their teeth, like animals.

Hope of a new dawn
God of yourself
You know the language of the stars
And the language of water

And the voice of torment

WEAVE YOUR CROWN OF GLORY FROM IT

—Olga Bruzzone de Bloch

"Poem to the woman"

This overview of the condition of the Latin American woman shows amply that, if we can still reproach Cuba for the persistence of the hetero-cop structure and, to a certain rather significant extent, of sexism, this country remains the only one of all this half continent called South America to have tried faithfully to combine feminism and socialism. A truth that is starting to get old but that bears repeating is coming to light: the equality of political rights is only a beginning, and they are often not applied, in the case of women as in the case of the decolonized peoples. An example, the Ecuadorian woman: since 1967, the law declares her the equal of her macho man; yet she remains controlled by marital tutelage, virginity is still sacrosanct, and she is obliged to accept that her husband benefits from absolute sexual freedom. She has been voting for forty-five years but continues to be the subordinate of all the males: the father, the husband, the boss, the priest. Peruvian women: so little represented in intellectual and political life, yet they benefit (on paper) from all the same laws as a North American woman.

Would massive participation in the market for employment and the workforce furnish a more concrete equality, since it is economic? Not any more than the preceding right: it happens that the participation doesn't even lead toward a very simple liberalization. The Paraguayan woman and the Argentinean woman, both so energetic next to their larval, passive male, exhaust themselves taking care of him like an eternal baby; and, like an eternal baby, this pseudo-macho oppresses them. In fact, in the traditions penetrated by Catholicism, the most retrograde element of Christianity, anti-sexual repression of women reigns masterfully, doubled by the greatest indulgence for the carnal "weaknesses" of men; divorce, contraception, controlling the birth rate, all remain abominations.

However, even in these archaic and disadvantaged regions, feminism is poking its nose through, feeling around the terrain, pushing its hidden buds through the soil. But it stands out very little among other questions that are ordinarily socialist; in these "revolutionary" circles, the fact that socialism neither resolves nor eliminates the problem for women has never been discussed.

The necessity of posing the problem of overpopulation obviously has one positive consequence: it disturbs phallocracy and locks it up in its own contradictions. Even in Islamic cultures, thus in the most profoundly misogynistic ones, even more so than in Catholicism, and in spite of the protective measures surrounding the male power, as soon as this burning question is brought up, a still-faraway possibility of emancipation materializes, perhaps.

The only appearance of a feminist tendency in North Africa was in fact brought out by an issue of *Socialist Objective* where, in 1972, Marie-Agnès Destaerke and Madame Bouveur relate that the UFA (Union of Algerian Women, an organization remote-controlled by the FLN,[16] like our UFF[17] is controlled by the French Communist Party) obtained an authorization to publish a text concerning contraception "in order to help regulate the birth rate." They admitted to the two French women who wrote the article in the *Socialist Objective*:

We have not yet seen a woman in the government, just as we have never seen one rise to a high position in the party. In the last ten years, we have seen only one woman promoted to the rank of general director of an office. However, today we have a considerable number of women with the necessary qualifications.

The abject poverty caused by involuntary procreation has finally made the FLN revise its Koranic options. It will become more and more difficult for this "socialist" male power to refuse promotions to women and the most modest reforms of the conjugal institution, so demeaning to the Muslim woman, to the extent that even a repressive leader like Boumédiène has to think about controlling the birth rate.

In thus reviewing the countries that have accomplished a popular revolution, and those of Latin America that are still stagnating in their backward economic and cultural situations (yet not without a vigorous revolutionary ferment under the surface), we observe that the variations in the feminine status are due as much to economic modifications as to the implantation of religious morals; we will see later, on a more complex level, that the situation is the same for the problem in the interior of the other camp, of Europe and North America. Here, the political regimes carry less importance than these two factors: the general economic stage of the country and the infusion of religion. All we have to do is look closely at the position of the powers regarding abortion or contraception, so diverse, to equal economy, according to whether the country has a largely Catholic or Protestant culture.

And China?

China is, in the socialist camp, a case apart that merits special attention. The book by Claudie Broyelle, *La moitié du ciel*,[18] with its strange subtitle, "Le mouvement de libération des femmes en Chine,"[19] brings an incomparable contribution to knowledge of the topic and gives the contours of a very specific problem.

Chinese women were the most oppressed women in the world; each one had to have a guardian, father, husband, brother, mother-in-law, even one of the same husband's older wives; all worked together to ensure that the woman would never be autonomous. This was a good reason for Chinese women to welcome with enthusiasm the advent of hard community life and to participate in it with fervor, first in the revolution, then toward productivity. With all the children cared for at the Children's Palace, the elderly parents at the Happy Houses, all professions are open to women: they are locomotive conductors, they are ministers in the government, generals, and so on.

In an interview granted on February 14, 1972, to *Le Nouvel Observateur* with Alice Schwarzer, the journalist with the MLF, Simone de Beauvoir declared:

> They (the Chinese) have eliminated the feudal family and, at the same time, brought huge changes in the condition of women. But insofar as they accept the conjugal family ... I do not believe at all that women are liberated in China. I think that you have to do away with the family.

Hasty judgment? Broyelle explains the Chinese family situation with enthusiasm. She insists that, with the facility of divorce and the large application of abortion and contraception, marriage in Red China is much closer to the true "free union" than was the case in Bolshevik Russia in 1917, with its so-called "free union"; the latter being, due to lack of control of procreation and efficient protection against venereal diseases, merely promiscuity leading to the insecurity of children and to a new kind of slavery, more atrocious even than the previous kind, of Russian women. Broyelle describes the care of children, shared by the entire community, the logical consequence being liberating the child from the mother if you want to liberate the mother from the child, as called for by so many European feminists, from the Italian Carla Lonzi to the Canadian-American Shulamith Firestone.

And, what is more, symmetrical to the sexist liberation of women, men's liberation develops also: while women are directing the construction of a dam, men don't hesitate to dedicate themselves to marvelous work with sewing needles and have found this charming formula: "The revolution needs embroiderers."

So, is all for the best in the best of all social worlds? Alas! The last part of Broyelle's book dampens any zeal that could be born from what precedes it. And it is so far from being a mere detail that the author of the preface, Han Suyin, declares the "keystone" of this essay to be precisely the oppressive chapter entitled "Concerning the debate on sexuality in China."

Very often, when I am giving talks in numerous Western countries, I meet men and women who seem convinced that "sexual relations" and "sexual freedom" (that is to say, sexual relations for women and girls outside the ties of marriage) are the best of the best parts of the liberation ... But I see now that I had not understood enough just how toxic this "sexual theory" is.[20]

The Chinese are now used to the Occident, including its intellectual supporters, criticizing them for their "puritanism." Broyelle is therefore going to try very hard to prove the merits of it, and even the "feminism."

So, we will see the confirmation of what we had already heard and often believed to be the tales of malicious reactionaries or petty, obsessed bourgeois people: not only are extramarital relations, without being forbidden by the law, so frowned upon that those who practice them lose face in the society, but also the sexual life of the Chinese, man or woman, is among the briefest in the world, since the age for marriage has been pushed up to twenty-five or twenty-eight. (Note also that any couple who continues sexual relations beyond forty years old is almost as discredited as those who copulate outside marriage.) To justify this late marriage, Broyelle declares: "It [late marriage] remains a measure of great revolutionary importance."

In fact, as she explains, it is necessary for the young Chinese woman between the ages of sixteen and twenty-seven to acquire financial independence through the practice of a profession, that she have formed a solid political culture, participated in many cultural activities, and so on, in order to approach marriage in perfect conditions of equality. Very well. But what about instinct during this time? It is completely left aside. It would seem to go without saying that, for Maoism, any pre-conjugal experience could only be negative for the woman, the naive prey for a misogynistic, contemptuous male. Better yet: one of the theorists, Deng Xiaoping, declares that "beauty must not be taken into consideration" in amorous attraction because "beauty does not escape the struggle of the classes."

In order to explain and justify such concepts at the end of the twentieth century, in the middle of the discovery of the fundamental importance of the sexual component to human evolution, for the individual as well as the collective, Broyelle doesn't hesitate to call to mind famous interviews with Lenin and Inessa Armand: "Isn't it better to oppose a pitiful marriage *without love* of petty-bourgeois-intellectual-peasants compared to *a civil proletarian marriage with love*?" Texts that, along with those featuring Lenin interviewing Clara Zetkin, even make French communists turn red with embarrassment (even though they are rarely susceptible of feeling any embarrassment at all).

Everything happens as if, under pious pretexts, Chinese Maoism is seeking to take over the sexuality of the young in order to divert it and direct it toward the task, undoubtedly very urgent and highly important, of building a more just society—that is to say, where everybody has enough to eat and where sexism is on the road to disappearing.

A catastrophe is on the way. Denied reality always turns around with tenacious severity against those who wish to ignore it, smother it. It is, in the more or less long term, corruption from the inside, by the repression and the negation of the instinct of pleasure, hypocritically identified (as in the worst moments of Judeo-Christianity) with love, which is an elaborate and complex sentiment (depending, in fact, on factors such as the social situation and the historic stage) and overidentified with marriage, which is an institution. The states and religions that believed it possible to manipulate Eros and silence it at times, give it voice at others, give it a seal of approval, label it, divide it, separate it between "appropriate" and "undesirable," all found themselves repenting—and bitterly. Because this negation of the real and this despotism exercised on the instinctual are inseparable, as we have seen, from the deep roots of sexism and the place of women in society, hence of feminitude.

Marcuse brought out well what is already discernible in Hesiod (*Works and Days*), that is, the male world's distrust, *because it is productive and constructive*, of beauty and woman, Eros, its promise of happiness—in short, all that relates to the "pleasure principle" in a capitalist or socialist authoritarian world. This distrust takes many variable forms that range from the declared puritanism of misogyny, in cultures of lack and extreme shortages, to the ambiguous tolerance of so-called consumption societies—let's just say "economies of abundance." But everywhere, the principle is the same.

China has created a very original form of this counter-to-nature concept that is so ancient. At the same time, it has liberated woman more than any other culture up to now, and all the while, in the name of this urgency of societies suffering from poverty, it locked up Eros, whose fate has always been linked, up to the present time, with that of the second sex. Basing itself on the secular (and oh-so-legitimate) fear of oppressed women with regard to eroticism always presented as a tax owed to the lord and master (Freud's famous "escape from sexuality"!), the Chinese revolutionary regime, for its goals of enlightenment, was able to maintain the feminine sex in a sexual obscurantism of which there is no other example since Lenin's aberrations, that were excusable in his time: the firm belief in the feminist and revolutionary benefits that surveillance of sexuality would constitute, its mixture with love and marriage, its status restrained and always elaborated in direct relation to the ideology of the regime. Admittedly, with such customs, the man must feel more cruelly hindered than the woman at the moment, for he knows what he is losing; the woman has not even imagined the reality. But the objective reality cannot be suppressed. A child to whom one offers candy as a rare treat due to good behavior might see the desire diminish, but his organism would still suffer grave effects of such a deprivation. To build paradise outside the light is to put into question the meaning of paradise; one could hardly fare well. How could the best of the socialist and revolutionary worlds where, up to twenty-five years old, only masturbation (to use Ginsberg's term) remains the sexual release for the young (and, after forty, the mature age), be the world that anybody would dream of building and living there, including women?

Let's review the most marking traits of what socialist countries of this last part of the twentieth century offer us; remember the degradation of Alexandra Kollontai's libertarian ideals in the USSR, the brutally sexist speeches of Boumédiène or the misogynist ones of Gaddafi, the paternalistic ones of Castro; and, in seeing where women find themselves today, women who fought, gave their blood, suffered torture and rape for this socialist state that they hoped would liberate them, or still yet, in the best of cases, find themselves tied to means of production and industrialization to a true erotic mutilation; then let's read Hélène Brion again, she who has been so forgotten today.

This old militant from 1913 proclaimed, in fact, in the revolutionary tracts of the Typographers Union, that she feared seeing the revolution use women's services in the way that, in the past, the progressive bourgeois class had used those in the working class to its profit, only to betray them afterward; the proletarian men were going to play the same traitorous role with regard to women that the first bourgeois revolutions played with regard to the proletariat.

The rest of the story showed that this revolutionary woman, become a shadow of the past, was right; that we are devastated when reading and listening to the leftist ramblings from those who, ignoring totally this series of irrefutable information about the feminine condition in the USSR, in the Republic of Algeria, in "decolonized" Africa, in Cuba, and even in China, ramble on disparagingly about the "principal struggle" (the class struggle) and the "secondary struggle" (the struggle of the sexes, diversionary).

Among the American "dark stories," the story is told of a conscientious little guinea pig scampering toward the laboratory, murmuring: "I have to hurry, or I'll be late for the lab experiments." The feminine sex that threw itself heart and soul into the "principal struggle" at the cost of rape, torture, and death for the lab experiments of socialism makes us think both of the prophecies of Brion and of this little guinea pig.

For a Planetary Feminist Manifesto (Continued)

The Rest of the World and Liberation Movements

We have just observed that the countries that have moved to socialism, whether it be of the Soviet type, the Algerian FLN, Cuban, or Maoist, have either maintained sexism or started it without questioning it; or otherwise they replaced it, in one lone case, by anonymity of an egalitarian sort but also frustrating and punitive; and that Latin American countries (whether they be of the fascist or socialist sort) demonstrate the same machismo, with maybe some nuances of difference toward the "second sex." What happens in the rest of the world? What is the situation for the liberation movements in the Occidental-American camp?

Germany, less often analyzed on this point, has expressed a very particular spirit of initiative in the frame of a general perspective, the "anti-authoritarian tendency." We owe the interesting idea of "boutiques for children" to them; the test trial of a totally new education system, free of the concepts of reward and punishment, led by a rotating team of parents working toward this double goal: to free the mother from the child and the child from the mother.

On the other hand, other feminists of the backward type have kept trying to integrate, like good socialists, the "secondary struggle" into the "principal struggle."

Here is what the women militants of the national convention of the extreme-left German party declared, according to the terms of the session described by Susan Surtheim in the *National Guardian*:

> We seek the liberation of all human beings. The fight for the emancipation of women must be part of the general fight for freedom. We recognize the difficulty with which our brothers will accept the end of masculine chauvinism, and as women, we are ready to assume completely our responsibilities and help them resolve this contradiction. Liberty now! We love you!

Is it impudent on my part to say it? I think that I see, in this fraternal lyricism, something of this mixture of artificial lightness and of teeth-clenching flatness displayed by the voice of the broker bragging about a housing subdivision. A blind man with his white cane, waiting for alms in the subway halls, a gramophone playing on his lap, makes the same voice—not his own—heard. I have trouble believing that women lucid enough to "seek the liberation of all human beings" can take their *own emancipation* as just a simple aspect of the problem. It's possible that these liberal women are following the lead of Evelyn Reed, member of the workers' party who spent a lot of time trying to show the socialists that struggle for women was a part of the class struggle (but that was in 1954!), or, quite simply, leftist bourgeois women whose social advantages blind them to the point of masking their sexist oppression; but, whatever the origin of the dark glasses, of the white cane and the joyous mechanical voice, there is one thing that is certain: they don't see a thing.

The liberals just kill me, said one of the most combative male students in May 1968. History is there to prove to them that they are always overrun by their own left. Why don't they just content themselves with being a part of the nice little right wing.

The rest of the story is instructive. In the December 1967 issue of *New Left Notes*, a typical masculine reaction showed what they must have thought about this feminine manifesto from the SDS (Students for a Democratic Society). Women, declared the letter's author, are not made to be leaders; they cannot separate themselves from men because they need them; they should be "more humble, more tolerant, more charitable." Women understood that they had been handing out canes (white) in order to be beaten, and they started rebelling against the objective, put forward by one of their own, to furnish "an effort for extra work during the time that was not already monopolized by typing and distributing the leaflets, fights with the police, and taking care of their revolutionary man."[1] This last remark makes you think of one of the ironic songs of "women's lib":

> My guy is a great militant
> He gives all his time to the revolution
> And I give all mine to him

And this comment from another American feminist, Martha Shelley:

> You can play the Che Guevara,
> You are my oppressor and my enemy!

In spite of the efforts of the most "politicized" among the women's liberation movements, like Juliet Mitchell, who regrouped the principles of the socialist revolution and women's struggles with more coherence than these reformists,[2] the observation imposes itself more and more undeniably: it is only by starting with their specific oppression that women will liberate themselves; they can only do it *against their former master* and not with the new ones.

Here is the current state of German feminism: In the Federal Republic of Germany, 9 million women work; out of those, there are 3 million office employees, 3.5 million factory workers. Statistics: 70 percent of wage earners, out of which only 9 percent are specialized.

The time for the liberation has come, but the combat did not take place. The combat will not take place only through the study of the means and methods of the repression, but above all in fighting against the thousands of imbeciles who have identification problems with Farah Diba and Jackie Kennedy; they do a poor job of it, ridiculously, by beating their children.

Ulrike Marie Meinhof, a member of the SDS (Socialist German Student Union), the extreme left party in the Federal Republic of Germany, made these statements, published by *Konkret* (September 1968), after a violent confrontation of the movement by its own militants: the men had refused to give the floor to women; tomatoes were thrown at Hans-Jürgen Krahl, the leader.

In Frankfurt, in Berlin, the Weiberrat (Women's Council) calls for a strike in the bedroom, begins a campaign for abortion, against Article 210 of the Constitution.

Again in 1968, it was the feminist Helke Sander who was the first in Germany to talk about "bringing the class struggle into the couple and its relations." She declared to the men that women could no longer wait for "their" revolution. Because, as she emphasized, "a revolution that is simply economic and political, based on the repression of private life, is of no help to us, as we have seen in the socialist countries." And she ended her speech, addressing the masculine comrades with the following unequivocal assertion: "Comrades, your behavior is intolerable!"

Regarding the issues of the problem of community, raising the children, the German women's input is equally interesting.

The Aktionsrat zur Befreiung der Frauen (Action Committee for the Liberation of Women), inspired by the work of Vera Schmidt, a revolutionary psychoanalyst of the 1920s, published by the Berlin commune Kommune 2, demands projects of a rather large scale: antiauthoritarian childcare centers must liberate women from the family breeding ground; they created a new kind of childcare centers (*Kinderläden*) that have multiplied in Berlin: ten in 1968, sixty-eight in 1970.[3]

We will turn later to a discussion of the glaring proof that the revolutionary feminist combat cannot be linked with the socialist combat such as it is without a demystification of the relation of the forces at present, and why it must form all kinds of alliances other than those with the mass parties, since they are of a masculine majority and direction. After having touched on the particular aspects of the feminine condition in the socialist camp and at the heart of the leftist groups in England and West Germany, it is a good idea now to retrace the broad lines of the current formation of women's liberation movements in America and the Western world, which will allow us to start work on a common platform for an international revolutionary feminist manifesto.

What is the origin of this current feminist tidal wave? America. The one in the north.

In the United States, the signal of this awakening was given by Betty Friedan in her book *The Feminine Mystique*, which we have analyzed elsewhere as one of the four cornerstones of theoretical feminism.[4] Graduating summa cum laude from Smith College, she conducted the most complete study of the demystification of Freudian concepts as they were put to use by the floor polish and vacuum cleaner markets, and she helped in unmasking the technological dictatorship, this same insidious and commercial despotism that Norman Mailer accused "liberated" women of promoting! Married, approved by her husband, to whom she dedicated her book and who told her, "If you want to convince people, show your human side, show pictures of your children" (later, she separated from him). She was the founder of the first feminist movement: NOW, the National Organization of Women, which spread throughout a host of American cities thanks to its reformist style.

In the film by Jean-Louis Bertuccelli presented in a private showing by the Association of Marriage Counselors of France about "women's lib," in the UNESCO auditorium in March 1971, numerous French women readers were able to discover the face with high cheekbones, showing signs of age, the beautiful slanted eyes, the shoulders, both tired and graceful, of this wise protester who demands the right to choose between the kitchen sink and the construction of a rocket for women, but who does not put into question the foundation of a world where one-third of it is dying of malnutrition, nor the family institution of which this sink is only a epiphenomenon.

At the end of a national conference in Washington, her "Declaration of the Rights of Women" adopted eight central rallying points, all liberal, that permitted the movement to be recognized by the political authorities. In general, it was a demand for a reform of the Constitution in a feminist sense; suppression of discrimination based on sex in the workplace, immediate revision of fiscal laws to allow tax deductions for household costs and childcare for working parents, the right of women to an education in accordance with their abilities, on an equal footing with men, at all levels of the educational system, the right for women to return to work after maternity leave without losing any of their seniority, the right of women to control their fertility with complete information on contraception, the abolition of laws penalizing abortion, and so on.

"Eight firm points, ... and pussy envy being what it was, years would go by before the last of those reasonable demands would become a legal commonplace ... but woe to the liberal politician who was not quickly conversant with them," comments Norman Mailer.[5]

Added to this campaign for laws are several actions that show signs of a more radical trend, such as the boycott of Colgate-Palmolive because of gender discrimination; but, Germaine Greer says:

> although they have never levelled an attack of any significance against the whole ludicrous cosmetic industry, when the same worthless ingredients make up all the preparations from the cheapest to the most fabulously expensive, and female insecurity is cultivated by degrading advertising so that these mucky preparations can be sold more quickly than ever.[6]

Sometimes, through one of those flashes of light that seem to give her a new dimension, Betty Friedan's intelligence reaches a truth that far surpasses her courteous rebellion; for example, when, after having treated the *SCUM Manifesto* as highly superficial, she predicts that if NOW's demands (NOW has female and male members) are not heeded, we could witness riots that would make the Detroit riots look like child's play;[7] or when, in *The Feminine Mystique*, she remarks that we are perhaps dealing with a "sick" society that distrusts the potential women represent.

But we owe the deepened inquiry into the meaning of this "illness" and the possibility of this apocalypse to others. Like all liberal movements, according to the observation of the nice gatekeeper that we mentioned, NOW was outflanked by its own left. Ti-Grace Atkinson came out to urge an extremist group that proposes annihilating, once and for all, sexual roles. She also works for a research group that analyzes the historic causes of women's condition. The convention of 1968, the year of general agitation in the world, flatly rejects the soft proposals of the 1967 manifesto that had brought about the phallocratic response published in the December 1967 issue of *New Left Notes*, quoted above. This hardening of feminine positions provoked, evidently, the fury of men who preferred by far hearing, as in Germany, "We love you!" in order to be able to one day ask their heroic, their dear companions in struggle to lay down their weapons and prepare the meals for the children at home. The women's lib movement started up, as much in England as in the United States.

The daily *Voice of the Women's Liberation Movement* came out, announcing this new style of struggle; the agitator Carol Thomas was arrested. *Toward a Female Liberation Movement*, edited by Beverly Jones and Judith Brown,[8] called the SDS militants "privileged women" ignoring all the true problems of women who were waging their own battles; it reminded them that women who become known in movements dominated traditionally by men only managed it by bowing down to male values. The political tactic defined by nine points would become the program for young groups of English revolutionary feminists seeking an example in Ti-Grace Atkinson rather than Betty Friedan:

1.—Women must refuse to join any movements other than their own. They cannot hope to restructure society before relations between the sexes are restructured. It is possible that the inequality of domestic relations is the cause of all evils.

2.—Women, often influenced by the fear of physical force, must learn to protect themselves.

3.—We must compel the means of mass communication to be realistic.

4.—Women must view their experiences in common until they understand, define, and denounce explicitly the multiple techniques of domination that men use in private and public life.

5.—Collectives must be organized so that women can be relieved of their burdens in order to give them time to grow psychologically.

6.—Women must learn their history, because they have a history of which they can be proud and that can give their daughters pride. There is a market for feminist literature, historical or otherwise. It must be nourished.

7.—Women who have scientific competency must conduct research on the differences in numbers in universities and the temperament of the two sexes.

8.—The demand for equal pay for equal work was pushed aside with disgust by the extremists, but it must be taken into consideration, because inequality is a means of enslavement.

9.—In this list that does not pretend to be complete, I mention the laws on abortion.

The author of *The Female Eunuch* correctly observes that point seven ignores "research conducted for the last fifty years."[9] We can add that this perspective itself is becoming quickly outmoded, with the progress in human sciences that brings out more and more, and on the most numerous points, the proof that what was taken as a fact of nature is in reality a cultural fact, man being the only animal that creates his own nature and re-creates it incessantly. On point six, we note a profound difference as well between Anglo-Saxon

women, always on the lookout for a tradition at the moment where
they rebel the most radically, and French women, daughters of the
revolutionary equation "What are we? Nothing. What should we
be? Everything," and who chant:

> We who are without a past, women,
> We who have no history,
> Since the dawn of time, women,
> We are the dark continent.
>
> —An MLF chant[10]

Judith Brown, a research assistant in psychiatry at the University of Florida, is one of the most appreciated American figures of
English feminism. She established a parallel in Part II of *Toward
a Female Liberation Movement* between the marriage of a woman
and the integration of blacks (an analogy that needs to be nuanced
as much as the comparison between the economic oppression of
the proletariat and the domestic oppression of women). She rec-
ommends feminine communities, single life, homosexuality, and
masturbation rather than integration though marriage. "We must
get our stuff together, begin to dismantle this system's deadly social
and military toys, and stop the mad dogs who rule us every place
we're at."[11]

In the beginning of the summer of 1968, at the moment when the
sun signals noon on the year's clock and at a time when the world's
youth was just starting to leave the barricades of the capital cities,
three shots rang out to signal the foundation of *SCUM*: Valerie
Solanas shot Andy Warhol, the filmmaker who, as she explained,
"was taking too much importance in her life." He survived; she was
sent to a psychiatric hospital; then she came out with the *Society
for Cutting Up Men*. The excess of black humor of this "bitch"

brings a comforted smile to men's lips, as Norman Mailer recognizes; he recognizes also that they are wrong, in *The Prisoner of Sex*. Valerie Solanas comforts, in the way that a well-made horror film, that is to say a commercial film, does; the monster jumps out at the moment when the atmosphere was becoming intolerable, so that the spectator can say: "It's only a movie." In Rome, the revolutionary homosexual group FUORI ("Outside") gives us the gift of a humorous poster: two passersby laugh their heads off when they see a parade with the sign "Gay Power" appear in the distance, but their smiles freeze when the procession arrives close to them; it is made up of poorly shaven brutes who bellow as they brandish billy clubs. The *Scum Manifesto* has an exact opposite effect on the male reader.[12]

Solanas's document, in fact, contains—like everything that is so extreme it seems crazy—a number of uncomfortable truths. Her declared praying mantis ferocity makes Solanas resemble somewhat the "king of the lepers" who, in the Middle Ages, took on for himself, to make it reality, what popular legend attributed to lepers: a hideous plot, with the alliance of the Jews and the infidels, to overthrow the royal throne. Solanas gives credibility on all levels to Pati Trolander, whom Normal Mailer cites, in the poem "Crotch Clawers":

> Self-fulfilling prophecy:
> Women are evil, sneaky and wicked.
> Shit.
> You are the one who asked for it.[13]

Here is what the monthly publication *Actuel* had to say about the *Scum Manifesto*:

Men are destructive larva, a lamentable genetic accident that a political massacre should abolish. Female power is waiting at the doors. The book makes its mark through its violence, a style, a logical frenzy. Men laugh after reading it; women are disturbed and reflective. You can shout insanity, crazy fantasies, mental debility all you want, but the book does hit a just resonance ... This book has done more for the cause than all the publications by militants, says the Lilith report.[14]

If the fool would persist in his folly he would become wise.

—William Blake

Here is a brief description of the author herself:

Valerie Solanas is always dressed in the same way, old jeans, a sweater and fur-lined jacket, a velvet cap on her head. She has the frozen face of a character out of Henri Rousseau's works. She ferments dreams and revolt. She could have been beautiful, but that doesn't interest her. Valerie Solanas hates men. Motionless and broody, she hung out for a long time in the lobby of the Chelsea Hotel, a meeting ground for the New York underground movement.[15]

Following are lines that show the general pattern of this document that goes as far in underground feminist literature as Sade did in erotic Jacobin literature.

The goal of women of a "civic and responsible mind" can only be to "overthrow the government, eliminate money, institute complete automation and destroy the male sex." Science proves that the species can continue perfectly to perpetuate itself without the help of men, if females accept to conceive only females. What is the male? "To call him an animal is to flatter him again; he's a thingamajig, a machine that walks around." Being near him "brings profound problems." Why? Because he is consumed by "guilt, shame, fear and insecurities, obsessed by fucking." His secret?

> The male is psychically passive. He detests this passivity and projects it onto the woman, defines himself as an active being and makes the torture wheel to prove it. His great show of force is fucking. Since he is wrong, he has to seek proof constantly. Fucking for him is a desperate attempt to show that he is not female. But he is passive and is dying to be a woman.

(It is curious to find an echo here of the wise Karen Horney who, along with Erich Fromm, represents the cultural branch of the American school of psychoanalysis and who, in writing *Our Inner Conflicts*, didn't even come close to Betty Friedan's most modest conclusions.)

The text explains further on that, after the elimination of money, "there won't be a need to kill men anymore because the only means of pressure on the female will have been removed." The problems of the functioning of the world that the victorious women will address will be the total revamping of education programs toward the sense of an accelerated intellectual level; the solution to the questions of "illnesses, senility, death"; the rebuilding of cities from the bottom up. The epilogue, of a beauty rather close once again to Sade's utopias, shows the male survivors ending their miserable days, wallowing in drugs or sniffing the air of the prairies with the toads, watching "the powerful female in full action," or going to the closest "suicide center where they will be gassed calmly, rapidly, and without pain," whereas the most reasonable ones won't try to fight but will instead sit "calmly" so they can "appreciate the show" and let themselves be soothed "by the waves of their irremediable abdication."

Pushing a truth to the folly that pulverizes it always makes unknown spaces apparent. Solanas went further than any reasonable sociologist in measuring the precipice that separates the sexes and delivers them into an idiotic battle, without any other way out than mercy, in a society that only one of the two built. It's possible that her insane cruelty, her well-argued and logical eloquence and cynicism, like that of all paranoiacs, played a role in the split of Atkinson and in the birth of "women's lib" that was the consequence of it. WITCH also comes out of this branch. WITCH is an acronym that stands for "Women's International Terrorist Conspiracy from Hell." They were blamed for a bonfire of bras, casting spells on banks, an invasion of Madison Square Garden dressed as magicians riding broomsticks—that made the stock market crash! It is also said that they have a deposit of dynamite in certain restrooms frequented by men. Finally, how could we not find echoes of Valerie Solanas in these most powerful words from Caroline Hennessey?

There's only one method of separating the human males from the over-compensating female-oppressing boys at this intermediate stage of the revolutionary game. The gauge is their tolerance for having their testes twisted. If he hollers, let him go—after you've twisted them off and given him a kick in the ass to send him on his way.

If he can grin and bear it, and look you squarely in the eye, the chances are his balls are so firmly attached that he doesn't hold them there with the glue of female oppressing and humiliating.

(Don't expect to find many of this type.)

   —*I, B.I.T.C.H.*, published in French as *Moi, la salope*[16]

"But how can women be so cruel?" asks, in tears, a character from a noir series crime novel. And his alter ego answers, "Because, at heart, they hate men. They would castrate you, Lambert, if they could, with impunity."[17]

Those who are surprised by this sudden explosion of hate between the sexes in the United States forget that the issue is hardly new. It was denounced more than twenty years ago by a few isolated voices, one of which, reprinted by *Les Temps Modernes* (at the same time that Simone de Beauvoir published *The Second Sex* and I was conducting research for *The Diane Complex*), declared quite clearly that women in America were "traumatized to the point of neuroses" by the resentment they brought out in men. The same author (Richard Neely) then analyzed the redirected expression of this resentment, through his noir crime series (where, well before *The Walter Syndrome*, he found it in *The Bride Wore Black*, the 1968 film by François Truffaut). Lost voices, voices stifled in the immense, gigantic hoax of the century: the denunciation, on a grand scale, of America as a matriarchy.[18]

"Yes, the argument that women were a social and economic class exploited by men, that women were finally the largest and most exploited class of all, ... was an argument that could begin to exist in the common awareness on a daily basis."

That was the opening salute from the fencing sword that Norman Mailer addressed to "women's lib" in *Prisoner of Sex*, an anti-feminist pamphlet.

If he could recognize that the *SCUM Manifesto* is the extreme of extremes and that it still represents the magnetic pole of "women's lib," it could be with the aim of compromising the movement altogether, along with this dreamer of "sexocide"; but it is nevertheless an undeniable truth. If, according to Reimut Reiche, the constituent seed of human and social life throughout the entire planet does not change at all after the reworkings of "socioeconomic organization" that the socialist revolutions were, it is, as we have seen, due to the unshakable sexism that presides in the *Mitsein*; but, just as you have to put aside Diderot and pick up Sade in order to rise to a true revolutionary consciousness, in order to conceive a future perspective where we explode this famous atomic seed of *Homo sapiens*, we have to put aside Kate Millett and spend a little time with *SCUM*.

Since the summer of 1968 that saw the birth of Valerie Solanas's manifesto and her "political program in science fiction form," women's lib has spread like a cluster of gunpowder prepared for the cannon, and the smell of dynamite crossed the Atlantic, reached London and Paris, made the Vatican sneeze, and shook up the windmills and tulips of the Dolle Mina like a storm, right up to the banks of the Northern European fjords.

> *I, B.I.T.C.H.*, have had it. With the system. With the establishment. With the men who run it. Especially the men.
>
> —the cover of *I, B.I.T.C.H.* and *Moi, la salope*

In late August of 1970—shortly after the Black Panther Huey P. Newton was released from prison and praising women's "just struggle"—the *New York Times* summarized the protests marking the fiftieth anniversary of the passing of the Nineteenth Amendment, granting the right to vote to women; women's lib was diffuse, divided, but firmly resolved, and projected a day of national protests against the oppression of the feminine sex, with parades, impromptu wild speeches, and guerrilla theater all planned.

Women brought "freedom trash cans" to publicly discard the most diverse symbols of oppression: cosmetic products, detergent, bras, ads for diets, knitting needles, and even birth control pills because they were sometimes considered as exploited up the consumerist society and egotistical male indifference. Discussions began in the streets, during the distribution of pamphlets; the "guerrilla theatre" simulated births, exposure of economic prostitution through psychological coercion upon hiring, and more.

The *Times* reminded readers that, after having demanded equal salaries and free access to abortions without charge, feminists were radicalized and declaring their intentions to beat down the patriarchal system. This charge got its source in the postscript to Kate Millett's book *Sexual Politics*, her doctoral thesis sold first in photocopy form; the postscript was by Dana Densmore, a radical militant, and was entitled *No More Fun and Games*.

Kate Millett, who had just posed the fourth theoretical cornerstone for the liberation of women, refused to accept the title, extremely journalistic, of "Mao Tse-tung of women's lib." It is certain that she finished building the theoretical blocks begun by Betty Friedan. Whereas the author of *The Feminine Mystique* is a well-to-do middle-class woman, an extremely competent researcher with a home, husband, and children, Millett came off as "brilliant, rejected by the masculine world." She belonged to a marginal universe, with a poor childhood due to a broken home, deserted by her father, her vague attempts at sculpture, her live-in relationship with a Japanese man, her refusal of marriage, and her support of "radical lesbians." Her doctoral dissertation, since published and translated, a best seller on both sides of the Atlantic, was described by her doctoral committee judge, George State, in the following way: "To read this book is like sitting with your balls jammed into a nutcracker!"

The most diverse groups were multiplying, with the most unexpected names: the "Redstockings," the "Sisters of Lilith," "Bread and Roses," and more. Among the tumult of "these furious voices," Ti-Grace Atkinson's rose above the others:

We need a *revolution in the revolution*. We have to find the truth of which many women are afraid.

If you examine the laws, you will see that marriage is legalized rape, a source of unpaid labor, that it removes woman's freedom of movement and that it absolutely does not guarantee the love of a man. Love is something else.[19] It is always understood with a notion of dependence; we want nothing to do with it. These individuals defined today as women must make the problem explode. To some extent, women must commit an authentic suicide.

With this extremist language, we are far from the 1967 manifesto and the first feminist group founded the same year in Chicago, with Joreen Freeman, Naomi Weisstein, and Heather Booth. The latter had begun to be radicalized when she gave an interview on the issue of abortion to *Mademoiselle*, where she declared that the revolutionary conscience began when one recognized that this problem "was social and not individual." Soon afterward, she founded the first liberation group with Chude Pamela Allen in New York. The tone of feminism had begun to change, even though this small group was formed at the same time as NOW. The left wing of the latter could only communicate, or otherwise merge, with the Booth and Allen tendency.

Such is the history of the American awakening. In the United States and in Canada, women had begun to decry their status in the fall of 1967. In the Canadian Nouvelle Gauche (new left), four young girls from the Student Union for Peace Action wrote an article: "Sisters, brothers, lovers, listen!" This text's starting point was the Marxist observation that a man's worth is that of a woman's in relation to man. They exposed, with the same bitterness as Carmichael or Juliet Mitchell, women's position at the heart of the movement of the New Left: quite simply the traditional one, an absolute submission to masculine leadership. Radical Canadian feminism had its starting point there.

Radical feminism gained ground in Great Britain. The author of *The Female Eunuch* tells how she took the floor "in front of a mixed, calm crowd." And nevertheless, surprise: "nervous, timid women expressed their opinions on the most subversive subjects in front of their husbands. Nurses are revolting, teachers are striking, skirts are at all lengths, women aren't buying bras anymore, they demand the right to abortions: the rebellion is gathering force and may become a revolution."

In Sweden, touched a long time ago by Betty Friedan's words, an awakening of a calmer type has regrouped intellectuals, housewives, and single women. Sweden is a country of an old feminist tradition, of which August Strindberg's gynophobic theater bears the traces. Women have been voting there since 1866. (That's the same year that Olympe Audouard's book *Guerre aux hommes* [War on men] appeared; it encouraged women toward violent methods.) Ten years earlier, this kingdom had granted single women equal rights with men, after the publication of a novel by the Scandinavian Fredrika Bremer, *Hertha*, "which, in 1856, was for the Northern European woman what *Uncle Tom's Cabin* had been for the cause against slavery in the US."[20]

This being said, and in spite of a growing number of Swedish women in the workplace (fifty-five married women enrolled in the Social Security system as currently working in 1962, compared to thirty in 1950), they continue to protest today against the lack of childcare centers that are meant to help out the working mother;[21] unlike American women, Swedish women complain less of being poorly welcomed in the workplace than of the lack of household help. Betty Friedan observes the fact and writes about it in *Woman:*

The Fourth Dimension: "In Sweden, they say that there can be no equality until men share the responsibilities of marriage with women, from the upkeep of the home to childcare, and until women become full partners of men in the society."[22]

The Group 8, founded in Stockholm by eight women, took charge of this awakening of the second sex, foreshadowed already by the film from a female filmmaker, a friend of the feminist Bibi Andersson: women, secretly enraged at having no control over the command levers, let off steam in their dreams and knock down all the men they meet through the use of judo. Study, debate, and writing groups boosted the movement that reported on its work at the international convention on August 12, 1971.

Among Nordic women, the "Dolle Mina," loud and in bright colors, deserve a special mention. The movement is mixed: one man for nine women, to the great indignation of the Americans who made an outburst at the same convention when the Dutch women brought this objective ally. These militants, among whom we find Sofia Vries, the famous feminist from Amsterdam, do not only preoccupy themselves with the emancipation of women; like the Danish, they rally also around socialism and harangue the housewives of the poorer districts. Their activities purposely take on a bolder path than elsewhere; they whistle at boys in the street and pinch their butts with the pedagogical intention of showing them what it's like to be a sexual object, undoubtedly to make them feel "this unhealthy mixture of narcissism and paranoia" that Norman Mailer refers to in the anti-feminist work cited earlier; they raise money to build a free abortion clinic and invade gynecologists' conventions, raising their T-shirts to show their tattooed abdomens: "My body belongs to me."[23] On Mother's Day, they organized a walk of single mothers. In Amsterdam, they founded a "House for Women," with a technical program of study and karate classes.

In Belgium, radical feminism took off with men at the start. The latter, in contact with rebellious military groups, had the idea of steering feminine study and research groups toward the issues of liberation, inspired by a theatrical representation: *The Nurse* by Armand Gatti. During the discussion that preceded this initiative, members of the Parisian MLF convinced well-intentioned comrades not to give in to the temptation to include men, with the goal of helping women speak out, past experience proving that women never express themselves sincerely and freely when men are present. So the men agreed to give the first push, then to back away. Since that time, exclusively feminine circles have started to function; a "Unified Feminist Party," "the Radical Lesbians," and mixed gender groups, like the "Marie Miner" that was always mixed and the FLF that has become mixed; a movement "for the legalization of abortion" broke out in Liège after the Manifesto of the 343 appeared in Paris; pop-up childcare centers appeared. In February 1973, in Ghent, a huge march for "abortus vry," free abortion, took place regarding the trial of Dr. Willy Peers.

Finally, in France, the Movement for the Liberation of Women was born almost simultaneously in Paris, Lyon, and Toulouse.[24] At the start of the fall semester in 1968, female student activists noticed that women's issues had never been included among the demands presented by the organizers of the demonstrations in May, and they decided to found a movement following the example of women's lib. This was written about in *L'idiot international* [The international idiot], issue no. 5.

> We are merely our husbands' servants. It is not our place to rise up proudly against our masters.
>
> —Speech by Saint Monica, Mother of Saint Augustine, addressed to women who complained of being beaten

The MLF activist who signed her letter "Actuelle" (Today), in the fourth issue of *Actuel*, summarized the beginning of the movement:

> Up until now, we were considered the domestic help, we had no other roles other than the ones imposed upon us ... Now, the time has come for a radical revision of the issues. All couples are bourgeois couples!
>
> Some adventurous souls who didn't enjoy these pleasures were prey to the flames. The virgins were considered like old women; lovers like whores; concubines like passing birds. After thirty, their market value was about zero. If they got involved in politics, they were advised to go take care of their vaginal problems elsewhere.
>
> American women were demonstrating loudly ... France, the country of coarse red table wine and the flannel belt, waited for May 1968 to break down the institutional framework of permitted revolts. But the issue of the liberation of women could not be found anywhere in the group demands.

When they came back to school in the fall, several intellectual women took up the issue, and they had to create pop-up child-care centers in order to start the movement up again at the various branches of the university in Paris—Censier, Nanterre, Vincennes, and the fine arts school, the last bastion to fall in the mini revolution of '68.[25]

It was thanks to the experience of these young women from the bourgeois class, thanks to their contacts with female workers, homemakers, and housekeepers from the working-class suburbs, and not thanks to God knows what intellectual prejudice, Marcusian or other, that the purely material objectives of their struggle—salary equity, demands for help in the home, etc.—were replaced, bit by bit, by the radical reworking of the couple and of the family in society.

The liberal bourgeois class, left-leaning people, leftists, in general, everybody who remained outside this movement, thought the following: this unexpected resurgence of a type of feminism from 1848 was due to the intellectuals' preconceived idea outside the "real" problems of the working class; the opposite was happening! When the girls from the MLF give in to the leftist intellectual tendency, they tend also to give a classical Marxist tendency to problems submitted to them, and not what is called (wrongly, besides) "pure feminist." It is the working-class women who agree to talk to them who also bring them back (sometimes unconsciously for them) to the issue of the specific oppression of women.

A good example was cited by a recent leaflet:

An employee in the post office has just explained the specific ways in which they are treated because they are women: methods of intimidation, discipline, infantilization, difficult psychological climate ... a problem always turned against her to bring her back to the conditions of exploitation (that were, besides, very hard). She tried hard to insist upon talking about what really bothered her; the girls didn't listen to her, obsessed by getting her to say what they wanted to hear.

—"For a Revolutionary Feminist Group"

So, we see the situation: the irony of the specialists, faced with what they judged to be an extravagance of "little bourgeois intellectuals," that is to say, the urgent need to reassess sexism above all, and no longer the economic capitalist structures, this irony fell flat. That is why the MLF, which started out as if in a dream world, criticized and scorned, persisted victoriously and developed in France, taking hold outside Paris, in milieus that were far from being uniquely those of teachers and intellectuals.

The first informal movement, uniquely based on a drive to

awaken, took off. It had no leader on high, no bureaucracy. It functioned on the base of bimonthly general meetings and diversified
groups, common interest commissions, or neighborhood groups
that complemented the original "consciousness raising" groups.
The members taught a small number of women quite simply to
get to know themselves as women, to appreciate each other, and to
develop solid emotional ties in accordance with the call to arms of
the MLF song:

> Alone in our misfortune, women,
> Talk to us, look at us!

Better yet: our imagination and humor take over:

Kidnap Ménie Grégoire; invent Madame Soleil, an astrologist; sleep
with the Pope; dress up like men; go to the hammam so that we can
caress each other as women; slap Isabelle (from *Hara-Kiri*),[26] who is
really too queer; laugh with our preferred lovers; cultivate our gardens
with little blue flowers; for all that, for all the rest, for the pleasure,
we're organizing for the cause. Let's raise our glasses and toast!

—MLF, January 1971[27]

The impact of unfettered fantasies over the real had to come
about. Ménie Grégoire was not kidnapped, but her show was interrupted by militants on March 11, 1971; little flowers were planted
in the gardens of Reuilly for a mock celebration of Mother's Day,
with guerrilla theater and open-air exhibitions of pictures; Professor Lejeune's lyrical and humanitarian proclamations—as filled
with emotion as the glass eye of an SS officer—were disrupted by
sausages thrown at him (after pieces of scrap meat were thrown,
accompanied by the cry, "Hey, mister, I just had an abortion"); and,

during an international march for unrestricted abortion, a wedding was interrupted at Saint-Ambroise church in 1972. And that's not counting the prehistory:

> Recent actions that were sometimes unanimous, sometimes by a group that was still free to do what it wanted as long as it was not censored by the General Assembly. Demonstrations in front of the Petite Roquette:[28] "We are all thieves, abortionists, whores"; stirring things up at various bogus and rigged conventions, at the general meeting of *Elle*, at the medical school (a meeting of physicians).
>
> —Actuelle

We can add to the list since then: the contradictions brought by the members of FHAR[29] to a roundtable presided by Évelyne Sullerot on "sexual freedom" at the Laennec Center,[30] as well as six months earlier, at the marriage counselors' debate where they were showing the film by Bertuccelli on women's lib at the UNESCO auditorium in March 1971; and above all, the punitive expedition at the Sexology Congress of Sanremo in April 1972, that was all over the Italian press and television and finally supported by the Three Marias in 1974.

> What man could lack confidence to the point of believing that fertility legitimizes love?
>
> —René Crevel, *Mon corps et moi* (*My Body and I*), 1925

The most spectacular action of the MLF, as we have seen, was the idea of the Manifesto of the 343 and the campaign that followed it, all the way up to the Bobigny trial. The manifesto itself was of a totally new kind: it began by simply announcing social facts and statistics (the number of abortions per year, the danger of their clandestine nature), then the signers declared themselves guilty of an act condemned by law, and finally ended with the simple solution of free access to abortion. Not one word about the motivations, no postulating, no explanation; never had any group produced such a lapidary text with the intention of provocation and demands. Its very simplicity was considered an enormous incitement. To dare to sign a text without saying how much they earned per year, for what reasons one could desire to end a pregnancy or why they did it, not mentioning anything about a partner (which moved Father Oraison the most, as we saw earlier)—what an outrage! The worst intentions were immediately attributed to the writers and the signers—the thirst for publicity, for example. That's normal. Montherlant cites somebody's reaction concerning the romantic suicide of a poor Russian émigré to France upon learning that his fellow countryman Paul Gorguloff had assassinated the president of the République: "Do you think that he meant it?" (Yes, Joe, that's France, too.)

In its comic caricature about the opinion of the average French man, reader of *L'Aurore*, and regular lottery player, the weekly publication *Minute*[31] gives us a surprising "Incredible Crusade of the Angel Makers,"[32] read with delight by women who still needed to get radicalized on this topic. This extreme case symbolized very well what existed as resistance—global, abrupt, cavernous—in this country of Voltaire, so strongly dechristianized, and among people who wouldn't dream of reading *Minute*, including those among the sympathizers, the liberals, those who pronounced the words "yes," "but," "if," "because," "however," "thus."

And to think that this passerby could give me my photograph: a son!
Two cents in the crack, and in nine months, my portrait in a nutshell.
—René Crevel, *My Body and I*

Fourier has more credibility than ever. This free disposition of the woman's body is scandalous and challenges the whole of society. In bourgeois society, frustrated and obsessed, this slogan was, and still is, interpreted as follows: "the freedom to let your instincts take over,"[33] that is, "permission to sleep with anybody." (It was enough to hear the bitter words of Professor Lejeune on March 5, 1971, at the main assembly:[34] "a certain movement that demands the emancipation of women, in reality it aims only at demanding *pleasure* ...). Today, we are starting to realize that the truth is not so simple and that this "free disposition" brings about all other kinds of consequences, including this one, of course; that it could be perfectly valid in the most rigorous of moral conduct to sleep not "with anybody" but with whom you please and not from whom you *profit*; to make of physical love a choice, a passion, a pleasure, an interest, an experience, anything except a fixation and a social situation, except a so-called source of revenue and a true source of alienation and servitude. But beyond this refusal to "abandon all morals," the free disposition in question puts all other behavior into play, those that concern not only women: freedom of reproduction or the refusal of reproduction, the freedom of style of erotic life that pushes aside all the prejudices against "deviations" and "perversions," and so on. That which consists, from Fourier to Marcuse, in fact, of the most serious questioning, of the interior, of our world, or of its structures of thought and its past.

It was thus on this "hot spot" that the MLF mobilized itself; and, just as I said earlier, this combat required so much attention and preoccupied it so profoundly that some militants, we must repeat, are worried today that they will see objectives for the future pushed aside in order to concentrate on these demands for free access to abortion. It is certain that this demand will be met one day, and that a real danger exists for the movement to fixate solely on this goal in the way that old feminism centered itself on the right to "culture," then on the right to vote. The example of black people is there to prove that these legitimate demands can become bones to throw to gnaw on for the revolutionary appetite. And strategy requires that the whole of a front should never be neglected for one particular point, nor that this point should be neglected in relation to the whole.

It is for this reason that, in November 1971, the militants drew up a document that seems to clarify the issue of the perspectives of the movement better than all the preceding discussions:

> We have to know if the movement will be a mass movement, in which potentially all the women of the specifically exploited group will take part, or if it will be another small group, because the leftist label that some strive to put on the movement will cut us off immediately from the mass of women. We are not here to follow men's politics and receive directives from the Unified Socialist Party or the Marxist-Leninists, with women in the middle. The leftists of the movement, manipulated by men, are trying to transform the movement into an annex of the political groups; they are transmitting the masculine conception of the liberation of women that need to be put back "into the right path."
>
> Women's struggle ... puts into question *all* the aspects of global society (into which the exploitation of class is integrated) as well as the privileged nature of the anti-capitalist struggle.
>
> —"For a feminist revolutionary group," November 1971

Italy has also awakened to radical feminism. As can be imagined, the challenge to abortion laws has known a passionate flurry of action, more violent still in this country, a bastion of Catholicism. Elvira Banotti's book on the subject (currently being translated into French) was deemed by critics as not only pernicious but also full of lies:

"It's all fabricated, from one end to the other," was said of this study that collected a set of facts even more unbelievable than in France. A series of debates took place around this book in Rome, where insults and even blows were exchanged between men and women.

Contrary to France, the new feminist movement in Italy is divided instead of being composed of one group, having diverse and even opposing interior branches, like that of "leftism" and "revolutionary feminism." (Not counting that of lesbianism, which, although in the minority, is so much more important in that it points a finger at a form of sensitivity and not an ideological thought.)

The names of these small groups are Movimento di Liberazione della Donna, which was founded in February 1971 and does not refuse alliances with masculine politics; the Fronte Italiano di Liberazione Femminile, more radical; and, at the extreme end, the Rivolta Femminile, which is the movement with Banotti and Carla Lonzi.

The latter expressed the point of view of these radical feminists in a sort of manifesto entitled *Let's Spit on Hegel* that has not yet been translated into French.

> Women should burn their shacks instead of spending their time stupidly cleaning them.
>
> —Françoise d'Eaubonne, *Le quadrille des matamores*
> (The dance of the braggarts), 1953

This fifty-page text (like the *SCUM Manifesto*) poses a fundamental challenge of the problems of women in patriarchal society, as its economy *structures* it, and as Occidental thought *reflects* it—particularly that of Hegel, who justifies sexism on the ideological and philosophical level. Carla Lonzi shows how two positions coexist for this thinker: one that identifies woman's destiny and the "principle of femininity" (what Freud confirms, let's add, by the famous words "anatomy is destiny"), and the other position, which estimates that servitude is "a human condition that carries out in history the evangelical maxim 'the last will be the first.'"

Carla Lonzi had the originality of emphasizing the connection between the oppressed woman and the adolescent against the phallocrat. This concept is undoubtedly steeped in the Mediterranean mentality of the complicity between the mother and the son against the father's despotism, a complicity that the Church has transcended at the theological level of an intercession of the mother based on the sacrifice of the son with the father. But this author's analysis rests on the possible connections between the movement for feminine liberty and the waves of youth protests. It is not, all the same, a return by the group to the sacrosanct family:

> In the countries of the socialist zone, the socialization of the means of production has not touched the traditional moral institution; it has even reinforced it in as much as it has reinforced the prestige and the role of the patriarchal figure ...
>
> The family is the pivotal point of the patriarchal order; it is founded not only on economic interests but on man's psychological mechanisms that, in every period, took the woman as object of domination and as a pedestal.[35]

After having reminded us of Lenin's errors regarding sexual matters, according to quotations from his interviews with Clara Zetkin and his correspondence with Inessa Armand (these very same deficiencies used by Claudie Broyelle to justify Chinese puritanism!), Lonzi declares: "No revolutionary ideology will be able to convince us any longer that women and young people find duties and solutions in the struggle, in work, in sublimation, in sport."

And, observing that the cult of male virtues, all having the motivation of fundamental aggressivity at their center, has made of the masculine subconscious "a repository of blood and fear," and that the role of reassuring and giving a sense of security has fallen to the woman, Lonzi proposes: "Let's abandon man so that he will feel the depths of his solitude." This proposal is in accordance with one of the declarations often heard at the MLF: the liberation of women goes along with the proof seen concretely, in real life, that they can live without men, at all levels.

> Dearest darling, while you are rejoicing about your domestic preoccupations, I am giving in to the pleasure of solving the enigma of the structure of the spirit.
>
> —a letter from Freud to his fiancée

In Hegelian interpretations, the world, according to masculine history, is born from two sources: work and struggle. Lonzi cites examples of the patriarchal filiation of a community at its head; in September 1970, as she was writing this manifesto, newspapers' headlines were all reporting the death of Gamal Abdel Nasser: "One hundred million Arabs suddenly felt like orphans." (And in November, after the death of General Charles de Gaulle, we could add the famous remark, "France is widowed.") The author concludes: "May we no longer be considered those who continue the species. We will give no more sons to anybody, neither to man nor to the state. From now on, we will give them to themselves, and we will reconstruct ourselves."

This Italian awakening is all the more interesting and poignant in the country of Catholic phallocracy, where free disposition of one's body is even further away than in our country, especially when the sacrosanct obligatory motherhood is concerned. An international study on women, published by Hachette ten years ago, remarked that Italian women were raucous, voluble, coquettish, and hypersensitive, due only to overcompensation for their lack of social existence and their status that condemns them to exist throughout their lives only through their fathers, their husbands, and their children. In summarizing a little broadly, it could be said that Italian women of today correspond more or less to French women of the 1930s and 1940s. So we can judge the impact that radical feminist agitation produces in a similar context.

One of the most sensitive countries in its reaction to this universal movement is Denmark, the country of old feminist traditions.

The president of the Danish Women's Council, named Edele Kruchow, declared to the journalist Yves de Saint-Agnès: "As enviable as our lot might seem, inequality between men and women still remains in the facts."

On the subject of salaries, she says the following: "It is in this domain that we note the most flagrant injustice. Denmark ratified the convention of the International Office of Work relative to salary equity.[36] However, the average salary for women remains 20 percent less than that for men."

This is why the Redstockings, an extremist feminist organization, began an original operation: to pay only 80 percent of the ticket price for public transportation; they called it "Operation Bus." That doesn't prevent them from devoting great debates to the primordial question of *koensroll*, that is, the respective roles of the sexes. Parades with signs, public aggression toward men, pushing the soldiers of the Royal Guard—such are the other undertakings of the Danish women with the ruby-colored legs. Another less effusive movement supports their demands, the Union of Danish Women. They are led by a twenty-eight-year-old feminist, as beautiful as a character in a Hans Christian Andersen Christmas tale, Grethe

Fenger-Møller, and she says the following: "We don't want to be considered like men but like human beings. Equality must be established at all levels, and specific roles must stop being attributed to men and to women."[37]

(In response to these "pretentions," the De Enlige Faedre, a masculinist association of "solitary fathers," was founded. It corresponds to the other Swedish movement, Männens Rättsförening, "Union for Husbands' Rights," that declares, as spoken by one of its defenders, Bo Eriksson, "The situation for man in Scandinavia is hardly more enviable than the feminine condition in Spain." No relationship with our MLH.[38])

All the women's movements held their first international convention (that is to say, American-European) on August 12, 1971. It was in Stockholm, in a vast building whose eleventh floor sometimes seemed too small to contain all the "angry women." The Germans, the timidest ones up to that point, declared that they would join the campaign for abortion started by the French. Projects were developed, among others an "international march for free access to abortion and contraception," that took place on November 20 of the same year.

"The feminist movement is not international; it's planetary," affirms *Let's Spit on Hegel*. The slogan is beautiful. We have to recognize that it is only a dream for the moment. Women's issues are planetary; but up to now, the movement includes only the majority of European countries and the northern United States. Women of the developing world and the majority of Latin Americans, the exploited of the exploited, have not yet emerged into human existence; perhaps another convention will see some Algerian women protesting against the setback for women's rights, rights so hoped for in the underground and jails by the heroines of the Algerian National Liberation Front.

In this same Mediterranean basin, the cradle of our most sinister oppression, as Germaine Tillion explains in *The Harem and Its Cousins*, a new and unexpected type of pop-up feminism has been born in Portugal. The following is what was expressed in a letter that I received well before the affair of the "Three Marias":

Feminism does not exist as an organization for the moment. It does exist, all the same, and this one is truly Portuguese, women who are particularly sensitive to the problem and who are starting to show themselves and to raise a little hell against the beautiful phallocratic order ... And they are already so representative that they boycotted the election of Miss Europe in Estoril ... Articles in the papers talked about it. It was not only the illegitimacy of their condition that they were questioning, but that of the entire feudal Portuguese regime. Thus, it was very politicized! Then, I also learned lots of interesting and strange things about women fishmongers, regular women here in France, with no fear of speaking loudly, who get together among themselves exclusively and decide to go to a popular show or to a bar in the evening without telling their husbands or lovers. They also have their own sort of club or association and take care of unemployed women and women who are ill. No help from the state: they pool their money and manage the whole thing." (Isabel D., August 10, 1972)

Thus, what is very interesting is that a certain popular consciousness raising—spontaneous, impromptu—of feminism for providing necessities for one another preceded the discourse of intellectuals here.

The "Three Marias" and Portugal

The next year, the scandal of the "New Portuguese Letters" broke out. As in the trial in Bobigny, where the accused, Marie-Claire

Chevalier, was reported by her "accomplice" (the boy who raped her), the three Portuguese women were reported to the police by the typographers who had collaborated in the "crime": printing this collective book that had just become a resounding success.

For having spoken openly and with an enraged sincerity about their oppression, their manipulative education, religious obscurantism, sexual assault, and alienating motherhood, they were accused of attacks on public morals and fined by the courts. Flyers were distributed: "They might be sent to prison for writing a masterpiece!" Quotations from their book were circulated: "I am telling you: in Portugal, woman is not only man's slave, but she also plays her role as woman-object with enthusiasm and conviction. I say: ENOUGH! It's time to form a block with our bodies."

Other countries are moved; intellectuals are mobilizing. The weekly *Nouvel Observateur* interviews them. Petitions are flying around Rome and Paris. On October 21, 1973, the MLF organized a "Night of the Woman" dedicated to them; three actresses, Delphine Seyrig among them, took turns reading long excerpts from this subversive work. On January 30, 1974, a candlelight march took place in front of Notre Dame to express feminist support for the "Portuguese writers," as Paris was in the habit of calling them.

And so it is that even in the regions of this "mare nostrum" where the phallocratic Occidental system developed, the system that Tillion summarizes and condemns so well, surprising explosions are being produced: Boumédiène must be thinking about controlling the birth rate, and on the other side of the Mediterranean Sea, in a fascist country, three women authors see a crowd of foreigners take up their cause, foreigners who, up to then, had adapted themselves quite well to the dictatorship of the Lusitanian puppet.

For a Feminist Planetary Manifesto (End)

Projected Goals

In the past, "sex" signified "woman." Sex and woman constituted the hidden face of the earth. The black continent. This is why the liberation of women is the same as the liberation of sex. (The excellent Professor Lejeune was not wrong on this point, as he accused the MLF of demanding the right to orgasm without terror.)

The liberation of women includes the defeat of men. But it is the liberation of man, male and female.

The liberation of women includes the formal proof that they can do without men at all levels. It would, however, be simplistic or poetic (in Valerie Solanas fashion) to imagine an institution of homosexuality and to reserve to a minority the task of procreating and the taste for doing it. There will always be heterosexuals of both sexes (including bisexuals, of course!), and always pregnant women who don't have abortions, always mothers, always children. Reproduction through ectogenesis, producing only females, is not a project. Procreation should be seriously and even energetically slowed down. There is no intention to stop it altogether. Not even in our dreams. Not even after the strikes against births that I am wishing for.

The liberation of women will end up in that for men—if not for those of today, at least tomorrow's men. It will end in the *restitution of space for the species*. It will end in the abolition of the repressive mechanism that makes the collective male unconscious "a receptacle of blood and fear." With the liberation of heterosexuals, just as of bisexuals and homosexuals. And, in the end, these labels will disappear.

But that's for tomorrow. For the time being, we won't escape the war of the sexes. We must get ready for it. The movements for the liberation of women must choose carefully the few masculine minorities that can form alliances with them, like the FHAR, the IHR, the MLH,[1] or certain marginal groups, against all the other men: accomplices of the phallocracy that they deny, "revolutionaries" that contest only its structures, and above all the "liberals," more pernicious yet than the pure-blooded sexists of the sorts like Lejeune, Chauchard, Pierre Debray, and Tilliette. "We must harass them and destroy them as a power, up to the silencing of the last of their voices. We must break up their leadership and reduce it to nothingness. We won't stop until we have destroyed the family unit, the heterosexual norm as base of the society, and sexist discrimination as a part of the working of the world," wrote a French revolutionary feminist.

For us, men are not the enemy. They are our legislators, our employers, our husbands, our lovers.

—Interview with the Pussy-Cats (*Elle*, November 29, 1971)

Our enemy is our master,
I am telling you as a good Frenchman.

—La Fontaine

In the issue of *Partisans* entitled *Libération des femmes: Année zero* (Liberation of women: year zero), several definitive analyses were published concerning the exploitation of women that had entered into the mores under the guise of family life. These analyses make it apparent that a fact of such a planetary order does not resemble a reform at all but instead can be called a revolution.

The Study by Christine Dupont

The most important, the most irrefutable of these studies was conducted by Christine Dupont. Thanks to her, for the first time, we can grasp the passage between the new feminism and this critique of capitalism that the traditional-style Marxist revolutionaries accuse it of neglecting.

> Even when the wild held no perils, Adam delved and Eve span and
> God the father was their daddy and walked with them in the twilight
> if they were good.
>
> —Germaine Greer[2]

The author of this study posits that the oppression of women, where capitalism as such was destroyed, is attributed to purely ideological causes; they are called "legacies," in the way that, to the great astonishment of traditional Marxists, religion stood firm fifty years after the October Revolution. But the thesis of "legacies" has nothing to do with Marxism as such, since that means attributing any phenomenon, religion or the oppression of women, to purely ideological causes. Would ideology, then, survive the material causes that it served to render acceptable?

This question of a theory necessary to explain the oppression of women outside the given economic structures (necessary because we note this oppression in *all* economic structures and *all* periods) has triggered essays by women separated by great distances who don't know each other: Margaret Benston wrote "The Political Economy of Women's Liberation," and the Cuban Isabel Larguía, undoubtedly little satisfied with Fidel Castro's advice for homemaking, wrote "Against Invisible Work."

Household Work, the Invisible Platform of Production

Christine Dupont defined the two sectors of feminine activity that serve as the base for society, a base as indispensable as the work men do outside: *reproduction*, first of all, which implies procreation and rearing; and housework, an exclusive sector, which serves as the invisible platform for *production*, that is, man's work outside the home. Without the preparation of his food, repairing his clothes, washing his clothes, and the arrangement of his living surroundings according to a minimum of hygiene and attractiveness, no proletarian would be able to sell his force for work; no merchant would be able to continue to sell and buy merchandise; no self-employed man would be able to pursue his career.

Now, when these services are sought from outside suppliers, they generate an expense much too high for a simple worker, whether he belongs to the manual sector or the intellectual of the work market, whether he is a manual laborer or an executive. No salary or treatment could allow him to live a long time with such a budget. Hence, marriage gives man the possibility of selling his work abilities under much more profitable conditions by economizing on the expense of a housekeeper, a restaurant, most or all of the laundry, without counting the economizing of time for sexual adventures. To this inestimable service that the spouse brings to the system of purchase of work, or to modern capitalism, a second service that is even more precious is added: procreation, which brings new future workers to the world. Finally, more recently, the woman adds to these two sectors her own personal contribution to *direct production*, to work, most of the time in jobs that make it most difficult to feed others because they are worse remunerated than the others, or part-time (this part-time work that the powers that be strive to take as a conquest of the modern woman and that is the best way of keeping her in the lowest zones of the economy).

Against so many striking services rendered to the market of work, what is the remuneration for women? In the first two specific sectors, it is about zero. Dupont shows that, in exchange for procreation and the invisible work of household burdens that permit man's visible work, the woman can only count on her own upkeep. She feeds, lodges, and clothes herself—that's all. She benefits from no increase in material advantages for such a great amount of work. She does not reach a higher level or promotion for procreating and rearing, whether it be for five children or only one, or keeping up with a ten-room apartment or a small room for two. To the contrary, a surplus of work for her brings about a decrease in advantages: leisure activities, freedom, material well-being. Her work status is the only one to not be remunerated and to be treated as capital for the society.

This paradox is so well implanted into social mores that the accountability of the state, when it thinks about reform, inscribes a statute of family aid as a supplement that takes only the couple into account. The couple, the base of this world, foundation of the family unit, atom of the society. And the opposition parties, in their demands, talk only of *familial* exploitation! (MODEF[3] is seeking the equivalency of *one* salary.)

"Free furnishing of work in the frame of a global and personal relation like marriage constitutes precisely a rapport of slavery," concludes Dupont, who joins Ti-Grace Atkinson in her judgments on conjugal rapport.

It's easy, as I have explained elsewhere,[4] to note on these bases that feminine oppression is thus at once *specific, communal, and principal*; specific, because this kind of obligation is not imposed on anybody of the masculine sex, and the social mores lead a woman almost inevitably to accept them under penalty of condemning herself to social insignificance, solitude, and often to poverty; communal, for the reasons just mentioned, since the great majority of women are either married, preparing to get married, were married, or live in a marital state; principal, because it reverberates into her other eventual exploitation, that of working outside the home. The wife of the worker, of the employee, of the executive, of the shopkeeper, of the professor, if she works, will not be exploited in the same way or at the same level; in most cases, the very choice of her work is determined by the husband's situation, the milieu where he works and where he has often introduced her. The number of children for whom she is responsible guides her work as well—will incite her, for example, to be satisfied with part-time work. Finally, the economic imperatives and fatigue of household work, if she is poor, will oblige her to make do with undeclared work or work poorly paid under various pretexts: absenteeism, secondary income, and so on.

We can't ignore, on top of it, this infernal cycle that so many working women suffer: the profits from outside work are canceled out by the obligatory domestic help she must hire—because only the man can obtain free domestic help through marriage or cohabitation. For the woman, if she seeks this same help, it will always be paid help. (I have personally known a "perfectly heterosexual" woman, who, due to the exhausting physical challenges of her conflicts between work and family life of a single mother and housekeeper, ended up accepting a homosexual relationship in order to raise her son and live in normally comfortable conditions, because she couldn't afford a paid domestic helper. Such a situation is rare.)

Logical consequence, as revolutionary feminists maintain: the first enemy for women is the "patriarchal" class rather than the "capitalist" class. Let's add even that the capitalist class and the leading class of the new socialist countries are still less woman's enemy than the power of societies that have not yet moved to capitalism or socialism: these societies, clusters of subcultures, represent the last places where the familial oppression of woman is doubled by an openly slave-driving social oppression, that of past centuries. Such is the status in the Third World.

"Phallocracy is pure negativity, that is part of the patriarchal ideology of the capitalist society," declares Anne-Marie Grélois in a private letter to the professor of philosophy and sexologist Michel Bouhy van Elzie, founder of the CERSI (Circle of Studies and International Sexual Research, in Liège). We can add that phallocracy is no longer only pure negativity; in the past, it had a reason to exist, as did slavery, as did war; it is thanks to this oppression of women that, as Virginia Woolf reminds us, "cities could be torn out of the jungle and marshes."[5] But today, still quoting from Anne-Marie Grélois, "the bourgeoisie needs to be phallocratic to maintain itself, and if you attack society at the socioeconomic level, you end up with a pseudo-socialist government, dominated by a totalitarian and phallocratic bureaucracy, the sign of the failed revolution."

This kind of truth was long treated as an individualist and petit-bourgeois error. That goes without saying.

I was very surprised when I wrote *The Second Sex* to be so poorly received by the Left. I remember a discussion with the Trotskyists, who told me: "Woman's problem is a false problem, there's no point in pursuing it." ... There were also Communists with whom I had a lot of trouble then and who made a great deal of fun of me. They wrote that the female workers in Billancourt didn't give a damn about the feminine problem.

—Interview with Simone de Beauvoir, *Nouvel Observateur*, February 14, 1972

The problem with the anti-sexist combat is that the injustice in which woman's condition is rooted is profoundly unequivocal, yet it's so complex that it sometimes takes on the appearance of an ambiguity.

This multifaceted oppression seems equivocal because the fires that swarm around this surface blind us one by one—at times, it is the sexual oppression, at other times the economic oppression; and she whose eyes are burned by one swears that only this one exists, and that the other is a "false problem," but these are only diverse aspects and not preferential ones of the same unyielding material, compact, unique, and hard like a phallocrat's heart: masculine supremacy. Such is the core material of the despotism, of the pride, of the greed that are the structures of the male society; it is through the deforming prism of faith that religion sees the "original sin" that transmits the same defect to all human society; and it was as a theologian that Louis-Ferdinand Céline wrote: "Seated, standing, supine, man is always his own tyrant." If we replace the word "man" with the word "male," we have one of Valerie Solanas's thoughts. The original sin is male supremacy.

Free Household Labor and Free Eros

Also, we must never let go of either of the two ends of the cord: when we explain and analyze the causes of feminine slavery economically as "invisible work," as Christine Dupont does, we must never forget the oppression of Eros, the sexual question, woman as object and degraded as merchandise or spectacle, condemned to reproduce in spite of herself; when we fight for our sexual freedom and for the free disposition of our bodies, we must keep in mind our condition as proletariat overexploited outside and "invisible worker" inside.

Is it thus impossible to determine where the passage takes place, so that we might establish a precise point at which to aim the force of the struggle?

In my opinion, this place of passage, this common denominator, is the sexual factor. But what has maintained the ambivalence is that the sexual is expressed as the *erotic* on the one side and as the *economic* and the *political* on the other.

This sexual factor has nothing to do with the amount of estrogen, as biologist dreamers such as Alfred Gilbert-Dreyfus would have us believe.[6] It is a fatality only in one sort of patriarchal and phallocratic society, whether it be capitalist or socialist, feudal or "primitive." It is maintained then by the simple difference of anatomy and its secondary traits: difference of physical force and, above all, the difference in the role of procreation.

The first difference fades more and more in developed economies, when skill replaces muscular force; besides, in all probability, it first appeared only with sexism reserving work in the interior and crafts for women. Much more important is the distinction in the roles of procreation. This is what remains identified by all the phallocrats as woman's "natural vocation," indeed, "her divine mission of maternity," and that leads a reactionary like Norman Mailer to proclaim that women could only attain true equality by "giving up their womb" (*The Prisoner of Sex*). The end of nursing and the advent of painless labor, and, even more, the control of fertility, have transformed considerably the feminine status today; they permitted the true condition for the first women's struggle since the establishment of phallocratism that can hope for its overthrow; but the origin of the oppression and degrading inferiorization has stayed exactly the same, with the division of the roles *according* to this sexual differentiation. The fact of being the only one who can carry a child continues to predispose the female human to all the alienating factors of maternity: why would the patriarchal system give up such a superb weapon of exploitation? At the most, in a state of late capitalism, they have to consent to according a better-paid position, greater liberty, improvements, reforms—indeed, increasing control of fertility, to the second sex. But: *Every woman born at this time, whatever the culture, whatever the class of society, is, as a result of her anatomy (absence of the phallus), destined above all other roles, all other possibilities, all other projects, to become the companion of the male and to reproduce the species.*

Such is the sole fundamental point in common between the woman of the developing area of Ubangi, the daughter of an American or European CEO, the child of Soviet collective farmers, or the little Israeli girl in the kibbutz, the youngest daughter of a worker in the Simca factory, the heiress of a hippie couple, or the offspring of a farm woman from the Cotentin region of Normandy.

If, on the contrary, the child is a male, he will be welcomed, for better or for worse, as a being with an indistinguishable destiny; he is not only the male, he is humanity's neuter gender. The idea of his future procreation is a detail taken for granted as a possibility, a probability; it has nothing in common with a future fixed in advance, to a primordial role that defines him as such, as a "male." This potentiality is a destiny solely for the female; we might as well say a fatality, heavy with all the condemnations. In this system, being a woman is, above all, this: being "condemned," as the infanta Inês de Castro said.

This definitive factor brings about two consequences that are the two branches of the system designed to seize the feminine individual and never let her go:

a) Erotic—The sexual is the natural outlet for the erotic field. Thus will be constrained to different subsidiary roles, and will find others forbidden to her, erotically, she for whom, in the words of Freud, "anatomy is destiny." According to the morals of her class or her country, her religion, her surroundings, she will be more or less chastised if she does not fulfill these directives: virginity until marriage, fidelity in marriage, accepting the sexual freedom of the man and her own frustration, childbirth against her will or solely in marriage, chastity outside the marriage—in fact, sexual distance according to the rules. All these rules of conduct are only some obligations among others, scattered throughout a number of human cultures. In developed economies and late capitalism, in a period of religious skepticism, these different behaviors can be very relatively observed with variable damages according to the age, the class, the economic power; they are not any less founded in principles that survive strongly rooted in the unconscious, as is proven by the condemnations of abortion that are carried out and applied (sometimes with a brutal ferocity) by people who have renounced all religious faith and who remain steeped in the ideology that they believe to be so far from them. These diverse sanctions that strike here and there, some of these behaviors or all at once, make up *erotic repression*. This does not strike only women, but it strikes women above all.

When it is maintained in a more or less invisible status quo, when it is under the surface and includes only private sectors from which the individual can escape more or less easily, when it concerns mores and customs more than laws, it can be baptized "oppression";

sexual oppression concerns, from the outset and as soon as they are born, all women, except in extremely rare cases. It consists of this obligation of identifying the primordial destiny to a sexual role, and in the immense majority of cases, with secondary obligations that make of it a discomfort, a burden, a frustration, or a degradation, and always an alienation. But even when the individual and collective chances together don't make a nightmare of it, this preeminence of the sexual role in the personal destiny ends up in perpetual invisible petty harassment, a constant warning to be watchful, a duty to observe without falter either a command or a ban. The most important, the most serious of this ensemble of great and small condemnations, is the enormous pressure exerted toward marriage.

This pressure exists also concerning the man, since patriarchal society needs family units as much as a living organism needs biological cells; it applies pressure at all levels, in laws, in customs and mores; if no country has dared to make marriage obligatory, it is because it is obligatory in fact if not in law. In this domain, a pressure and even a repression is applied even stronger, for once, for the man than for the woman, regarding one of these antisocial behaviors that avoid marriage or that separate him from it: it's about the two general attitudes regarding homosexuality.

The one toward woman only brings about an increase in feminine oppression as such: there's not much difference between those that act on the lesbian and on the single woman. The lesbian is sanctioned less as "deviant" than as a woman alone, a woman without a male.[7] The situation is very different for men.

The FHAR (Homosexual Front for Revolutionary Action) and the IHR (International Revolutionary Homosexual) were often told, "The homosexual is repressed, the lesbian is oppressed."

But *all* women are oppressed. The lesbian suffers her increased oppression like an invisible force that she attributes ordinarily to the faults of her surroundings, to prejudices, even to herself; it is often difficult for her to make the distinction between what society calls her "solitude" (since the other woman doesn't count as a companion) and her feminine oppression (the gap between salaries, difficulty of access to well-paid jobs or leadership roles, the inferiority of tasks and social as well as political activities). For the man, on the contrary, whether he is the most obtuse or the most conciliatory, it is difficult to deny his repression, since the police interfere with him and his way of loving, since he is the object of serious conferences treating his "sickness," the target of taunts and persecution, sometimes beaten up. It is, however, this harassment or these frustrations, so different according to sex, that establish the common origin of the patriarchal iniquity: for women, sexual oppression because they are women, oppression intensified when they are lesbians (since lesbian equals woman alone, object of spectacle); to men, repression, and the worst: erotic repression.

We conclude then that all women undergo, to different degrees, a *sexual oppression* that can turn to repression according to the mode of sexuality; *erotic repression* cracks down on her if she is a single mother, has had an abortion, is adulterous, sometimes a concubine, sometimes "adventurous," or even divorced; the same erotic repression concerns the free woman or the victim of an accident, treated so quickly as a whore, and the man homosexual; for the female homosexual, it is a matter rather of an intensified oppression, with a repressive tendency; as for any other woman without a man, even if her "conduct" was irreproachable for the bourgeois morals or "saintly" for Christian morals.

Sexual oppression of the phallocratic system is thus made up of three stages, and its highest stage, *erotic repression*, concerns rebellious women or those who are victimized, and homosexual males— because all of them, male or female, are in a state of transgression.

b) *Economic and social*—This sexual factor that the phallocracy renders determinant in a woman's life contains a second consequence: socioeconomic oppression.

How Sexual Oppression Is Expressed on the Economic Structure

This oppression exerts power on two levels: first, that of the *female worker* at times overexploited, at times reserved for menial tasks, even at the highest points, as is proven by the growing salary gap and gains as one moves toward the summit, then, on the second level, as *housewife* furnishing the invisible work.

It is, in fact, here that the delicate passage of sexual oppression and social oppression operates; the Marxists were right to attach it to the class struggle, but they only saw one part (that of the worker, not of the housewife), and that, in addition, they want to identify with the totality of oppression, denying sexual oppression as such, whereas it does survive, as we have seen, in socialist countries.

The problem is that, up to the present time, Marxists have examined the most spectacular aspect of this oppression: the exploitation of the female worker and the undervaluing of feminine work. They didn't catch what Christine Dupont exposed in the text analyzed earlier: the production of invisible work, not only free and practically made obligatory by the requirement to invest the sexual in the marriage; but still indispensable to work that is proletarian, liberal, and commercial—in short, to all work producing or diffusing the merchandise of consumption: indispensable to the system, capitalist or other.

So this is how the feminine problem is posed: a human category assimilated to a sex, identified with sexuality in the capacity of reproductive function, brings about, on the one side, a massive frustration of the resources of Eros (*erotic repression*), and on the other side, systematic obligation of a certain type of work outside visible, remunerated work but indispensable to it, at the worst expense of she who pays the price, the homemaker and child-raiser (*socioeconomic repression*).

Hence, at all levels, including that of exterior work studied by the theorists of the class struggle, the specific oppression of woman is of a sexual origin and comes back to the sexist, patriarchal society.

Departure for a Long March

Cross-Referencing Erotic Freedom and Women's Causes

We have just seen, in the preceding pages, that women's causes are tied closely to that for Eros, and that the second sex couldn't liberate itself without liberating the entirety of sexuality, meaning: its possibilities of eroticism not identified with the reproductive function.

"I am hardly saying," says Vivian Gornick[1] (after having shown how man oppressed himself by wanting to subjugate women) "that the sexual role system has been equally damaging to both men and women. To be in overt control ... could never—*never*—be comparable to the position of total powerlessness which has characterized female life although, by default, and in a curious way, it has characterized much of male-dominated society as well."

We couldn't say it any better. The fact remains that, in sacrificing one of the two sides of his original bisexuality, homosexuality, man condemned himself to suffering the same erotic repression as unlucky women, or as the rebels against the repressive morals of females condemned to celibacy or maternity.

Masculine Homosexuality and Repression

It's not that the erotic repression of this kind of women and the erotic repression of male homosexuality are identical everywhere —far from it.

In certain small clusters of subcultures, the homosexual can be perfectly tolerated because he is invisible, or even sanctified in certain cases, but the status of the woman is always much more openly inferior. On the other hand, in socialist countries, the male homosexual is much more repressed than in the capitalist camp, whereas the feminine status is improved—improved but not transformed in depth, as I have repeated—it occurs even though, on the sexual plane, it is more disadvantaged to the extent where socialist power needs children and sees itself more or less disposed to reinforcing the family structure, which is always accompanied by a painful puritanism. In drawing rather large brushstrokes, we can say that the woman is more exploited economically in the capitalist camp but can conduct her struggle for sexual freedom more openly than in the socialist camp, but nowhere is she the economic and social equal of man, since the family has not been abolished anywhere, even if it has been reduced to forms much more restrained in China than elsewhere, to the benefit of the communal lifestyle and the perfect detriment, once again, of erotic life.

Now, we must keep repeating it: the freedom of the sexual is tied to woman's freedom and to the revolution. That consequence comes from the following: *You can't liberate the sexual alone but must liberate the body altogether, of which the sexual is a part*; and the free disposition of the body—not only of the sexual organs—is capital for the woman and puts the entire society into question; that is the only and true revolution, and it cannot take place without dismantling the entire economic system.

Xavière Gauthier emphasized this aspect of the failure of the Surrealists well in *Surrealism and Sexuality*; and their petit bourgeois, terrified, recoil when faced with a veritable liberation of the sexual that would have brought about the liberation of woman—of the woman that they venerated so highly—the aspect of their failure that integrates itself with other failures of a political nature: "All submission to sexual norms of the society is accompanied by a general submission to that society, no matter what blasphemous proclamations accompany this submission."[2]

"The militants of the MLF blithely dismiss the delicate question of love." Is it so, oh Father Oraison, that the Church's distress is so great when faced with the increasing loss of its clientele that it comes down to invoking its age-old enemy, Eros, even when it's in the majority? (Namely: heterosexual love.) Why didn't you get excited, rather, at the "thirst for purity" that these "repressed female Christians" revealed and these women "enamored with the absolute" manifesting their distancing from the masculine "brutal grip" and from what Saint Monica called "the abuses of the conjugal bed"? When faced with two ridiculous choices, you should have chosen the traditional; it would have been better accepted by the public.

It is as important for freedom to be able to make love as to be able to refuse it.

MARIANNE: How about you? How are you?

JULIETTE: I'm okay. (To herself.) Not to have to make love.

MARIANNE: You know, I like that better than working in the factory.

JULIETTE: Me too, I wouldn't want to work in the factory. (To herself.) What I say with words is never what I'm really saying. (Interior voice.) I'm waiting ... I'm watching.

—Jean-Luc Godard, *Two or Three Things I Know about Her*

Calling into question sexual norms as a part of rebelling against society does not belong exclusively to the Surrealists; different failures marked these different methods; but always, at the beginning and at the end, the terrible question of the free disposition of the body came up, consequently of the disposition of women by themselves—hence that of humanity in its entirety by itself.

To a certain extent, Wilhelm Reich's honorable failure resembles that of the Kollontai legislation that believed a total liberation of Eros possible in the early days of the Soviet Union. That was in keeping with Marx's denunciation of "bourgeois morals," not with Freud's, which was both less limited and much less exact concerning the oppression of women. The great poverty of the Russian masses after the October Revolution, the high infant mortality rate, and the impossibility of demanding a supplementary effort of frustration among the youth and the working class lacking consumer goods meant that the totalitarian liberation of Eros was lived some time afterward in disorder and chaos, but in a more or less satisfying way; at the first sign of return to a possibility of consumption, it was all over; sex had held, for the Russian man of this period, the role of written poetry for the French from 1940 to 1944: a substitute for food. Traditional morals triumphed thus in Soviet Russia with the return of sex to the fold, that is, to the family unit. The woman kept her role as *producer*, which was an emancipation with relation to the past, but without being able to leave behind the ancient role of unpaid *reproducer* and furnisher of invisible, domestic work that is found everywhere, in all the countries of the world; her largest participation in the world of outside work gave her a dignity that she had ignored up until then but doomed her to a crushing multiplication of activities, all the while removing, through the ban on abortion, any chance of erotic pleasure since contraception was nonexistent. It was the beginning of the revisionist deviationism;

the revolution would transform everything, except life. For enlightening reasons—reasons of *enlightenment*—the pleasure principle was sacrificed once again to the reality principle.[3]

Freudian theory, such as Wilhelm Reich pushes to its logical, desirable consequences, finds in the eventual realization the barrier that limits all theories in advance of their time, and still more: the failure of therapeutic psychoanalysis reduced to its own forces. The best-conducted analysis, the most successful abreaction of the patient ends, in the best of cases, only in returning a driver's license to the treated individual, not a car; only the revolution can give him a car. Freud's major book, *Civilization and Its Discontents*, which serves as the basis of Marcuse's work, was able to describe the ills of the Occidental world brilliantly; a revolutionary power that would strive on these bases to change or abolish morals recognized as abusive and duplicitous without transforming them at their profound depths, radically, not only *conditions* of life but the *true origins of these conditions*—this power would know the same failure as the competent psychoanalyst that healed a patient (traumatized by social injustices to the point of neuroses, let's say), without changing anything about the social injustice—thus, without having conducted the revolution. In both cases, we find the hoax of the driver's license without the car. And the revolutionary government will be obliged to return pitifully (and, what is more serious, with hypocritical justifications) to the same mystifying morals, those of the former exploiters: the glorification of monogamous marriages, reinforcement of the family unit, diktat of sexual stability, of monosexuality, and so on.

It's not because they were bad, insincere, and corrupt that the revolutionary heads barred the route, in Russia, to the liberation of Kollontai, nor was Fidel Castro when he asked women to return to their pots and pans; nor was Boumédiène, who saw sexual attacks multiply in Algeria due to its exacerbated Koranic puritanism, its legislation of absolute repression of Eros, and the notorious halt of emancipation of women. It's that, with all the nuances included in the difference of the situations, in all the places where the power of the people is seized by an economically underdeveloped society, in order to effectuate its development, we see all the instinctual forces of the individual used in a collective effort that frustrates him and, to a large extent, castrates him; and in this exploitation, the woman is overexploited at the very moment when the recognition of her rights and her equality is proclaimed most forcefully. "Woman must be twofold revolutionary, says Castro. But who will prepare the meals for the children not yet of school age?"[4] There is no hypocrisy but an unsolvable contraction. Unsolvable in a state, be it revolutionary even, of male power: that is to say, implying a certain kind of thought, of belief in power and in technology as social and vital development, of necessary leadership and maintenance of sexism.

This frustrating labor to which the man of underdeveloped societies is condemned, that a revolutionary power would develop, appears necessary to produce the goods for consumption in the fastest way possible. (And in order to, in the fastest way possible, accelerate the massacre of nature and the pollution of the air and water.) Hence, household work, the invisible platform of productive male work, must experience a parallel encouragement, or rather a reinforced obligation. So, here we see the pleasure principle sacrificed to the principle of reality and productivity, with the "delay of satisfaction" that Marcuse described.[5]

Repressive Morals and the Productivity Principle

The hateful denunciation of the "uselessness of the feminine sex" that characterized the ancient Greek world dissipated; nevertheless, its origin can clarify Marcuse's thoughts: "Woman's beauty and the happiness she promises are fatal in the work world of our civilization." (An observation that rejoins somewhat Theodor W. Adorno's, according to which love should prefigure a better society.) In this case, one would find a satisfactory explanation for this surprising sudden stop to a beginning of sexual liberation—at least in theory and in the mores of the upper classes—that the Council of Trent gave to the protests of the Renaissance. Because the beginning of modern times and of industrialization is contemporary with this same council, which made a sacrament of marriage under pressure from the devout. And if the feminine sex, the most oppressed and the most duped in the development of this civilization, showed herself here and often elsewhere as accomplice to her own alienation, it is not so much that the second sex is the most indoctrinated, the most conservative, the most abundant with "Uncle Toms" that collaborated with slavery; it is also because women, these famous "temptresses" reviled by the ancient morale, then by the Christian church, knew instinctively and from experience that they would be the first victims of the no-less-famous "yielding to instincts" so feared by the Church, then by bourgeois morale in favor of production, and that, condemned to representing all Eros for man who had chosen to renounce his homosexuality of yesteryear, they preferred the reassuring hardship of their traditional oppression to the horrifying fate of a return to the past by "yielding to instincts." That is why, slowly reassured, bourgeois moral codes that had taken over so many points of the ancient misogyny changed their point of view radically on one precise point: woman, accused in the past of being "insatiable" like fire, of being a Messalina in power that a strict conjugal despotism had to neutralize, saw herself suddenly attributed a nonexistent libido and accused even of "evading sexuality" by Freud. Isn't it better to choose the lesser of two evils?

As long as marriage or, at best, heterosexual monogamic love is represented as the only link that is both private and social, society, even endowed with a relative abundance, won't be able to differ much from yesterday's model. Overly repressive, dedicated to the principle of production and of reality, it can only offer secret softening of the repression, piecemeal moral reforms, a sex fair in Copenhagen instead of a radical questioning of lifestyle. But, as long as male power prevails, it goes without saying that nothing will change in this area, and that even the origin of conditions of life, which we discussed earlier, has no reason to be reexamined. Morals are condemned, in the power of these ancient hands, to conserve aggression, instincts of destruction, and violence as primal drives, the imprint left forcefully on the flesh and on nature, and for sole impediment of this "dynamism": a self-punishing guilt. It is impossible, without an absolute triumph of the feminine, that these elements, handed down from the most ancient antiquity, might be replaced by yesterday's ideals become fundamental needs: beauty, peace, and happiness, tied to incessant and spontaneous artistic creation and to the reactivation of all the erotic zones of the body, repressed since infancy in oblivion due to superrepression.

How would that seem possible in a society like ours that is not really one of consumption that boasts falsely of this title? The end of the vital necessity of a conflict between the two principles of pleasure and production—this is what would permit satisfying all human needs, in an environment healed of all its wounds, if productivity at all costs were replaced by productivity corresponding to the simply necessary (in the limits of relaxation and pleasure essential to the human), and, above all, to the suppression of the *false* needs that mask *true* desires. No revolution ever stretched to this effect, because they all carried with them, like a defect, the male principle that the new rulers believed to be a "relic" of the abolished structures, but it took root at a much deeper level: that of the sexism that identifies man as the masculine aggressive, creative, builder, and organizer, and the woman as the feminine custodian, passive, emotional, sentimental, and above all eternally fertilizable and nourishing (from which we get the incredible mess we are fighting today, thanks to this phallocratic dichotomy).[6]

One Marriage, Two Losers

In marriage, man and woman are both losers, but the woman is both more alienated and more reassured; the economic advantages of freedom and of direct participation in production are neutralized for her, in single life, by the affective and sexual desert that she fears by tradition and, above all, by the perpetual questioning of lifestyle according to the temporary companion who helps her flee this desert, not counting the dangers of possible pregnancy in a society where abortion remains a crime. The woman needs particularly advantageous economic conditions, or a taste for independence and a fearlessness in the face of all dangers, to confront such problems in place of the relative comfort offered by marriage: the little fortress-ghetto where one man alone protects you from all the aggressions, the violent acts, the contempt, the insults, the tricks, and the bad behavior of *all* the others. That is why she will accept almost universally this status of *fille au pair* who agrees to exhaust herself in nonproductive, free work in exchange for room and board alone, or who will nearly go crazy trying to maintain this work (and raising the children) while working outside in a position, underpaid in 90 percent of the cases.

Revolutionary feminists are demanding that study groups be formed for this problem "that would permit us to examine the ambiguous politics of capitalism and patriarchal/capitalist relations," they say. Because the invisible work of the housewife is obtained by *patriarchal ideology and oppression*:

- marriage;
- the push to motherhood;
- the "nature" of the woman;

on which capitalist oppression attaches itself:

- economic dependence on the husband;
- barriers to paid work, underpayment;
- or double workday.

The capital problem of this constraint rests in the sexual repression of the man and, consequently, more still of the woman. The question of household exploitation intersects thus the liberation of Eros.

The Goal of Our Long March

If we follow one of these two vectors, either the problem of sexual relations that are situated in France between the prison of marriage vows or the monitored freedom of the single woman, or the second vector, the problem of specific economic exploitation of woman by unpaid work in the home, we will see that one inevitably overlaps the other. Sexual freedom, no longer under conditions, but total, would end all social obligations to marry, for man as well as for woman. At the same time, heterosexuality would disappear as the norm imposed and the structural base of the society, along with sexism and unpaid work in the home for women—it would be the end of the phallocratic patriarchy.

It would be, at the same time, the triumph of the feminine as a second drive incessantly repressed by the historical male development.

It would finally be the massive end to runaway population growth and to intensive productivity to satisfy false needs that distort true desires, hence the end of the massacre of nature, of apocalyptical pollution and the destruction of the environment, the care of which will be picked up again by the sole bearers of life's sources, women.

The revolutionary spirit will be surpassed by the number-one requirement of the modern world: *mutation.*

Such is the goal of our long march.

THE TIME FOR ECOFEMINISM

New Perspectives

In September 1973, a movement was born in France—a movement closer to the Belgian Unified Feminist Party than to the French MLF. The new group, the Feminist Front, was formed by several women from an MLF group, others from the subgroup Evolution (founded in 1970 after the "Women's Estates-General" and in reaction to it), and, above all, by independent women from all parties and all movements. The group's statutes adhered to the 1901 law for associations, and, accordingly, the new movement marks a tendency that is much more legalistic and even reformist.

In contrast with the Italian movement, which remains somewhat divided, there is no antagonism between this new front and the MLF, which it supports in some of its activities and invites to participate in the front's work. Its dream (rather utopian still, it must be admitted, given the average age, the settled nature, and the bourgeois status of its current members, notwithstanding the continuing possibility of an infusion of new blood) is to serve as a link between all the women's movements and associations, leading toward a massive "sorority" (the Americans say "sisterhood") that would further women's causes and their liberation in a determinant fashion. The front believes in means as moderate as those espoused by Betty Friedan: parliamentary representation, obligatory home economics courses for boys as well as girls, professional promotion, and equal salaries. A woman's right to choose abortion is supported without qualification, and the right to divorce is upheld against certain reactionary projects, but the sexual revolution still causes a great discomfort for these prudent ones—or for these prudes.

Another group has arrived on the scene even more recently, formed from a group of the revolutionary feminists and also adhering to the statutes of the law of 1901: the League for Women's Rights. This new group is much more radical, although just as resolutely legalistic. Its goal is to fight on legal grounds, enclosing the male society in its own contradictions, with the help of a collective of women lawyers and judges, in order to have women proclaimed a group susceptible to racist treatment and thus able to protest against discrimination on constitutional grounds.

We do not yet know the future contributions of these groups that have so suddenly and so quickly emerged after three years of MLF existence. But, thanks to the first group, an attempt at synthesis is possible between two struggles previously thought to be separated, feminism and ecology.

Even though Shulamith Firestone had already alluded to the ecological content inherent in feminism in *The Dialectic of Sex: The Case for Feminist Revolution*, this idea had remained at the embryo stage until 1973. It was picked up again by certain members of the Feminist Front, which first included it in its manifesto, then removed it. The authors then separated themselves from such a timorous new movement and founded an information center: the "Ecology-Feminism Center," destined to become later, as a part of their project of melding an analysis of and the launching of a new action, *ecofeminism*.

Regarding this question, I would add the idea "from revolution to mutation," which inspired the title of a portion of this work. Nor would it be superfluous to recall one of the questions posed earlier by the revolutionary feminists, a group within the MLF: "We need to know nonetheless if the movement will be a mass movement to which all women will potentially belong as a specifically exploited group, or if it will be just another subgroup."

It is in keeping with this spirit that militants, as much from the Feminist Front as from the League for Women's Rights, concentrate their strength on mobilizing and sensitizing as many of their "sisters" as possible about the relatively restricted and immediate objectives, working toward reasonable goals that can seem "reassuring" (outside the acronym MLF, which has already become "frightening" for many), all the while not forgetting (at least for the League, younger and more dynamic than the Feminist Front) the eventual targets: the disappearance of the salaried class (beyond equal salaries), the disappearance of competitive hierarchies (beyond access to promotion), the disappearance of the family (beyond the control of procreation), and, above and beyond all of these, a new humanism born with the irreversible end of the male society, and that, by definition, must work through the ecological problem (or rather the extreme ecological peril).

For the moment, certainly, the mobilization of women around "specifically feminine" issues can take, even on a legal level, a tone of exigency that widely surpasses the ancient demand for "rights."

We want, say these followers of the most recent feminism, to depart from what certain subversive German groups call the "anti-authoritarian quagmire," without meanwhile sinking into bureaucracy or elitism; we also want to reach the workers and set up bases in the provinces; but as immediate and concrete as these projects are, we know that, above all, we need urgently to remake the planet around a totally new model. This is not an ambition, this is a necessity; the planet is in danger of dying, and we will die along with it.

Besides the authoritarian socialists or leftists of various degrees whose drone I have situated here as "principal struggle and secondary struggle," there are analysts and agitators, possible companions in struggle much more enlightened than these neo-Stalinists; they never cease calling for the "totalization" of the combat and protesting that everything that is "fragmentary" compromises the final goal, to destroy the Carthage of the system. These activists do not place themselves in the minefield of the "class struggle"; rather, they emphasize the necessity of a global awareness. It is not a question of forwarding one's particular demands but of introducing new areas of consciousness:

> It is logical that individuals begin with the real experience of their own alienation in order to define the movement of their revolt; but once that is defined, nothing other than integration into the cultural firmament of the system is possible for them ... Those of you who are normal, stop limiting yourselves to your normality; homosexuals, stop limiting yourselves to your ghettos; women, stop limiting yourselves to your femininity or to your counter-femininity. Invade the world, exhaust your dreams.[1]

There is a lot of truth in this exhortation, for it was by limiting themselves to their supposed "counter-femininity," that is, the demands for such and such a right, that yesterday's feminists imagined themselves to be the magic transformers of their feminitude; that they buried themselves, having gained, for all practical purposes, nothing but air. I completely agree that women's struggle should be global, totalitarian—even when it presents itself from a modestly reformist aspect—or not be at all. But the authors of *Grand Soir* are committing the same error as the society they are fighting by conflating the category "women" with "homosexuals," "the mentally ill,"[2] and other minorities in revolt against their alienation. In so doing, they forget that the question for women is not that of some minority but that of a majority reduced to the status of a minority, and the only one to be treated this way—and, what is more, the only one of the two sexes with the ability of accepting, refusing, slowing down, or accelerating the reproduction of humanity, with whom rests at the moment, even if they are not totally aware of it, the sentence of death or the salvation of humanity in its entirety.

The sole totalitarian combat capable of overturning the system, instead of simply changing it once again for another, and of shifting finally from the spent "revolution" to the mutation our world calls for, is women's combat, that of all women—and not only because they were placed in the situation described in the preceding pages, because the iniquity and absurdity outrage their very souls and demand the overthrow of unbearable excess—that is legitimate, but it remains sentimental. The point, quite simply, is that it is no longer a matter of well-being but of necessity; not of a better life but of escaping death; and not of a "fairer life" but of the sole possibility for the entire species to still have a future.

U Thant (the former UN secretary-general) and the French scholars from the Museum of Natural History, the European Council, and the *UNESCO Courier* have said it again and again to all the highest international authorities; Konrad Lorenz sums it up: "For the first time in human history, no society can pick up the reins." (Obviously, since he is thinking, like everyone else, of a male society; that is, a society composed of representation, competition, and industrialization—in short, aggression and sexual hierarchy.)

The World Futures Conference that took place several months ago in Rome and received a great deal of press—more than the war in the Middle East—has repeated it, even if France is keeping silent.[3]

What were these Cassandras shouting from the rooftops? Quite frankly, that the point of no return had practically been reached, that one cannot stop a vehicle careening at a hundred miles an hour toward a brick wall when one is only sixty feet away from it, and that everything could end with a very virile "Prepare to meet your maker!" or "Keep clear of industrialized zones!"

Why this flight? To what extent does this colossal declaration of failure coincide with the feminine wish to snatch the car's steering wheel from the hands of male society, with the intention not of driving in its place but of jumping from the car?

These new perspectives of feminism do not detach themselves from the MLF, but they stand apart within it, due less to the more classical and not *underground*[4] language or the acceptance of a fledgling organization and the concerns of the feminine "masses" than to the global objective, an answer to the critique of "parcelization" referred to earlier, and that would even be a new humanism: *ecofeminism*.

The reasoning is simple. Practically everyone knows that the two most immediate threats of death today are overpopulation and the destruction of natural resources; fewer are aware of the entire responsibility of the male system—the system as male (and not capitalist or socialist)—in creating these two perilous situations; but very few have yet discovered that each one of the two menaces is the logical outcome of one of the two parallel discoveries that gave power to men fifty centuries ago: reproduction, and their capability of sowing the earth as they do women.

Until that time, women alone possessed a monopoly on agriculture, and the men believed women were impregnated by the gods.

Upon discovering the two possibilities at once—agricultural and procreational—man launched what Lederer has called "the great upheaval" for his own benefit. Having seized control of the soil (thus of fertility and later industry) and of woman's womb (thus of fecundity), it was logical that the overexploitation of the one and the other would result in this double peril, menacing and parallel: overpopulation (a glut of births) and destruction of the environment (a glut of products).

The only mutation that can save the world, therefore, is the "great upheaval" of male power that brought about first agricultural overexploitation and then lethal industrial expansion. Not a "matriarchy," of course, or "power to women," but the destruction of power by women, and finally, the way out of the tunnel: egalitarian administration of a world being reborn (and no longer "protected" as the soft, first-wave ecologists believed).

Ecology and Feminism

I had already defended this point of view, before the birth of the Feminist Front and before reading Shulamith Firestone, in 1972, in a letter to *Nouvel Observateur*, after an ecologist conference where the absence of women was particularly blatant. This declaration brought me numerous, unexpected letters. Some advocated a demand for "women's power" and accused me of reverse sexism. Pierre Samuel, in his otherwise just and honest book, *Ecologie: Détente ou cycle infernal* (Ecology: détente or vicious circle),[1] referred to my work as "dangerous exaggeration," and, in the end, he aligned himself with the concept that was to become the one behind the Ecology-Feminism Center founded by the dissidents from the Feminist Front.

But is worldwide catastrophe really at our doorstep? Stopping short of the noble remarks of somebody like Jean Lartéguy, who, faced with the figures I was citing on television, shrugged his shoulders and said, "Oh, specialists are always mistaken in their predictions ..."[2] A lot of people say, "Someone will invent something." All this talk allows them to put the Horsemen of the Apocalypse in a bottle, like goldfish.

Consider, however, this remark: "Ecology is going to replace Vietnam among the essential preoccupations for students." Who said this, and when? The *New York Times* ... in 1970. That year, the son of the female physician Marie-Andrée Lagroua Weill-Hallé, who founded "family planning," rallied Americans in an effort to struggle against collective suicide, the correlation of which he saw clearly in the problem his mother fought.

Ecology, the "science that studies the relations of living beings among themselves and the physical environment in which they are evolving," includes, by definition, the relations between the sexes and the ensuing birth rate. Because of the horrors that menace us, the most intense interest is oriented toward the depletion of resources and the destruction of the environment, which is why it is time to recall that other element, the one that so closely ties together the question of women and their combat.

Should we consider some technical details?

In America, the alarm was sounded in 1970 by the anti-establishment youth of Earth Day, who moved immediately to eco-terrorism—they bury cars and fight physically with loggers. Cellestine Ware, in her feminist book *Woman Power*, says that "they want to breathe in accordance with the cycle of the cosmos." No— they want to breathe, period. Judge for yourselves:

Irène Chédeaux[3] tells us that, each year, America must eliminate 142 tons of smoke, 7 million old cars, 30 million tons of paper, 28 billion bottles, and 48 billion tin cans. "Each one of the 8 million New Yorkers breathes as much noxious material as if they had smoked 37 cigarettes, and they know now that there are more rats in the dumps than humans in the city."

Shall I give you other details about the state of affairs? Fish are dying en masse in the Delaware River (oh, Westerns and Fenimore Cooper!) because Sun Oil, Scott Paper, and DuPont dump their waste there; but that undoubtedly is nothing next to the fact that Lake Zurich is dead, suffocated by human waste, and that Lake Geneva will not last much longer; still nothing next to the fact that the Mediterranean, called the "great pure one" by the ancient Greeks, has become such a garbage can that, in Marseille this summer, I had to drive along the coast for miles before finding a beach affording a little cleanliness. In the United States today, numerous enterprises declare that 10 percent of their investments is absorbed by pollution control. A derisory effort, given the catastrophic dimensions of the damage. We owe this modest result, and the more striking ban of a pipeline four feet in diameter that was to cross the Sahara, to the struggles of the various groups of "conservationists," the one best known for its radicalism being the Sierra Club. In January 1970, President Richard Nixon devoted a large part of his State of the Union Address to the ecological question. Soon after, a law was passed ordering the airlines to devise a plan by 1972 that would reduce the fumes from combustion by three-quarters. Jean-François Revel[4] relates how, in that very country, these endeavors, because of their anti-industrialism, have been labeled "communist maneuvers" by certain fanatics. This was the most beautiful confirmation of a prophet: Cyril M. Kornbluth, the author of *The Space Merchants*.[5]

A totally new sort of protester has just emerged: the eco-guerrilla. At night, students saw down and remove billboards that disfigure the countryside. The newspaper *Actuel* reminds us that, in Berkeley in 1967, young engineers founded Ecology Action. They called themselves "apolitical"; we can imagine how political interest groups might react to their goals:

To suppress absurd practices: new models of cars every year ...

To control necessary but potentially dangerous practices: the treatment and distribution of food, the construction and organization of housing, the production and distribution of energy.

To eliminate destructive practices: social regimentation, covering the earth with concrete, asphalt and buildings, the dissemination of waste, wars.

"It is quite simply called a revolution," comment those signing the article. But *which one*?

In the meantime, the abomination is growing every day. The air is charged with 10 percent more carbon dioxide gas than at the beginning of this very recent era called industrial. There are "12 microbes per cubic centimeter[6] in the Alsace region, 88,000 on the Champs-Élysées, and 4 million in a department store." A rat placed on the ground at the Place de la Concorde dies after ten or fifteen minutes in the Paris of 1971. This leads us to assume that soon, since air pollution is rapidly increasing, a three-year-old child will have to wear a gas mask.

We have already seen the conditions for demographic inflation; let's return to them.

If, according to the calculations of Édouard Bonnefous,[7] world population multiplied by 2.6 between 1800 and 1950, but the total population of cities by more than 100,000, thus eight times faster, there was an insane jump from 1950 to 1960: this time, the world urban population experienced a growth ... of 35 percent. Deforestation follows the progress of technology: the Sunday edition of the *New York Times* devours 190 acres of forests!

When I was a child, the Garonne and the Seine were considered the only two truly polluted rivers in France. Today, 6 million tons of waste contaminate the hydrographic network of our dear country, and the rate is increasing. In other words, in the year 2000, there will be as many pounds of refuse as humans on the planet. That is as bad as anything in a horror film. *Le Figaro* may well have called the Rhine "a big sewer," then, in a more prudent vein, a "great collector"; words change nothing about the thing (let's use the word "thing" as a discreet euphemism for the word "shit"). But we should refrain from accusing the camp of capital too quickly: if our lakes are agonizing or have become closed, dead seas (Annecy; Léman in Switzerland; Lakes Michigan, Erie, and Superior in America), we can savor this consoling assessment: 224,000 miles of running water in the Soviet Union are hardly in better condition. The underground layers of fresh water? That is capital on which we cannot write checks forever; for, with population growth, the need for water increases. This was the subject of a recent science-fiction novel by Jacques Sternberg: tap water, throughout the world, was replaced by a flow of revolting insects—a hazardous product had increased the size of every microbe or bacteria to monstrous proportions! How frightening is Dracula next to these images? A horror story for children. And it is so true, the menace is so precise, that, in light of the imminent lack of fresh water, all industries are researching means of desalinating seawater. (But to what avail, if we have to remove the pollution from it, too?) Alas! Where is the spirit of the Emperor Julian, who said, in 358 AD, "Water from the Seine is very good to drink"? He was not a "technologician."

Let's look at our own South. The Aquitaine National Petroleum Company has harmed the surrounding farmland so much with its sulfurous gas that it was recently ordered to pay damages and interest to the Béarnese farmers who had taken it to court. This was not their only worry; they also had to fight against the establishment of a large aluminum factory that, enclosed with

Aquitaine Petroleum in a small valley, doubled the risks of atmospheric pollution.[8]

The catastrophic situation of urban agglomerations is becoming known everywhere. Paris holds the record for air pollution per square meter; every day it receives this celestial manna: 100,000 cubic meters of sulfuric acid. There is one city more poisoned—Tokyo, about which scholars have told this prophetic joke: in 1980, the average Japanese citizen will have to wear a gas mask to go about daily business. I can picture the samurai removing the mask instead of performing hara-kiri with a sword.

Here again, pollution strictly speaking joins with the destruction of the natural environment. The air is barely more than a layer of smut in big cities, but their waste increases the aggression against human health. It sounds like a bad dream when we read that New York discards 250 million tons of nonnuclear waste every year: old cans, car carcasses, plastic material, burned gas, disgusting refuse of all kinds. The image is in keeping with the habitual sadism of the main character in the comic strip *Pravda la Survireuse*,[9] who contemplates a huge pit filled with old car shells from atop her motorcycle and says, like some romantic beauty leaning over one of the lakes of yesteryear: "What a beautiful sight!" Thus, filth in the air, approaching the atmospheric ceiling; filth on the earth, rising ever higher; we live between two layers of waste, like cave dwellers between the stalactites and stalagmites.

What solution can be found for such an absurd nightmare?

Revolution? Yes, but not "our daddy's." The most antiquated quote from the socialist song "Juin 1848" is undoubtedly:

Under the seals, who is holding nature hostage?

It should be replaced by:

In deadly infection, who will change nature?

The answer cries out: "It's you, it's us, it's me!" But I, but you, but we are irresponsible: we cannot act otherwise, aside from infinitesimal behavior changes; foremost among the responsible parties is the technological civilization, super-urban and super-industrial, the insane race that launched the unstoppable wheel toward profit, in much the same way that the Gauls sent burning wheels hurtling down steep slopes; but that was in order to fertilize by slash-and-burn techniques, whereas our technological culture ruins and murders the nourishing soil under the wheel's fire. As the crime worsens, so does the madness: the overpopulation of the executioners who, at this moment, are engendering the future victims of their collective infamy.

The global population at the end of the Roman Empire is estimated to have been 250 to 300 million, less than the population of modern-day China. Apart from China and India, which always had the second highest birth rate, the rest of the human species was distributed mainly throughout the Mediterranean Basin. Epidemics, famine, and natural disasters varied the demographic levels, and global growth was insignificant. It took sixteen centuries before the world population reached 500 to 550 million in the seventeenth century. Therefore, we can evaluate, roughly, the level of growth in the following way:

- 250 million in sixteen centuries (twice the original number).
- By 1750, we had reached 700 million.
- Thus, 200 million in one century only.
- Next, growth increases. The discoveries of civilization, work to decrease mortality rates, and greater longevity gave us, in 1950, 2.5 billion inhabitants.

- New figures: 1.8 billion inhabitants in two centuries, that is, 900 million a century instead of the 200 million of preceding centuries.

"The situation was dramatic enough that it demanded preparations," says Elizabeth Draper in *Birth Control in the Modern World: The Role of the Individual in Population Control.*[10] But the expansion has only intensified; we can no longer count by centuries, but by decades; in 1960, we already numbered 3 billion (twenty years before the expected date, since experts predicted 3 to 3.6 billion by 1980!) The rate of growth is 500 million in ten years—in ten years, the world population increased, between 1950 and 1960, by the number of the total population in the seventeenth century!

The 3.6 billion expected by 1980 had undoubtedly been exceeded in 1969. What is appalling is that we have been told that the current population will double in thirty-five years!

But the overpopulation is not happening everywhere at the same rate. Cities with more than 100,000 inhabitants are first: they are growing eight times faster than the others. The frightening jump from 1950 to 1960 was even higher among the urban population; it increased by 35 percent.

"We have to build quickly, no matter what, no matter where, no matter how ... Profits are high and immediate. To make new factories work, we need workers living near them. We are building cities that are cities only by name: housing projects, shops, drugstores, supermarkets, cinemas. Advertisements are everywhere: the worker must consume. If he does not consume, production will drop. If production drops, he will lose his job. If he loses his job, he will not be able to pay the rent, the bill for the washing machine, etc.," explain Colette Saint-Cyr and Henri Gougeaud.

We find ourselves back in the demented universe of *Space Merchants.*

Let's look at the American example—Robin Clarke, UNESCO expert, gives the following details:

During the course of a lifetime, an American baby
will consume 100 million liters of water,
28 tons of iron and steel,
25 tons of paper,
50 tons of food,
10,000 bottles, 17,000 cans, 27,000 caps,
(maybe) 2 or 3 cars, 35 tires,
and will burn 1,200 barrels of petroleum,
will discard 126 tons of garbage,
and will produce 10 tons of radiant particles.

This means, the expert concludes, that the birth of an American baby carries twenty-five times more significance for ecology than that of a Hindu baby.[11] It remains for us to evaluate, which Robin Clarke did not think of doing, the chances for survival of such a distressing world economy where, according to the region, one individual will consume, during the course of sixty or seventy years, twenty-five times more than another, for it is possible that the rebellion of the developing world, fed up with being the Buchenwald of the planet, will change the statisticians' figures. Even if there is no rebellion from the developing world, where will this American baby, in adulthood, find to consume, burn, and throw away all that Robin Clarke predicts, since it has already been predicted that the earth will become a desert in twenty to thirty years, at the rate we are going now? ("In 1985," announces Professor René Dubos, "the entire planet will be nothing more than a barren desert.") Will massive death from malnutrition put an end to the exponential rate of demographic growth? And of urban concentration?

It was the Marquis de Sade, one of the greatest scientific geniuses of all time, who, on the eve of the French Revolution, had already declared in *Justine* that the concentration of people in the cities contributed to the acceleration of mental health disorders and sexual obsessions. We have seen that this hyperconcentration is due to overpopulation, whose dangers Malthus, much later, would expose. (In a more muddled fashion, Restif de la Bretonne, in *The Corrupted Ones*, is saying the same thing.)

Earlier, I discussed "the stress of the white rat"; it's time to come back to it now. John Calhoun, a researcher, had the idea in 1958 of installing a colony of Norwegian rats in a barn in Maryland that he had set up for them. First observation: in a space of 900 square meters, 5,000 rats lived in harmony, but the population did not exceed 150 new births.

The second stage that he observed: increasing the number of adult rats in divided quarters brought about aberrations in both sexual and social behavior. Young rats set about practicing collective rape of an isolated female like vulgar gangs in the crowded projects in Sarcelles or Billancourt. Others were observed engaging in hypersexual behavior, practicing all the possible forms of the instinct, as if trying to overcome the anguish from overpopulation. Others finally became perfect gangsters, or other sorts of outlaws, isolating themselves from sexual as well as social contact in order to engage in nocturnal murders. Ordinary wars to gain power multiplied into absurdity. The females finally stopped building their nests and suffered a stress of fertility.

We must, of course, mistrust analogies made too hastily. On the subject of does who lose interest in their fawn after a delivery under anesthesia, an argument brought up by opponents of painless childbirth, Simone de Beauvoir answered in a decisive, albeit very simple, manner: "But women are not deer."[12] If female white

Norwegian rats do not recognize their offspring following an intensive concentration of "urban" habitat, we can scarcely compare this fact to that of the young Israeli mother growing accustomed to nursing not only her own child but also her comrades' babies in the kibbutz daycare center, in an interesting goal of disrupting filial bonds. What takes place at the level of animal collectives can never be transposed directly to the human level without a careful examination of the differences in structure; it is the absence of this principle that makes a sociological essay like Lionel Tiger's *Men in Groups* so flawed.[13] But here, without falling into the same trap, we can envisage a definite similarity between the experience of the Norwegian rats and that of our urban concentrations. The German ethnologist Paul Leyhausen is of this opinion. Like Sade, he finds an important factor in urbanization that contributes to the rise of mental illness. The number of suicides increases, as do the problems of alcoholism, mental deficiencies, juvenile delinquency, and nervous breakdowns. The growing difficulty of isolation and exhaustion due to overcrowding and transportation contributes to a weakening of resistance of the nervous system that, it seems, could be communicable. We already know all that, you say? Yes, but never before has something considered a bother, a hassle, an imperfection of modern life reached such critical dimensions; the throbbing of a cavity in a tooth has become cancer of the jaw. Sexual crimes are starting up again in London; abominations previously beyond the scope of our experience—kidnapping, gang rape—are appearing in Paris; New York, to name only the one city, protects itself against the madness by *imitating it* with a series of "little, insignificant murders."[14] To the destruction of the environment corresponds, at the current birth rate, the destruction of interior man. And also—finally, some light shed on the issue—the stress of the white female rat.

In an article entitled "Why We Abort,"[15] a woman who signs the article as Christiane says:

> Rats, in cases of overpopulation, suffer fertility stress. Men have lost contact a little with their instincts and totally lost the power of spiritual command over their bodies; women, thanks to their underdevelopment, less so. Perhaps we can say they are beginning a kind of stress. And, what is more, that the demand for free abortion is a profoundly intuitive cry of alarm. Perhaps we should lend an ear.

It is no longer "lending an ear" that is necessary, but rather shrieking out loud. The world is beginning to accept the idea of abortion for other reasons that make women violently demand their right to exercise control over their own bodies, over their future, over their procreation; it is thanks to worry over the exponential rate described and analyzed earlier that the male society is experiencing some tendency to question itself and to accept demands that are brought about by totally different motives. For once, the interests of the oppressors and the oppressed coincide. But what is remarkable about this situation is that this interest, if it is met, will lead to the realization of a situation more favorable for an oppressed caste— women—than for the caste of the oppressors; and the latter group knows it quite well. That is why they hesitate to accord something they themselves must desire: a stop to an insane growth in the birth rate that, along with the destruction of the environment, signs a death warrant for everyone. At the same time, obtaining this fortunate halt by giving women freedom of access to contraception and abortion is, for men, the conviction that "women won't stop there" and will begin to control their own lives; this is, recalling Fourier, a scandal of such violence that it is capable of undermining the bases of society. Hence the hesitations, the contradictions, the reforms and obstacles, the steps forward, the leaps backward; this comic grimace on the face of power conveys the extreme interior opposition that is ripping male society apart, at all levels, in all countries.

> Making money, getting rich, exploiting man and nature in order to climb to the highest places on the social ladder ... As long as a society organizes its production for the goal of converting the resources of man and of nature into profits, no equitable and planned system of ecological balance can exist.[16]

It is evidence itself. At the base of the ecological problem are found the structures of a certain power. Like that of overpopulation, it is a problem of men; not only because it is men who hold world power and because, for a century now, they could have instituted radical contraception; but because power is, at the lower level, allocated in such a way as to be exercised by men over women. In the domain of ecology as well as that of overpopulation, we see conflicts contradictory to capitalism harshly confronting one another, even though these problems far surpass the scope of capitalism and the socialist camp suffers from just as many, for the good reason that, in both, sexism still reigns. Under these conditions, where the devil can we find—even in the case of prolonged pacific coexistence of both economic camps—a possibility of implementing an "equitable and planned" system on a planetary scale, whether it be ecological or demographic? Konrad Lorenz is right: no (male) society can pick up the reins.

The first problem: stopping new births. Male society has begun to be afraid, and, in turn, Poland, Rumania, and Hungary have adopted the solution of "liberalizing" abortion; in the capitalist camp, England followed on October 24, 1967; Japan penalizes a surplus of births. Four American states, New York among them, "have followed in the path of the frank and massive yes."[17] On the other hand, in Roman Catholic countries, we find a sole timid overture in France; in Spain, even therapeutic abortion is forbidden—let the mother die, so long as the fetus lives, even if it only has a minute chance of not following its mother in death. These examples represent some of the principal contradictions of a civilization panicked at the necessity of consenting to what will prolong humanity but also toll the first bell for its old putrid patriarchal forms.

If these problems are men's problems, it is because their origin is masculine: it is male society, built by males and *for* males—we must repeat this tirelessly.

It would be derisory to play at the little game of historical "ifs," or it would bring us back to the land of a charming science-fiction novel about parallel universes. What would have happened "if" women had not lost the war of the sexes at the distant time when phallocracy was born—thanks to the passing of agriculture to the male sex? Without what August Bebel calls "the defeat of the feminine sex" and what the modern Wolfgang Lederer, author of *Fear of Women*,[18] calls "the great upheaval," what would have happened? We would do well to keep ourselves from entering further into this fantasy: "Ah! If the sky fell, a lot of sparrows would be caught," my grandmother used to say. One lone negative response emerges: perhaps humanity would have vegetated at an infantile stage, perhaps we would have never known either the jukebox or a spaceship landing on the moon, but the environment would have never known the current massacre, and even the word "ecology" would have remained in the little cervical box of *Homo sapiens*, like the words "kidney" or "liver," words that never cross the lips or the pen if no suffering or pain is felt from these organs.

"Pollution," "destruction of the environment," and "runaway demography" are all men's words, corresponding to men's problems: those of a male culture. These words would have no place in a female culture, directly linked to the ancient ancestry of the great mothers. That culture might have only been a miserable chaos, much like the ones of an Orient that, as phallocratic as it may be, brings out much more "anima" than "animus." It seems that neither of the two cultures would have been satisfactory, insofar as it would have been sexist also; but the ultimate negativity of a culture of women would have never been this, this extermination of nature, this systematic destruction—with maximum profit in mind —of all the nourishing resources.

Returning to the famous stress of the white rat, it is interesting to note that, in the animal kingdom, as in the human kingdom, it is the female who tends to refuse procreation and not the male, although the instinct of preservation should be present throughout the species.

If we consider the behavior of the males in power in our society, what do we see? Conscious of the peril of overpopulation, they strive to make us believe that it is a "developing world problem" and concentrate their efforts on the most disadvantaged spot of the planet, and consequently the one that consumes the least. (Pierre Samuel, in Écologie: *Détente ou cycle infernal*, notes that the United States alone, with 6 percent of the world population, consumes 45 percent of global resources!)

The most material interest explains the attitude of the West: the caste of the masters profits most from growing itself and limiting the expansion of the disadvantaged, its future Spartacus revolting warriors; we saw this recently when Aimé Césaire stood up in protest against a proposed law designed to favor contraception further (already largely accessible) in Martinique; the black member of Parliament disdained the text for its manipulative intentions. He asked: "Why Martinique and not France?" Certainly, the women in Martinique had every right to answer Césaire, telling him that it was up to them and not a man to decide, much as was the case in Harlem a few years ago,[19] but the attitude of Césaire, the political leader from Martinique, was logical. For a long time now, the developing world has known that overpopulation is not a fact of wealth or of assurance that the elderly will be taken care of, but that, on the contrary, it is an element of misery and of morality; they continue to over-procreate through ignorance, material shortage, and heightened oppression of women. It is understandable, additionally, that for the enlightened ones, there is a legitimate distrust of the gifts of European family planning, whereas they would be welcomed with enthusiasm if the Occident began to benefit largely from its own discoveries in this respect.

The Catholic hetero-cops with their "right to life" movement or the preachers of the "moral order," Jean Royer and Jean Foyer,[20] are powerless in the face of this evidence: the scandalous revolt of women regarding their bodies is moving in the direction of the most immediate interest of humanity, of the future, of procreation itself. The true holders of power themselves, who are neither for Jesus Christ nor for Jehovah, but for power, know it, too; it pains them, but they know it. Neo-Malthusianism began to be a necessity well before what motivated the women's revolt and the Manifesto of the 343. When the arteries of capitalism age to the point where they need increasing doses of family planning like Novocain—oh, blasphemous planning, oh, economic anti-liberalism!—the time is near.

"The planet is going to overflow!"
　　　　—Slogan shouted by demonstrators outside the "Right to
　　　　Life" conference at the main assembly hall in Paris

Before capitalism, the last arrival, aging and resistant, before feudalism, before phallocracy, there was feminine power, which never reached the dimension or the stature of matriarchy. Feminine power was founded on the possession of agriculture; but it was an autonomous possession, probably accompanied by sexual segregation; and that is why there was never a true matriarchy. Men controlled the pastorate and the hunt, women agriculture; these two armed groups confronted each other; such is the origin of the supposed "legend" of the Amazons.[21] When the family arrived on the scene, woman could still treat from power to power, as long as agricultural functions continued to make her sacred; the discovery of the process of fertilization—of the womb and of the soil—tolled the last bell. Thus began the iron age of the second sex. It has certainly not ended today. But the earth, symbol and former preserve of the womb of the great mothers, has had a harder life and has resisted longer; today, her conqueror has reduced her to agony. This is the price of phallocracy.

In a world, or simply a country, in which women (and not, as could be the case, a woman) found themselves truly in power, the first act would be to limit and space out births. For a long time, well before overpopulation, that is what they have been trying to do.

The proof is the existence of contraception folklore, where the most frighteningly dangerous procedures border on pure superstition. (Note: not only to avoid having a child but *so that the husband would stay away from the conjugal bed*, oh Freud and the "feminine tendency to evade sexuality"!) These contraception rites, obviously, were never cited by male scholars, whereas lists of opposite rites— those for fertility—exist everywhere. It is only on the planetary scale (not even national) that man deigns to notice overpopulation; woman notices the rabbit effect at the family level. What methods did she have at her disposal to make it known?

The selfish handmaidens so strongly denounced by the brilliant Henry Bordeaux and the Catholic novelists writing between the wars, after whom the "Right to Life" clique takes up the cause, much to the benefit of advertisements for Nestlé,[22] the selfish French mothers who declared they would only jeopardize their lives two or three times by foaling; we can bless them today for the feeble, very feeble, brakes they managed to apply: where would we be in a world peopled thirty years earlier and faster by the heroic devout women, the readers of Father Bethlehem's sanctioned press?

Yes, we must repeat it to obsession, cry it, spread the word: *Just like the class struggle, demography is man's business.*[23] In the areas governed by Catholic misogyny, it is doubly so: the transmission belt between male power at the top and us is, by definition, the men who control the exploitation of our fertility: the husband to whom we must submit, of course, but also the priest, who can only be a man, the doctor or the judge, who, nine times out of ten, is a man; all these civil servants of male power are males.

To summarize: if the class struggle, demography, and ecology are all the problems and affairs of men, it is due to "the great defeat of the feminine sex" that took place throughout the planet in 3000 BC. After the demise of the Amazons and agriculture, the guarantor of power, shared for a certain time between the sexes in the Hittite, Cretan, and Egyptian civilizations, little by little, the wealth of the earth became masculine at the time when woman, tied to the family, no longer had recourse to vanished Amazonian ways. Patriarchal and masculine power peaked in the Bronze Age, with the discovery of what would later become industry. Women were then put under strict surveillance by the victorious sex, which still suffered from fear and distrust of them; they were exiled from all sectors other than the family ghetto; not only from power and from work outside the home, but even from areas in which man seemed to have no fear of competition: physical sports (ancient Greece, except Laconia), theater (feudal England, Japan), art and culture, higher education (practically the world over, apart from a few oft-cited exceptions). Pariah relegated to rabbit-like unions, and, in the best of situations, a luxurious ornament for the victors; finding the sole refuge, in all cultures, to be religious sequestration, escaping from many by devoting herself to the phantoms of the deity; today, she sees more and more profoundly and in more and more places that only men control the "revolution" and profit from it, no matter how much help she gives them in hopes of escaping an oppression she believes to be caused by an economic system and *which is oppressive only due to the male characteristic of the system*. After the victory of a class or a category, *she* only benefits, at best, from slight improvements in conditions, reforms, advantages—a few coins that fall from the coffers of the upheaval—that is, if she happens to be on the right side; but power has only changed hands, never its structure; as we have seen, never do we find a deep challenge to the rapport between the sexes, a humanist and ecological question among others.

"Seated, standing, lying, man is always his own tyrant." Céline would have been surprised at the connection of his thoughts to Marx: man's rapport with man is measured by man's rapport with woman. If some men, always and everywhere, end up the ultimate profiteers from a revolutionary change, it is precisely because they apply to others the measures of force that *all* men as a group apply to *all* women as a group—even if, on occasion, it happens that Mr. So-and-So grovels to his own wife.

How, then, do we approach the problem of maximal profit that sacrifices the collective interest to private interest, or the race for power that takes the place of collective interest in revolutionary instances? How can this problem be resolved as long as mental structures remain as they are: that is to say, informed by fifty centuries of masculine planetary civilization, overexploitative and destructive of the resources?

The proof that no revolution directed and accomplished by men can achieve the necessary mutation is that none has ever gone further than replacing one regime by another, one system by another in accordance with the existing structures, and that none has ever even envisaged the sole possibility of going further, of departing from the infernal cycle of "production-consumption" that is the alibi for this enormous mass of work—useless, alienating, mystified, and mystifying—the very base of male society wherever it exists.

No, imagination is never in power. We keep falling into the same patterns, into the same fatal stereotypes; much like the sentiment expressed by the people when Louis XIII's favorite birdcatcher replaced the Constable Concino Concini: "Nothing but the cork has changed; the wine still tastes the same."

A few years ago, in a science-fiction collection entitled *If This Goes On*,[24] only one of several tales on the theme of a total change after a catastrophe[25] envisaged the following scenario: industrial production ended, scientific research limited to a small number of well-confined laboratories, collective efforts directed toward the areas of reflection and thought, art, and nonproductive activities. Astronauts returning to Earth after long years away despaired at finding Earth taken over by what they deemed an irremediable decay—until the day they noticed that all the discoveries of the past had been carefully preserved and transferred to a restricted number of depositories but were only used on rare occasions; for example, a very rare remedy was fabricated and a supersonic jet sent to get it in emergency cases, to heal a sick child; the rest of the time, transportation was by horse or bicycle. Importance thus was shifted from the speed of the transport to its motivation. The civilization of gadgets had disappeared and had given way to a humanism that was not retrograde after dispensing with technical devices devoid of common sense. The author of this "utopia" was a woman, the only woman in the collection of short stories: Marion Zimmer Bradley.

In 1972, Gébé, an artist who seemed not to be aware of this tale translated from American English, produced his filmed utopia: *The Year 01*.[26] Work in general stops; the workers leave the factories, office workers leave their offices, and hawkers shout in the streets: "Open your windows and throw the key into the street." Then they start working again at a considerably slower pace, just enough to meet the immediate needs of the people; there was no need to kill the capitalists, for they took care of it themselves; the sky was darkened by CEOs throwing themselves from skyscrapers. The answer to the inevitable question "But how do you occupy so much leisure time?" was given with simplicity: "We think, we reflect, *and it's not a sad thing to do*." As long as humans shudder at such an unhappy prospect—the possibility of thinking and reflecting about themselves—they are still stuck in Pascal's time: competition, aggression, and all the horrors of male society will triumph.

Without a doubt, from the immediate feminist viewpoint, this new "Village Seer" that Jean-Jacques Rousseau–Gébé offers us is hardly satisfying; everything therein is truly profoundly changed, except the rapport between the sexes; woman remains the sole object of erotic desire; she is still this white woman who mends the former chief editor's pants, this black woman who grinds the manioc while the men discuss the Year 01 in Africa; another finds she has not gained much by milking cows instead of typing. All the same, however, for the first time, and unknown even to the author, a truly anti-male conception of the world was shown to us in the form of a public product, a film; the "utopia" (in the classical sense: yesterday's utopia, tomorrow's truth) that the feminine alone can implement. That is to say, women above all, but not only women: their objective and natural allies, young people, these youths from both sexes who will carry deep within themselves the strongest protest against the outdated world of the father, once they have thrown away the aftermath of its macho-leftism.

Because women who call for an alliance of the child and the woman are right: the feminine is that part of the world separated, put aside, put between parentheses, that suffers the economic and cultural dictatorship of the father; the first and most insurmountable taboo, the most severe anathema leveled at incest is for the one that sanctions the amorous rapport between mother and son; the other bans are secondary. Why? Because it is the wall that phallocracy felt it necessary to raise against women's power. Above and beyond the stories of sexual jealousy born of the Freudian triangle, modern anthropology has been able to discern, in obligatory exogamy, the dictatorship of the patriarchal society and its fear of women, its misogyny that becomes gynophobia in the face of this terrible menace: that the mother and the child would unite against the father.[27]

A massive end of productive work is not a utopia; it has been shown that 7 to 10 percent of present production would suffice amply to meet food, clothing, and housing needs. Even though *The Year 01* does not emphasize the ecological necessity of this solution, one scene ties pollution to the demented inflation of industry—the one where the fisherman, stammering from emotion, cries into the telephone: "I did it, I caught a fish!" It is a real cause for celebration: "We welcome the first fish of the Year 01!" When we learn, thanks to our Cassandras preaching in the futurologist desert, that more marine species have disappeared in thirty years than in the entire geological period following the Pleistocene epoch, we can ask the question: Which is worth more, fish or gadgets?[28]

The current consumption-production cycle inevitably linked to industrial expansion, fruit of the mental structure of phallocracy, can be broken down in the following way: 80 percent of superfluous products, about 20 percent of which are entirely useless, must be thrown on the market at the price of poisoning and destroying the patrimony in an ascending curve; to do this, work time roughly equivalent to 80 percent of a human life must be available—in other words, equivalent to practically total alienation. That is not all—these superfluous or useless objects must have a short life span and be replaceable, which increases the poisoning and destruction. Finally, supreme alienation: since the products must be consumed, desire to acquire them must be inspired by a techno-promotional circuit; that is, fabricated from start to finish. Since the producer is also a consumer, he will thus be alienated and fooled at every level, inside, outside, and all around, as Gébé would say. A scam aimed at time, which is the framework of life, at sensitivity, which is its valuable side, a gigantic, planetary, monstrous frustration; there you have the results of the cycle born 5,000 years ago, beginning with the caging of the second sex and the appropriation of the earth by males: "progress."

This root of the problem remains totally unnoticed in 1974 by modern revolutionary movements.[29] Even for the anti-conformists of Marxism, the ecological problem comes back to the evils due to capitalism (and it is certain that, in a system of profit, the two are closely connected, but the presence of the problem in socialist systems proves that it is not identified solely with capitalism), in much the same way that the inequity in the rapport between the sexes is defined as a superstructure that would be changed by the substitution of one economic regime for another. In instances in which youths have become involved in the protest only through some political label or other, they are subsumed by the system that they fight without knowing it, since they do not recognize, beyond the socioeconomic aspect, its profound and primordial motivation of war between the sexes. But, to the extent that youths' sensitivity belongs to the battered feminine, oppressed and repressed in the world order of the father, where even their economic position situates them, in general, on the same plane as women—supported by the father who expects a service, a return on his investment—youth of both sexes come more and more to the realization that their cause is not only that of the mother but also of all women the world over. The day when the male options of macho-leftists (including for girls, we must repeat) have been entirely eradicated by the consciousness of an emergency, of a burning necessity—to explode the consumption-production cycle instead of giving it a new form doomed to the same failure and leading to the same death—feminism will have won because the feminine will have triumphed.

The case is clear—we are in no way pleading for an illusory superiority of women over men, or even for the "values" of the feminine, which exist only on a cultural level and not at all on a metaphysical one. We are saying: Do you want to live or die? If you refuse planetary death, you will have to accept the revenge of women, for their personal interests join those of the human community, whereas males' interests, on an individual basis, are separate from those of the general community, and this holds true even at the level of the current male system. For proof, we have merely to consider the contradiction between the supreme instances of its power, pushing women into production (and they have announced that "1975 is the year of women"), and the private interests of the males living under this same power, who furiously resist the idea of depriving themselves of their personal maids. We have merely to consider the contradiction between the effort of this same power to diffuse and aid contraception in the goal of using, for its production, the feminine time taken away from the nourishing function, and the same indignant resistance from individual males against the fact that their females could control their procreation!

This brings me back to the beginning of this book: awareness of feminitude, of the misfortune of being a woman, is taking place today in a contradiction and an ambiguity that announce the end of the same misfortune. Starting at real-life events, at radical subjectivity, her experience as a species treated as a minority, separated, reified, *looked at*, a woman of my generation discovers that her "little problem," her "secondary question," this so-minute detail of the subversive front, indeed, her "fragmentary struggle," is no longer content to link with but identifies directly with the number-one question, with the original problem; the basis, even, of the indispensable need to change the world, not just to improve it, but *so that there can still be a world*.

What revenge for the sole human majority to be treated as a minority! Until now, it was difficult for women to comprehend the source of the misfortune of feminitude; they limited themselves to demands for "fragments" of world management before getting to the roots, free sexual disposition, which suddenly revealed a sense of totality. She who, until now, had been not man's "companion" but at once the alchemical crucible of his reproduction, his beast of burden, his scapegoat, his spittoon; with whom he sometimes amused himself by covering her in stones and by proclaiming her to be his holy grail; the one who always brought about in him, by virtue of a constant threat of victory, a hostile distrust that has gone as far in certain cultures as the hatred that engenders ritual mutilation (Africa) and death (sexocide of witches in the Middle Ages, of the "debauched" of the Mediterranean Basin or the Orient) and that has evolved into a true "gynophobia," as Lederer puts it, she has now become, in law and in possibility, if not in fact, what she was in pre-phallocratic times: the sole controller of procreation. As soon as this right can be freely lived through massive contraception and uninhibited access to abortion, the disappearance of half the human nightmare will depend on her as she implements the "stress of the white female rat."

This immense power that will be returned to her, that is already coming within sight, has nothing in common with the one that organizes, decides, represents, and oppresses and that still remains in male's hands; it is exactly in this area that she can most efficiently bring about its defeat and sound the death knell of ancient oppression. In short, according to a slogan of the "Ecology-Feminism Center," we have to tear the planet away from the male today in order to restore it for humanity of tomorrow. That is the only alternative, for if male society persists, there will be no tomorrow for humanity.

Her very life threatened, as well as the one she passes on (that she chooses whether or not to pass on), she who is the keeper of this life source, in whom the forces of the future are realized and through whom they pass, is thus doubly concerned with finding the fastest solution to the ecological problem And, what is more, she represents, in the purest Marxist fashion in the world, this producing class frustrated from its production by male distribution, since this source of collective wealth (procreation) is possessed by a minority, males, the feminine species being the human majority.

The specialists themselves recognize it; along with Edgar Morin in the ecological conference of the *Nouvel Observateur* (where no women appeared), they admit that "we are starting to comprehend that the abolition of capitalism and the liquidation of the bourgeoisie merely give way to a new oppressive structure." Reimut Reiche had already brought out and explained this fact in *Sexuality and*

Class Struggle, that the "core" resists all revisions of the order. That core, as I have shown here, is the phallocracy. It is at the base of an order that can only assassinate nature in the name of profit if it is capitalist, and in the name of progress if it is socialist. The problem for women is, first, demography, then nature, and thus the world; her urgent problem, the one in common with youth, is autonomy and control of her destiny. If humanity is to survive, she must resign herself to this fact.

Consequently, with a society finally in the feminine, that will mean nonpower (and not power to women), it will be proven that no other human category could have accomplished the ecological revolution, for no other was as directly concerned at all levels. And the two sources of wealth diverted for male profit will once again become an expression of life and no longer an elaboration of death; and the human being will finally be treated first as a person, and not above all else as a male or female.

And the planet placed in the feminine will flourish for all.

1971–74

APPENDICES

A. How Women Don't Control Their Own Destiny

We need to describe, before we can trace it, the important and complex chart of handicaps due to feminitude that distinguish specifically women's lot from men's in our culture; hence, we will enumerate the inevitable variations after this summary.

One element remains constant: women's situation develops along these two vectors, one horizontal and the other vertical: *sex* and *social category* (the rapport to production).

The following observation strikes us as the first result: the nature of the possibilities starts with a rise on the social scale, which does not necessarily mean, besides, an increase in monetary means; a teacher, a freelance journalist, an artist can have more trouble living off what she earns, and with less stability than a salaried employee; she is perhaps freer than the latter to the extent that a greater choice of possibilities presents itself according to the various factors of her background.

In the most disadvantaged category, the *working-class woman*, we see the following different relationships to sexuality:

(a) *Married or living with a man*.——The absence of *moral* standing, that means the disapproval of the surrounding people, the repression of respectability, no longer plays a role these days in the same sense as at the beginning of the century; the moral status of a woman changes to the extent where she is a man's companion, and even in the working classes, always more conservative, not much difference in this aspect is made between "false" couples and "real" ones.

The principal handicap of this category is, then, the absence of *social* standing that extends to all women of the lower classes as also for the men with whom they share the same lot in life (it is not specific in itself, then, but reinforces the rest) combined with the *absence of freedom* allowed to all housewives, above all those who are poor and in charge of children; added to this is the absence of freedom due to work outside the home (even though, here, there is a certain dialectic contradiction: the woman who works outside is exhausted but does attain more control with her husband) and the inevitable tendency of living in a ghetto: in a closed circle, during her rare leisure time, with the same few people, doing the same things, etc.

(b) *Alone*.——The same picture with a *greater freedom* of action and a lack of *accrued* social regard (a woman without a man).[1]

(c) *Divorced*.——The same picture, with a heightened *lack of freedom* when she has children, and greater freedom without children; attached to a decrease of *moral* regard, much stronger in the lower classes today than in the case of cohabitation or children outside of marriage, and still very strong in the petite and middle bourgeoisie.[2]

(d) *Lesbian*.——This case is much more frequent than one would think in the poorer classes and translates into a growing number of girls from the working class living together. Here, the lack of freedom hearkens back to that caused by poorly paid work; this independence that is greater than in the preceding condition (two women together "manage" quite well and share the household work, and they don't have children) is counterbalanced, not so much from social disapproval, since feminine homosexuality can easily remain invisible, as by the impossibility of being protected and respected, as any woman without a man is at risk from other men.

In the case of a lesbian with a child, it is usually a case of a divorce, the men of the working class being less likely than the middle class to accept in their wife what easily seems to be a "vice."

(Finally, numerous cases of lesbianism exist among prostitutes; they find consolation for their atrocious daily life in love for the same sex. Pimps tolerate it even less than working-class men. I remember a manuscript, memoirs of a crook, in which each chapter contained a defense of the high contribution of pimps to public decency; because, according to the author, they maintain respect for good moral standards and repress the "girls'" vices, their dishonesty, their laziness and, above all, lesbianism; what would honest citizens do without this collaboration from the "milieu"?)

(e) *Whore.*—Lesbian or not, the prostitute does not belong to the working class, even though today a certain *social recognition* (projects for retirement, social and health protection, etc.) makes her appear as a sort of marginality within the feminine proletariat. When they practice their profession part time, they are usually from the middle class, generally married and mothers (see Godard's film *Two or Three Things I Know about Her*). Today's call girl is the courtesan of the Second Empire. Her ghetto is practically as absolute as the prisoner's in the common law system.

(f) *Country/Farm women.*—A woman alone won't last long in the country, with the exception of some strange eccentrics, a weakened reminder of the ancient "sorceress"; she will go to work in the city. A *low-wage worker*, if she remains alone, she will benefit from greater freedom than a housewife but will only find short-term romantic liaisons that an emotional frustration will counterbalance with a lack of social standing, all pushing her into marriage at all costs: the mass media, press, film, and television all conspire incessantly to that end.

Today, if we look at the *homemaker* or *housewife* of the working classes, we find a marked ghetto due to total economic dependence on the husband; to be protected, she has to become a prisoner. Among the middle classes, her lot improves considerably, and her level of fatigue is reduced, but the restriction on her liberty is not diminished: her servitude corresponds exactly to the number of children of a young age, even if she can hire domestic help. *Divorced*, her obligation to the ghetto diminishes sharply; if she has no children or if her children are older, she benefits from the most significant liberation from her feminine condition; this is why the social condemnation exerts itself—even though less sharply than among the working classes—in order to remove desire of this liberation from women, and to make them believe that it is a "solution of despair."

The *prostitution of the housewife* that I discussed earlier is always possible in poorer households, or in certain members of the middle class, trapped in an impossible situation: deserted by her husband, nonpayment of alimony, illness, etc. All the handicaps pile up on her at the same time: the loss of social standing is still the highest in the lower classes, less able to keep this "second profession" a secret, a "profession" that her husband often encourages. A new element is added, that of danger: not protected, even though integrated into the society through her home and her children, the call girl or the occasional prostitute can be sequestered, beaten, and subject to racketeering. *La punition* ("The Punishment") by Xavière[3] is a good example. This hell is a common occurrence of the feminine condition.

(We cannot repeat enough that one of the strongest means of pressure exerted on all women to constrain them into marriage is that one man saves her from all the others—in theory.)

The personal life of the salaried worker, of the working-class woman, of the woman in the countryside, etc., will not vary, from beginning to end; in the case of *independent or freelance work*, professional success becomes possible, a promotion is sought, and finally the individual variations become stronger: intelligence, her character, family, the place she lives, and the choice even of place to live. Social standing is acquired, even if she is in poverty, and the former moral denigration suffered by the woman of the middle class is no longer in play. The only remnant is the tendency of the ghetto, especially if she has children, when the woman is obliged to reconcile familial tasks with performing in her profession; and finally, in the case of divorced women or lesbians, in certain milieux (above all in the middle class of areas away from Paris), a drop in moral standing is always to be feared.

Finally, at the top of the social ladder, we see the absence of freedom disappear, along with the disappearance of moral or social denigration, in all the imaginable categories; but—especially according to the chosen career—the danger of a new ghetto of a different type appears, of a certain amount of leisure, but that equivocates to a draining, an exhaustion, a limitation that only very strong personalities can push aside, to the extent where feminitude, that always plays a role even at this level, forces the woman to count more than ever—because the stakes here are enormous—less with one man than with the man's world more still: the very one from which one man alone (marriage) is supposed to protect her at the beginning.

Some ethnic and social variations, sometimes local ones, are removed from this general background; for example, certain antiquated traditions still exist that attach social standing to the single mother (in the Ariège region in France, in certain Romanian villages): they expect a woman to prove her fertility before she can be married; certain limited social categories (artistic milieux) attach a snobbery to homosexuality; on the contrary, in Italy, even in the middle classes, lesbianism meets with much more disapproval than male homosexuality.

These reflections are useful to express, in a very schematic way, to show sexual inequality not identifiable to social inequality; for a man, his destiny will simply be more and more controllable as he moves up the social ladder, without any consideration of sexual status: single, married, divorced, father, or sterile—except in the case of *homosexuality*, the only one where he is disadvantaged (in general) in relation to women, his status being much harder to hide; on the other hand, in his case, there does not exist, even if you think of the homeless man, or the legionnaire, any typically masculine situation that places him in the abjection legitimized, organized, and accepted of feminine prostitution and of daily rape, of the perils and the horrors that she represents, and that made Kate Millett say, "Whores are our political prisoners."

B. The New "Feminine Mystique"
("What Is Meant by Politics?")
(Liberation Movement)

"Being a communist is being free already." Mireille Bertrand, a member of the political office of the Communist Party affirmed this, on Saturday the 29th at the main assembly meeting for the Movement for Women's Liberation to one thousand women from all over. Their average age: thirty-two. "Why things are changing at the workplace just as in life—nothing happens without you." That's what was written on the invitation from the Communist Party to this day of the woman, and an invitation to vote for it at the next opportunity. Étienne Fajon was presiding over the meeting. He was clearer. "The Communist Party is the party of the emancipation of women."

We went, and we saw and heard women, like Marie-Claire, sixteen years old, who said: "I want to live, too, I want to be free to live, and I want things to change." We liked Marie-Claire a lot, as well as many others. Women like us, but not entirely. In talking with some of them, we had the impression that we lived in two different worlds. What were political issues for us were personal problems for them. What we wanted to change starting today were, for them, issues to deal with later. These differences gave us a lot to think about. What follows is an imaginary debate between the ideas apparent and the presentations and discussions on Saturday and our own thoughts.

Women in the Communist Party: *We are proud that the number of women in the workplace has increased. In the USSR, 40 percent of scientists are women. In France also, the number of female executives has increased two times faster than the number of women in the working class. The liberation of women begins with their entry into the working world.*

Women in the Liberation Movement: Okay. If I wanted to work, it was so that I didn't have to ask for money from my parents or, eventually, my husband. That's true. And also to have friends at work—to see things outside, outside these four walls of pots and pans and the kids. But I don't have the impression of being free or of having taken a great step forward. Not at all.

Communist Party: *But you do agree that women are more exploited than men. So we have to fight first for salary equity and work conditions.*

Liberation: But if a party tells me, "Work for the common program, you will have the same rights as men," isn't this party setting me up to share the same alienation as men? Do we want to resemble men? To enter the field of competition? Is the goal to become a man? And what does the man do anyway? When he has a position of power, he oppresses others. And if we move up the ladder, we will probably do the same thing. That is what we refuse. Our struggle must be collective. To be free is not simply to take orders and receive rights catalogued in the common program.

Communist Party: *Being a communist is being free already.*

Liberation: That is a beautiful sentiment that, for us, means something else besides what Mr. Bertrand explains. It is not solely to push the common program. Our demand from life is greater. It goes beyond what is proposed in the common program. Our current demand is to end the oppression of woman by man.

Communist Party: *There is nothing more absurd than to want to pit women against men. Fulfillment in work and love can never be reached that way. The essential issue today is to liberate the woman from exploitation and have her participate in political life. Socialism is knocking at the door today, engage in politics more, and more, always more engagement.*

Liberation: What are politics? We are in a situation that is not satisfying, and there are things that we want to change right away—above all, things that we have in mind. And in the mind, even with the most attractive projects for a future, woman is never equal to man. It is because of this inequality that has existed for centuries that women say there is a specific oppression of women.

Communist Party: *You are talking about motherhood. But in a socialist state, the state organizes childcare issues, activity centers for children, and so on.*

Liberation: That is all well and good. That improves women's conditions at work. We get the impression that we are rallying our energy for the profit of a productive system. On the one hand is the family; on the other, work.

Communist Party: *The family is the natural base of society. We are not against cohabitation, but today that would be trying to create a little group in the middle of a repressive society.*

Liberation: We are also exploited in the family. How many men are there who truly share the household work, who take care of the children, who accept that their wife wants to make love and says so? Very few yet. So why do you tell us, "Those are personal problems, let's take care of that later, shall we?" Among those who are fighting today to change the system, many of them—and often women—are attacking this exploitation by the family. That can only contribute to destroying the bourgeois society, by attacking the mentalities that it produced and that it uses to protect itself. In all that, there is nothing personal. The same holds true for the free disposition of one's body and the right to abortion.

Communist Party: *We defend the right to abortion, but that is not the main problem. If you are a responsible person—that is, if you don't need to abort too often, in any socialist society …*

Liberation: Yes, still the others who decide. However, the woman knows very well how to say what she wants if she lets her body speak, if she talks about her own emotional and intellectual experience. Talking with your activists about emotional experiences is not possible. It is the party that talks and not the body. For you, the body has no voice.

Communist Party: *And, nevertheless, you have seen very well that the women of the Communist Party express themselves easily and eloquently on the podium and that they are the first to fight in the factories and elsewhere.*

Liberation: But each fight is not inscribed in the body. However, today, when nothing has been decided, the language of feminine affective content, shamed for a long time, shows a creative energy and can be a formidable driving force—a force that can also act on man's way of thinking.

Politics, then, becomes closer to us, and we have no reason to be silent to put things off until tomorrow. Denying this oppression, not favoring an autonomous organization of women where this oppression can be defined and fought, amounts to distancing half the sky from the revolution.

(The remarks imagined here from the Communist Party are drawn from the Communist newspaper *L'Humanité*, from *France Nouvelle*, or from interviews with activists from the Communist Party at Saturday's meeting of the Movement of the Liberation of Women.)

Liberation, November 1, 1973

C. A Rose for Valerie

"Bent under the arch of strident sap, a young woman points at her vaginal lips with a polished fingernail to chill metaphysical thirst."

It is in the spirit of this beautiful quotation from Gilbert Lely singing Sade's text that the gravestone for Valerie Solanas must be sculpted.

Locked up in a psychiatric hospital for having fired three shots at a filmmaker who swindled her; released, then locked up again for having attacked another man; the author of a short book of around fifty pages that blows up with the sound of a thunderclap the muted silence of the women's lib cocoon makes people believe that a movement is coming, a horde of castrators crazy for blood, provokes the immediate and classical desertion of a party that it has just served with such fervor; then released again after having spent long months in solitary confinement, with no mail (either from her lawyer or her editor), she committed herself to this death of a scorpion caught in a circle of fire; the SCUM exterminator exterminated only herself.

So many writers have dreamed of replicating the spirit of Sade's writings and have only, at best, seized a few snippets! It was the hand of a little *underground* American, half-prostitute, half-actress of parallel cinema and who had never read the Marquis de Sade, the only one who could benefit from such a heritage. Like the prisoner of Vincennes, Valerie was locked up "like a wild beast"; like him, she saw the aura of a massacre attributed to her, whereas she never killed anybody (well, yes, at least she tried, which was not the case for Donatien); like him, she could have attributed André Chénier's poetic cries at the foot of the guillotine to herself at the end of her days:

> Dying without emptying my quiver?
> Without piercing, without trampling, without mashing in
>   their muck
> These executioners scribbling laws!

A second-degree literature turns away from her many of those who cannot breathe on her heights. Sade has had the reputation of being a "misogynist" and the reasoned reproaches of the reasonable feminists, as if one is supposed to take that into account, in pages that describe massacres and tortures and all the bottom of the infernal depths that burrow into the soul of just any grocer, insults leveled at the "beautiful sex"! You might as well revoke the interest of complex and remarkable voodoo cosmogony in the name of the raw chicken that its followers eat so crudely, panting like panthers. Readers, and above all female readers who stop at this particular aspect of Sadian desire, forget the immensity of the goddesses of crime like Juliette and Clairwell, of whom Sade, alone in his period, painted the unheard portrait, women and above all men who express indignation at the Solanian "project" of castrating and exterminating 48 percent of humanity (up to the total suppression of the monetary sign that strips women of power over the other) miss the profound humanism of his inspiration: after having abolished money, vanquish death. "Millions of women ... will resolve the problems of old age, of illness and of death and will completely reinvent cities and housing."

Émile Marenssin declares in *La bande à Baader*:[4] "The only radical demand of the communist society is the abolition of death." This swan song of male society that is the communist ideal, the exterminator, the blasphemous, the implacable Valerie brought it back herself.

Like all poets, and particularly the "poètes maudits" (the misunderstood poets), SCUM has the gift of ubiquity. It multiplies, it spreads, it becomes a torrent of cursing magic:

> SCUM will attack buses, taxis and distribution services ... will destroy
> useless objects, cars, shop windows ... will move against television
> antennas ... At the same time, it will fuck the system in the ass, will
> destroy, will kill, SCUM will recruit ... the murders will always be
> conducted with discernment ... In place of strike picket signs, it will
> be long knives that SCUM will plant at night.

She who most certainly never read Pascal seems to plagiarize him: "Man is horrified at the idea of having free time during which he would find nothing else to do other than contemplate his grotesque person." Her political views have a geometrical accuracy: the first and, undoubtedly, the only one, she discovered that the conflict is not situated finally between men and women, but between women who have gained consciousness and those who refuse to do so. Man, at any rate (such as he has created himself by his own society), is called to be swept away in the near future. When Yevgeny Yevtushenko, in 1964, proclaimed that "the real men of today are women," he merely expressed in a clumsy and sexist way (the one that I had used myself fifteen years earlier and that unleashed mockery, not by its clumsiness and its sexism, but on the contrary, by the packet of truth that it contained)[5] the modern, self-evident fact that is the following: if there is the least hope of salvation from a desperate situation, it can only come from women.

And it is with this admirable remark concerning women who refuse to gain consciousness: "She lends her body without thinking, wipes her ape-like forehead wrinkled by the effort, pushes the failing ego up the ass, compliments the abject toad," that Valerie Solanas rises up to the pinnacle of the highest literature and replaces the organization by a powerful deflagration in a flash. The accent placed on the urgency of the rescue, everybody—and she was the first among them—took it for a call to genocide. This question of massacre is only a trifle. The gold that remains at the bottom of Valerie's Sadian crucible is this ray of light that we would like to see inscribed everywhere, her radiant words: "IF WOMEN DON'T MOVE THEIR ASSES QUICKLY, WE ALL RISK DYING TODAY!"

—*Françoise d'Eaubonne (Tombstone for SCUM, in preparation)*

D. A "Feminist Front" Leaflet

Leftist Machismo Is Still Machismo!

In May 1968, in office 453 at Censier University, where the Action Committee worked, "We are on the way" wrote the three arguments, of which the principal points follow:

1) The feminist movement, taking a true challenge of patriarchal society as its point of departure, has finally contributed to the end of feminine alienation. *Women* ... have quite simply emulated the traditional charges of the *alienating functions* and the responsibilities that are just as alienating of the masculine state.[6]

2) By limiting themselves to legal and economic demands, by *layering an absurd and impossible war between the sexes on top of the authentic class struggle*, feminism has missed the revolution, misled its followers, and created a confusion of language more alienating yet than the univocal language of the lords and masters of the feudal period.

3) Far from attacking the sexual-cultural stereotypes that alienate couples and families, feminism has piled them all up together with pleasure, all topsy-turvy and with no regard for the

contradictions. Always running after the latest fashion, *in cloth-ing and appearance as well as in political thought*, feminism has made women the accomplices, voluntary or not, to the crimes of the consumption-oppression of the Third World, of children, and of the marginalized.

Here is what we feel about these three arguments from one of the most active and famous committees for leftist action:

a) More than one of these criticisms ("by limiting demands to the legal and economic realms ...") would be correct if applied to what we call "mama's feminism." Wasn't there another at the time? Was it already dead? So be it. However, how many of these eloquent critics came to invade one of the first meetings of the Women's Liberation Movement (MLF), shouting out, "Power is at the end of the phallus"? We'd like to know that.

b) The radical feminism of the MLF is, however, the first to strive to move beyond the "legal and economic limitations" and to focus on the sexual-cultural stereotypes in question. Why, then, have the leftists maintained the ostracism in relation to it that they leveled against past forms of feminism, if not that, like all men in politics, THEY ARE HOSTILE TO ANY FORM OF FEMINISM?

c) The style itself is revealing. The writers don't contrast an "inauthentic class struggle" with an "authentic class struggle"—instead, they feel obliged to write "absurd," "impossible," and "war." These Marxists break ranks thus with Bebel, who wrote: "Woman was a slave before slaves existed," and Engels, who declared: "Women will never be liberated unless they first liberate themselves sexually." What is more, they are in total contradiction with the history of the facts that shows us the struggle between the sexes leading sometimes in fact to a war, and even a war of extermination (sexocide of the "sorceresses," the bloody revolt of Vlasta and her Amazons in the Middle Ages, etc.).

The very style of their repudiation exposes the passionate emotion in these men's positions.

d) The term "fascinated women" replacing "feminism" (that should be completed by "yesterday's feminism") in the first argument proves a philosophical idealism that is absolutely apolitical and anti-Marxist. It isn't because women were "fascinated" by the virile privilege that they entered en masse into factories and offices, and they benefited very little, or exceptionally, from the responsibilities (alienating or not) of the "masculine civil service structure": they furnished *underpaid* manual labor to a mass of masculine professions, not of their own free will and by desire but by economic imperative, this imperative imposed by a male society, and uniquely by it.

e) The reference to clothes and to fashion in the third argument completes the picture of this phallocratic mentality that doesn't think for one instant to turn to auto-criticism (if women have become "accomplices, voluntarily or not" of an unjust society, whose fault is it?) or to a simple question: Why in the world would this accursed feminism, being dead well before 1968, lash out still against a cadaver? Could it be a fear of a rising phoenix?

Conclusions: Whether they are reformers or revolutionaries, revisionist communists or leftists, the most anti-establishment of men, taken as a group (not individually), are always masculinists, phallocrats, and machos. All the speeches about the "principal struggle and the secondary struggle" and on the "primary importance of the class struggle" can do nothing to change this fact.

LEFTIST MACHISMO IS STILL MACHISMO.

Women can expect salvation only from themselves. But this time, in a totalitarian perspective, and not in limited and partial demands—in the total and irreversible toppling of male society.

We can only liberate the "Third World," children, and the marginalized by liberating *ourselves* from the male chauvinism that is the base of this society of consumption-oppression.

—*FEMINIST FRONT*

E. To See Clearly (Combat for Man)

There are words that we can never repeat enough, because they make up the starting point for all our actions and engagement. So let's repeat, one more time, these comments:

> In ten years, at the rate things are progressing, man's situation on their planet will be desperate. In other words, we will have destroyed all the sources of life, from animal, vegetal, and even mineral sources (fresh water becoming increasingly scarce). In short, in ten years, we will have either won or lost the "battle for nature," if we are not able to fight vigorously to put an end to the "vicious cycle."
>
> —Cry for action released in January 1969 by French scientists meeting at the Museum of Natural History

I don't want to be the bearer of bad tidings, but given the information I have as secretary-general, only one conclusion is possible: the member countries of the UN have ten years to put aside their quarrels and engage in a global program designed to stop the arms race, to clean up the environment, and to control the demographic explosion. If not, the fear is that the above problems will attain such proportions that we will not be able to control them.

—*Declaration to the UN in 1969 by U Thant, secretary-general of the UN*

Faced with the rapid growth of pollution in all the areas of the biosphere, we appeal to all the organizations, all the associations, and all the people concerned about nature to carry out an energetic campaign of information during the decade of 1970–1980 in order to persuade the populations about the gravity of the planetary dangers that will inevitably result from this pollution and affect our civilization.

—The experts at the UN, UNESCO,
and the European Council, 1970

All the accords in the world will remain useless if the fundamental problem is not confronted head-on. All the earth's pollution has one cause: man. The world's population will double well before the year 2000. No matter the quantity of ingenious solutions that scientists find to deal with it, pollution will be a part of life. We will be like rabbits in a cage, with a limited ration of food, living in our own garbage, increasing our numbers at an insane rate and carrying on a fervent struggle for water and food to stay alive.

—UNESCO Newsletter, August/September 1971

It isn't enough to read these excerpts, or to agree and go on to other things. We must study them at the deepest level, see only that, consider the problems relative to saving nature and to the survival of the human species as being THE ONLY IMPORTANT QUESTIONS, *and give it all our attention. This is the only condition that will enable us to pursue valid action.*

—Combat for Man, Autumn 1973

Notes

Foreword

1. Modified from Carolyn Merchant, ed., *Ecology: Key Concepts in Critical Theory*, 2nd ed. (Amherst, NY: Humanity Books, 2008), 24–8. Used by permission.

2. On Françoise d'Eaubonne's founding of the Ecology-Feminism Center in 1972, see the chronology in Françoise d'Eaubonne, "Feminism or Death," in *New French Feminisms: An Anthology*, ed. Elaine Marks and Isabelle de Courtivron (Amherst: University of Massachusetts Press, 1980), 25. On the Center's "launching of a new action: ecofeminism," see Françoise d'Eaubonne, "The Time for Ecofeminism," trans. Ruth Hottell, in Merchant, *Ecology*, 201–14. The original French version is Françoise d'Eaubonne, *Le féminisme ou la mort* (Paris: Pierre Horay, 1974), 215–52; *Écologie et féminisme: Révolution ou mutation?* (Paris: Libre et Solidaire Éditeur, 2018).

3. D'Eaubonne, "The Time for Ecofeminism," 212.

4. Johann Jakob Bachofen, *Myth, Religion, and Mother Right*, trans. Ralph Manheim (Princeton: Princeton University Press, 1967); Friedrich Engels, "Origin of the Family, Private Property, and the State," in *Selected Works* (New York: International Publishers, 1968); Robert Briffault, *The Mothers*, abridged edition (New York: Atheneum, 1977); August Bebel, *Woman in the Past, Present, and Future* (San Francisco: G. B. Benham, 1987).

5. D'Eaubonne, "The Time for Ecofeminism," 210.

6. D'Eaubonne, "The Time for Ecofeminism," 209.

7. D'Eaubonne, "The Time for Ecofeminism," 212.

8. Ynestra King, "Feminism and the Revolt of Nature," (Humanities Press, 2001), 14.

9. Sherry B. Ortner, "Is Female to Male as Nature Is to Culture?" in *Woman, Culture, and Society*, ed. Michelle Zimbalist Rosaldo and Louise Lamphere (Stanford, CA: Stanford University Press, 1974), 67–87.

10. On the debates between ecofeminism and deep ecology, see Ariel Kay Salleh, "Deeper than Deep Ecology: The Ecofeminist Connection," *Environmental Ethics* 6, no. 4 (Winter 1984): 339–45; Marti Kheel, "Ecofeminism and Deep Ecology: Reflections on Identity and Difference," in *Covenant for a New Creation*, ed. Carol Robb and Carl Casebolt (New York: Orbis Books, 1991); Jim Cheney, "Eco-Feminism and Deep Ecology," *Environmental Ethics* 9, no. 2 (Summer 1987): 115–45; Warwick Fox, "The Deep Ecology-Ecofeminism Debate and Its Parallels," *Environmental Ethics* 11, no. 1 (Spring 1989): 5–25; Michael Zimmerman, "Feminism, Deep Ecology, and Environmental Ethics," *Environmental Ethics* 9, no. 1 (Spring 1987): 21–44; Ariel Salleh, "The Ecofeminism/Deep Ecology Debate," *Environmental Ethics* 14, no. 3 (Fall 1992): 195–216; Ariel Salleh, "Class, Race, and Gender Discourse in the Ecofeminism/Deep Ecology Debate," *Environmental Ethics* 15, no. 3 (Fall 1993): 225–44. On the debates between ecofeminism and social/socialist ecology, see Janet Biehl, *Rethinking Ecofeminist Politics* (Boston: South End Press, 1991); Laura Schere, "Feminism, Ecology, and Left Green Politics," *Left Green Notes* 9 (August–September 1991); Janet Biehl, "Ecofeminism and the Left Greens: A Response to Laura Schere," *Left Green Notes* (November–December 1991); Discussion between Lori Ann Thrupp, Daniel Faber, and James O'Connor (on Faber and O'Connor's "The Struggle for Nature"), *Capitalism, Nature, Socialism* 1, no. 3 (November 1989): 169–74; Discussion between Ariel Salleh, Martin O'Connor, James O'Connor, and Daniel Faber, *Capitalism, Nature, Socialism* 2, no. 2 (February 1991); Mary Mellor, "Eco-Feminism and Eco-Socialism," *Capitalism, Nature, Socialism* 3, no. 2 (Spring 1993): 43–62.

11. Recent titles include Ivone Gebara, *Longing for Running Water: Ecofeminism and Liberation*, trans. David Molineaux (Minneapolis, MN: Augsburg Fortress, 1999); Mary Judith Ress, *Ecofeminism in Latin America* (Maryknoll, NY: Orbis Books, 2006); Marti Kheel, *Nature Ethics: An Ecofeminist Perspective* (New York: Rowman and Littlefield, 2007); Jytte Nhanenge, *Ecofeminism: Towards Integrating the Concerns of Women, Poor People, and Nature into Development* (Lanham, MD: University Press of America, 2011); Greta Gaard, "Ecofeminism Revisited: Rejecting Essentialism and

Re-Placing Species in a Material Feminist Environmentalism," *Feminist For-mations* 23, no. 2 (Summer 2011): 26–53; Anne Stephens, *Ecofeminism and Systems Thinking* (New York: Routledge, 2013); Robert Musil, *Rachel Carson and Her Sisters: Extraordinary Women Who Have Shaped America's Environ-ment* (Rutgers, NJ: Rutgers University Press, 2014); Carol Adams and Lori Gruen, *Ecofeminism: Feminist Intersections with Other Animals and the Earth* (London: Bloomsbury, 2014); Maria Mies and Vandana Shiva, *Ecofeminism: Critique, Influence, Change* (Atlantic Highlands, NJ: Zed Books, 1993, 2014).

Introduction to the New French Edition

1. This wording and methodology is a nod to Maria Mies and Vandana Shiva, *Ecofeminism* (London: Zed Books, 1992).
2. As Jade Lindgaard said on the podcast *Présages*, "Que peut-on faire politi-quement de ce désastre?" March 26, 2020, found at urlz.fr/dsEI.
3. With this choice of adjective, we reference a dichotomous and hierarchal social construction of masculine and feminine values.
4. Although we see the virus as a catalyst, we also mean to evoke Arundhati Roy's "The Pandemic Is a Portal" (*Financial Times*, April 3, 2020) here.
5. The radical ecofeminism we call for aims to affect change at the very roots of oppression, whether in terms of gender, age, ability, class, race, or oth-erwise. We enlist in this movement because we see it as a double refusal of reformism: first with regard to feminism, for "the master's tools will never dismantle the master's house" (Audre Lorde), and also with regard to ecology, for "sustainable development" in an ecocidal system does not seem viable to us. In addition, the radical ecofeminism we demand does not focus primarily on "women" but rather on every being that dies at the hands of the patriarchy, from murdered trans people to animals killed by the thousands in slaughterhouses.
6. Carolyn Merchant, *The Death of Nature* (New York: Harper, 1980).
7. Françoise d'Eaubonne, *Écologie et féminisme: Révolution ou mutation?* (Paris: Libre et solidaire, 2018), 93.
8. Our proposal of the androcene is intersectional. It is embedded within colonial-centered theorizations of the "Capitalocene" (Jason Moore), the "Plantationocene" (Donna Haraway and Anna Tsing), and Malcom Ferdinand's most recent contribution of the "Négrocène" within French ecological literature.

9. Informal conversation with Vandana Shiva for the podcast *Écoféminismes: Défendre nos territoires*, Arte radio, November 2019.

10. Here we refer to the notion of "situated knowledges" developed in part by Sandra Harding, Donna Haraway, and Patricia Hill Collins.

11. A person whose perceived gender corresponds to their sex assigned at birth.

12. A person who belongs, in a real or supposed way, to a group subjected to a process of racism. This adjective highlights the socially constructed nature of differences and their essentialization.

13. "Sometimes perceived as heroines, sometimes as victims, credited with a favorable image, the 'beurettes' are far from being docile bystanders of unconditional integration. Permanently subjected to a paradoxical tension that compels them to distance themselves from a cultural difference of which they are constantly reminded, they strive to forge a path of personal accomplishment for themselves." Nacira Guénif-Souilamas, *Des beurettes* (Paris: Hachette Pluriel, 2003).

14. Gloria Anzaldúa, "La conscience de la Mestiza: Vers une nouvelle conscience," Les Cahiers du CEDREF, no. 18 (2011): 75–96.

15. A "settler" is a person who lives on land that was originally inhabited by native peoples. In North America, this term references the first immigrants, mainly English and French, who imposed their cultures and traditions through violence (settler colonialism), but also designates all the other people who have immigrated there since.

16. In addition to the theorizations of a patriarchal capitalism expounded on within this preface, "Racial Capitalism" is the theory developed by Cedric J. Robinson in his 1983 book *Black Marxism: The Making of the Black Radical Tradition*.

17. For an overview of the author's life, see Caroline Goldblum, *Françoise d'Eaubonne et l'écoféminisme* (Paris: Le Passager Clandestin, 2019). Her memoirs were also published in five volumes: Françoise d'Eaubonne, *Mémoires irréductibles: De l'entre-deux-guerres* à *l'an 2000* (Paris: Dagorno, 2001).

18. Several researchers contest this and maintain that the term appeared simultaneously on various continents, as Émilie Hache cites in her brilliant preface to *Reclaim: Recueil de textes écoféministes* (Paris: Cambourakis, 2016), 28.

19. The first occurrence of the word is on page 75 of this edition, before appearing again in the title of the part "The Time for Ecofeminism," on page 187.

20. Expression borrowed from Denise Brial, director of the documentary *Une irréductible rebelle: Françoise d'Eaubonne* (Atalante, 2006).

21. The (very sparse) archives of the Ecology-Feminism Movement are at the

library of Angers. A detailed examination of them would perhaps allow us to better understand the activities and the history of this group.

22. Intended to provide information for the activists of the association (assessment of past and future actions), this "bulletin n° 4" is dated summer 1974. It is reproduced in its entirety in the second part of Caroline Goldblum's book, *Françoise d'Eaubonne et l'écoféminisme*, 72–4.

23. Goldblum, *Françoise d'Eaubonne*, 93–7.

24. D'Eaubonne, *Écologie et féminisme*. Published four years after *Feminism or Death*, this essay can be considered the culmination of the ecofeminist reflection begun in this book. It reiterates and develops the warnings formulated in 1974 but also outlines a societal project founded on cooperation and the challenging of hierarchies governing patriarchal and capitalist society.

25. "We have to tear the planet away from the male today in order to restore it for humanity of tomorrow. That is the only alternative, for if male society persists, there will be no tomorrow for humanity," 221.

26. Vandana Shiva, *Monocultures of the Mind: Perspectives on Biodiversity and Biotechnology* (London: Zed Books, 1993).

27. *Le pouvoir aux femmes, c'est le non-pouvoir!*, pamphlet from the group Écologie-Féminisme, August 1977, in d'Eaubonne, *Écologie et féminisme*, 198.

28. "World-systems" theory, inspired by Fernand Braudel and developed by Immanuel Wallerstein, Oliver Cromwell Cox, Giovanni Arrighi, and Samir Amin, affirms that a country's economic circumstances are inseparably linked to those of others and must therefore be understood in light of global dynamics that we refer to today as globalization. Thus, the so-called underdevelopment of countries of the "South" is induced by an unequal and unjust structure that has maintained and perpetuated a hegemony of countries of the "North" for centuries, beginning with the first colonial period.

29. That said, the author's focus on "phallocracy" can be disconcerting. Her frequent use of the term (to which we generally prefer the term "patriarchy") denotes an essentialization of categories typical of the radical feminism of the 1970s. But d'Eaubonne regularly evokes a nonbinary vision of gender and even of sex, and she goes so far as to suggest that gender is a social construction of the phallocracy (p. 174).

30. P. 84.

31. Maria Mies, *Patriarchy and Accumulation on a World Scale: Women in the International Division of Labour* (London: Zed Books, 1986, [2014]).

32. The term "capitalist patriarchy" is a key term in (eco)feminist theory.

However, the term was first introduced by Zillah Eisenstein in her 1978 anthology *Capitalist Patriarchy and the Case of Socialist Feminism.*

33. Paola Bacchetta, professor of feminist and gender studies at the University of California, Berkeley, and anti-racist feminist activist, recalls that "in the 1980s, *Feminism or Death* was an important text for the feminist movement in Paris. The activists knew the text, and d'Eaubonne was also a well-known figure of the movement" (conversation with Paola Bacchetta).

34. To delve deeper into this question, read the article by Isabelle Cambourakis: "Un éco-féminisme à la française? Les liens entre mouvements féministe et écologiste dans les années 1970 en France," *Genre et Histoire*, no. 22, 2018.

35. In the materialist feminist tradition, essentialism is *the* trap into which no feminist should ever fall. Thus, positing a link between nature and women has dangerous consequences: the naturalization of the body or the glorification of "the Woman" as naturally more connected to the earth. This timidity has long robbed the movement of all political or theoretical legitimacy. We reaffirm here that the connection between wounded bodies and hurt lands is above all social.

36. Mary Daly, *Gyn/Ecology: The Metaethics of Radical Feminism* (Boston: Beacon Press, 1978). Mary Daly wouldn't have had access to translated excerpts of d'Eaubonne's writing. She would have had to wait until the 1980s for the first and rare English translations of her work, which were Elaine Marks and Isabelle de Courtivron, *New French Feminisms: An Anthology* (New York: Schoken Books, 1980); and the 1994 translation of the last chapter of *Feminism or Death* published in Carolyn Merchant's book *Ecology: Key Concepts in Critical Theory* (New York: Humanity Books).

37. See the bibliography at the end of this book.

38. Dorceta E. Taylor, "Women of Color, Environmental Justice, and Ecofeminism," *NWSA Journal* 9, no. 3, *Women, Ecology, and the Environment* (Fall 1997), 1–17.

39. To speak of the "South" in relation to the "North" makes no sense. These entities are social constructions used as analytical tools, but within the same country or the same city, there is always a North and a South, the latter serving as a reserve of workers and resources for the former.

40. P. 33.

41. P. 108–9.

42. Samir Amin, *L'accumulation à l'échelle mondiale* (Paris: Anthropos, 1988).

43. Questions which will be raised in the ecofeminist analyses of Maria Mies and Vandana Shiva, *Ecofeminism.*

44. "Abya Yala" is the name preferred by native populations, more specifi-cally the Kuna, for Latin America. Through this act, they refuse to refer to themselves by a name derived from Amerigo Vespucci. Self-determination through language is a powerful political act, especially when words are always imprinted with colonialism.

45. On this topic, see the works of María Lugones ("La colonialité du genre," *Les Cahiers du CEDREF*, no. 23 [2019]: 46–89) who critiques the foundational article of Aníbal Quijano, "Race et colonialité du pouvoir," *Mouvements* 51, no. 3 (2007): 111–18.

46. "Reclaim" is a recurring term in the ecofeminist movement. It signifies the idea of regaining, rediscovering, "returning to" forgotten practices and sen-sations, with a relationship to the living world buried under centuries of capitalism. "Reclaim" is not an invitation to move backward but rather a way of reinventing imaginaries and practices starting from the wounds and the vulnerability of the world. It is an inventive power, a regeneration and vital force that unites all living things.

47. See the bibliography at the end of this book.

48. "Blindness" here refers to "colorblindness," an anti-racist concept intro-duced in the United States that has not yet been analyzed in France. It adopts a blind universalism that considers humanity as one without distinguish-ing by race. In doing so, it absolutely denies systemic discriminations in this regard and does not manage to develop a strategy to combat them. D'Eaubonne does not ever seem to fall into colorblindness, since she grasps the weight of social relationships of race between individuals and within societies, but she simultaneously completely ignores the political produc-tions of the South on this subject.

49. Myriam Bahaffou, "Écoféminisme décolonial: une utopie?," *AssiégéEs*, no. 4 (September 2020).

50. Jeanne Bisilliat, *Femmes du Sud, chefs de famille* (Paris: Karthala, 1996).

51. Further reading on this topic: Rodney William, *L'appropriation culturelle* (Anacaona, 2020).

52. The afrodescendants, Chicanas, Latinas, or the descendants of indigenous peoples have fought for agricultural rights, have defended their lands, have opposed the construction of oil pipelines or mines, and have preserved the spread of nonindustrial food. They identified long ago the complicity between patriarchal power and global ecocide.

53. Ngũgĩ wa Thiong'o, *Decolonising the Mind* (London: Heinemann Educational, 1986).

54. This devaluation also gave rise to subversive possibilities of parenthood, to a political power of maternity, explored notably by Fatima Ouassak in *La puissance des mères: Pour un nouveau sujet révolutionnaire* (Paris: La Découverte, 2020).

55. Chandra Talpade Mohanty, "Under Western Eyes: Feminist Scholarship and Colonial Discources," *Boundary* 2, 12/13 (1984): 333–58.

56. P. 119.

57. We read, for example, on page 173 : "La situation de la musulmane est particulièrement tragique à cet égard. La lutte militante, le dévoilement, avaient jeté en Algérie les bases d'une certaine émancipation ; cependant l'attitude intérieure des héroïnes que dès l'enfance avait *perverties* (dans le véritable sens du terme) leur soumission au mâle demeurait très ambiguë." To move away from the stereotype that Islam equals oppression of women, which is still very present in France, read Zahra Ali, ed., *Féminismes islamiques* (Paris: La Fabrique, 2020).

58. Edward Said, *Orientalism* (New York: Pantheon, 1978).

59. P. 112–17.

60. Gayatri Chakravorty Spivak, *Can the Subaltern Speak?* (New York: Columbia University Press, 1988).

61. D'Eaubonne, *Écologie et féminisme*, 165–83.

62. A slogan used by activists of the transnational movement of women and feminists for climate justice and by certain NGOs that work with women and the climate.

63. The women water protectors of Standing Rock, the Sacred Stone Camp resistance against the Dakota Access Pipeline (DAPL), has become emblematic of widespread indigenous-women-led climate activism across the globe.

64. It is important not to overlook the indigenous women that compose larger indigenous island resistances to rising tides that threaten the total submergence of their homelands and violent displacement of their peoples and cultures. The Pacific Climate Warriors are just one example of such activism.

65. In *Écologie et féminisme*, d'Eaubonne calls for a global ecofeminist "mutation" more than a revolution, since she was critical of the masculinist connotations the term "revolution" was saturated with at the time.

Introduction

1. *Histoire et actualité du féminisme* [Feminism, its history and current state] (Paris: Alain Moreau, 1972).
2. Rolande Ballorain, *Le nouveau féminisme américain* [The new American feminism] (Paris: Denoël-Gonthier, 1972).

The Tragedy of Being a Woman

1. Translator's note: This translates as "Deep down inside man, that is."
2. These worthless quarrels cost Lina her sanity and threw Michèle—war heroine—into self-destruction.
3. Paul Verlaine.

Majority or Minority?

1. Nicolas Restif de la Bretonne, *Ingénue Saxancour, ou la femme séparée* [Ingenue Saxancour, or the wife separated from her husband] (1789).
2. Françoise d'Eaubonne, *Y a-t-il encore des hommes?* [Are there any men left?] (Paris: Flammarion, 1965).
3. Translator's note: Dauphiné is a former French province in the Southeast quarter of current-day France. Grenoble was the capital.
4. And so much more so that it denies itself! At present, the refusal of lucid women to procreate corresponds to the healthiest resistance to this genocide through suffocation brought about by rampant population growth. It is impossible to worry about future generations without seeking to limit them as much as possible for the simple possibility of existing.
5. Aragon.

Work and Prostitution

1. Fanny Deschamps, *Ils parlent d'elles* [Men talk about women] (Paris: Grasset, 1968).
2. Here we come back to the emperor of all misogynists and even of all gynophobes, Proudhon, who declared first that a woman did not even have any

value in the eyes of God if she was not beautiful. (Then, later, he claimed that true femininity was in backbreaking housework and, if possible, stirring manure in heavy shoes as badly dressed as possible.) And even closer to our times was this observation by Denis Diderot: "Praising the intellectual and moral character of a woman is almost always a sign of ugliness." Old outdated stuff? Let's look at Jean Cau, who, in *Ma misogynie* (Idée Fixe, 1972), picks up the exact same ancient insults with no fear of making a fool of himself. (A Cau always finds a greater Cau who admires him.)

3. Pierrette Sartin, *La femme libérée?* [Liberated woman?] (Paris: Stock, 1968). I felt the effects of the same reaction from my grandmother when I was preparing my own high school exit exam and I read the *Life of Verlaine* by François Porché that was discussing the sexual relations between Verlaine and Arthur Rimbaud. Even though she was a frequent traveler, a revolutionary, an admirer of Voltaire, she suffered a "migraine" and had to go to bed.

4. Pierre André, in *Les Femmes en Union Soviétique* [Women in the Soviet Union] (Paris: Spes, 1961), reports that young girls are dreaming more and more of a husband who earns enough for them to become "housewives." It is significant to learn that, in the poorer Parisian suburbs, "as soon as a job is particularly dreary and repetitive, they say: *that* is a job for a woman or a person of color." (Survey from *Elle*, October 4, Méridien Hotel.)

5. This is the argument used by Stephen Hecquet (*Faut-il réduire les femmes en esclavage? Oui* [Should women be reduced to slavery? Yes], 1957) to prove that woman is the strong, sturdy sex and should be treated as such for the greatest profit of man, the luxury sex.

6. "His wife is in the gallows, and everybody knows that he is the one who stole," wrote Gustave Flaubert in a letter to Maxime Du Camp, talking about a suspicious servant.

7. *Sociologie de la sexualité* (Sociology of sexuality) by Helmut Schelsky, a professor in Hamburg. The examples cited are far less numerous than mine in my book, *Histoire et actualité du féminisme* (Feminism, its history and current state), without counting the symmetrical exceptions of the male sex (see *Eros Minoritaire* [Minority Eros]). It is important to note this precise positioning for an author who, elsewhere, declares that if we ever arrived at a perfect equality between the sexes, "it would be impossible for us to conserve our cultural heritage" (92).

8. Schelsky, *Sociologie de la sexualité.*

9. "Is habit second nature, or nature the first custom?" That is the question

Blaise Pascal asks. It is comical to see so many "liberated" intellectuals stuck on the notion of essentialism today when considered next to this fideist from three centuries ago.

10. Christiane Rochefort, *La complainte* [The complaint].

11. Sartin, *La femme libérée?*

12. Translator's note: "Cour des comptes," with independent jurisdiction, is between Parliament and the government.

13. Alexander Solzhenitsyn, *Cancer Ward*, 1968.

14. Sartin, *La femme libérée?* Hearing this, two people left the factory in protest.

15. Évelyne Sullerot, *La femme dans le monde moderne* [Women in the modern world] (Paris: Hachette, 1970).

16. Andrée Michel and Geneviève Texier, *La condition de la Française d'aujourd'hui* [The condition of today's French woman] (Paris: Denoël-Gonthier, 1964).

17. Madeleine Guilbert, *Les fonctions des femmes dans l'industrie* [The function of women in industry], 1966.

18. Guilbert, *Les fonctions des femmes.*

19. Noël Lamare, *Connaissance sensuelle de l'homme* [Sensual knowledge of man] (Buchet/Chastel, 1964). Lamare collaborated on *Le livre noir du divorce* (The little black book of divorce) or is quoted therein; this passage is one of the most charming in this book dedicated to showing "the insidious and demagogical feminism" of the French judicial system!

20. *Le livre de l'oppression des femmes* [The book of women's oppression] (Belfond, 1972), 35.

21. *Le livre de l'oppression*, 28. This story was told by a young girl in 1972. In 1930, when I was in a coed class at Hattemer, I heard the same thing from the school director, shaming the boys because I made better grades than they did. My mother went to this school, too, and was a student of Marie Curie, who, in her youth, had to force her way into the College of the Sciences, where the male students were blocking the way. (In the medical school, they burned the first female students in effigy.) The continuation and historic permanence of the misogynistic discourse.

22. *Le livre de l'oppression*, 28–9. Here, you can admire the way sexual repression meets anti-feminism.

23. *Le livre de l'oppression*, 29.

24. See, for example, Edmond Haraucourt, one of the rare few who supported Oscar Wilde, this critic of the "tarts."

25. A variation: "So, when all is well with *your* ass, all is well with *you*." Let's

note that the same phallocrat, in the opposite case, reproached his wife for her frigidity.

26. Herbert Marcuse, *Eros and Civilization* (1955).

27. Marcuse, *Eros and Civilization*.

28. Translator's note: The French franc was revalued in 1960, with each new franc being worth 100 old francs; 90,000 old francs, then, became 900 new francs. In 1974, 900 new French francs equaled about $180.

Rape

1. Even the spelling of this sentence that I have just written is revealing. The comic effect of the past participles *"violé"* (raped) and *"engrossé"* (became pregnant) comes from their masculine form. We know it: the word "to be," in French, is masculine; it is applied to the male and to the female. This language that hates the neutral gender replaced it with the masculine, whereas biologists' most recent observations concur that it is the woman who is the species, and that the man *is differentiated from her* much more than she differentiates from the man.

2. *Le torchon brûle*, no. 4 (August 1972).

3. *Le torchon brûle*, August 1972.

4. *Le livre de l'oppression des femmes* [The book of women's oppression] (Paris: Belfond, 1972), 169.

5. *Le torchon brûle*, August 1972.

6. Some Catholics, during the Resistance, proclaimed the right to commit suicide to escape torture, basing their argument on the right that the Church gives to women to commit suicide to escape being raped.

7. A good example was given in December 1973, by the case of the rape of a young organizer in the Committee to Help Immigrants, by a Caribbean man, reported in *Libération* by Annie Cohen-Solal. Leftists asked the girls to avoid making too much noise about it, for fear of discrediting their work against racism; they bolstered their pleas with strong arguments about the "sexual destitution of the poor immigrants."

8. *Tout*, no. 12.

9. *Le livre de l'oppression*, 93.

10. Translator's note: Mouvement de libération des femmes (Women's Liberation Movement).

11. *Le torchon brûle*, August 1972.

12. *Le torchon brûle*, August 1972.

13. Cf. d'Eaubonne, *Y a-t-il encore des hommes?*

14. The fable of the woman "naturally consenting" and of her "secret desire" is disproven by a flood of facts that simple observers know well: for example, the number of young girls being treated for their fear of having sex, the number of them who write to advice columnists, asking: "Am I a monster then …," and the numbers of women who become obsessed with priests, doctors, homosexuals—in short, all the men who can both give them access to a world of men and protect them from the male order. That is what Freud calls (naively) the "tendency of women to evade sexuality."

15. Several years ago, in Toulouse, I took part in research concerning conjugal rape that was particularly prevalent among the working classes and immigrants. The women researchers had had a woman hospitalized; her husband found her and raped her in her hospital bed, even though she was hemorrhaging badly.

The Stress of the Rat

1. Elizabeth Draper, *Birth Control in the Modern World: The Role of the Individual in Population Control* (New York: Penguin, 1965).

2. Since that time, scientists have established the mathematically verifiable calculation of the population in the year 2020, if the current rate of growth is maintained: *10 billion!* Obviously, that is impossible. What worldwide catastrophe could reestablish the possibility of being?

3. Cf. Conclusion: *Ecologie et féminisme* (Ecology and feminism), where I give details of this conclusion.

4. This text was already written when *Anti-Oedipus: Capitalism and Schizophrenia* by Gilles Deleuze and Félix Guattari appeared. It puts forward the same thesis.

5. Carla Lonzi, *Sputiamo su Hegel* (Rivolta Femminile, 1974), translated as *Let's Spit on Hegel* in *Italian Feminist Thought: A Reader*, ed. Paola Bono and Sandra Kemp (Oxford: Basil Blackwell, 1991).

6. Lonzi, *Let's Spit on Hegel*.

7. Yet we mustn't exaggerate. A fanatic about virginity and conjugal fidelity, the female believer becomes skeptical about the edicts forbidding practices that avoid pregnancy. "A number of *Christian mothers* only have two or three children," observed Simone de Beauvoir (*The Second Sex*).

8. The proportion of women in these professions is still so small that it is insignificant.
9. Lonzi, *Let's Spit on Hegel*.

Regarding Abortion

1. Translator's note: The "Manifesto of the 343 Salopes" (sluts). A group of 343 women, many of whom were famous, published a document on April 5, 1971, in the weekly *Le Nouvel Observateur*, declaring that they had all had illegal abortions. At the time, it was a crime in France that could be punished by imprisonment.
2. On April 26, 1971, during a debate/discussion, the *Nouvel Observateur* club was surprised to see the participating delegates from the MLF (Movement for the Liberation of Women) leave the stage, saying that they preferred to hear from the women in the room rather than the "specialists" spouting their knowledge.
3. Translator's note: A line was missing here in the published text.
4. Translator's note: A parody of the French national anthem, changing the lines: "They are coming into our midst to cut the throats of our sons and compatriots."
5. Cf. The correspondence between Claudel and Gide where Claudel explains to Gide that if you start to allow excuses for homosexuality, you will soon find masturbation, cannibalism, and rape of children.
6. Simone de Beauvoir, *La force des choses* (Paris: Gallimard, 1977).
7. Considered as a crime against humanity is "serious violation of the physical or mental integrity of the group," immediately next to "measures meant to hinder births in the group"! Such are the beautiful gems of the male logic: to ignore the contradiction between these two terms, to the extent where the only way of respecting "the physical and mental integrity of one of the members of the group" (a woman) is precisely to take measures to "hinder" an unwanted birth.

For a Planetary Feminist Manifesto

1. It's not an issue of returning to Bachofen's belief in a "matriarchy." But Simone de Beauvoir herself recognizes the "very high place" that woman occupied in ancient antiquity. In *The Crisis of Psychoanalysis* (1970), Erich

Fromm declares that Bachofen's thesis, even though false, showed an incomparable productivity of thought in the nineteenth century, and that having ignored it explains, to a great extent, the aberrations of an innovator like Freud when he takes up the feminine problem.

My research has brought me to the belief that it was the defense, armed, of agricultural riches, that is at the origin of the supposed "legends" of the Amazons and their battles against male hunters and shepherds, sexual segregation being necessitated by masculine taboos against feminine sexuality. (Cf. My contributions: *Le complexe de Diane* [The Diane complex, 1950] and *Histoire et actualité du féminisme* [Feminism, its history and current state, 1971]. Note that, just as this book was being published, *Time* magazine brought out a striking confirmation of my thesis by a report from W. Jesco von Puttkamer, a German ethnologist, who has just discovered the traces of this supposedly legendary ancient civilization of Amazons in Brazil.

2. See my book, *Éros Minoritaire* [Minority Eros] (Paris: A. Balland, 1970).

3. With one exception: the periods of military government and the state of war. Hence Louis XIV, a devout hetero-cop, accepted the warrior homosexuality of his generals on the declaration by the Marquis de Louvois that homosexuality "was very good for leaving women behind and having a good time with one's lovers"; and Napoléon Bonaparte, the Corsican fanatic of sexism and familial oppression of women, worried very little about the morals of his legal adviser Jean-Jacques-Régis de Cambacérès and those of his soldiers.

4. Massimo Consoli, *Appunti per una rivoluzione morale* (Ragusa: La Fiaccola, 1971).

5. Soviet women have garnered much success in applied sciences and take part in the military, and are the only women in the world to do so, along with Israelis and Vietnamese; however, they have invaded the medical profession only because it is one of the worst-paid in the USSR; their paltry participation in the high spheres of political command has often been reported and decried; and daily life ties them tightly to their family, just about as much as for any other Occidental woman.

Another example: according to *Women in the Soviet Economy* (Norton Dodge, 1966), women working in construction receive neither professional training nor tools and equipment.

Also, a friend returning from the USSR in the summer of 1972 confirmed the observation cited earlier to me, that young Soviet women aspire more and more to marrying a man blessed with a good position so that they will be able to stay in the home. In that country, women are more protected against rape; it is punished by fifteen years in prison, and even simple improper gestures can make men lose their jobs, be excluded from the party, or be prevented from joining it. But prostitution has been spreading very openly for several years and seems to be increasing. Tirades about the intellectual inferiority of women or their biological inferiority are not at all rare or scandalous, even in highly intellectual circles. On September 12, 1967, a session of the "Union of Writers," where Solzhenitsyn was being criticized, compared him to Svetlana Stalin, emphasizing that the danger came from the "talented man"; concerning Svetlana's book, it was only a matter of "women's jabbering." Solzhenitsyn, *Les droits de l'ecrivain* [The author's rights], Collection Combats (Seuil, 1972).

A last detail: contraception remains solely for men, the pill impossible to find, and Western tourists often find theirs stolen.

6. Reimut Reiche, *Sexuality and Class Struggle* (London: Verso, 1970).

7. Guy A. Smal and Joseph W. Mbuyi, *Femme Africaine reveille-toi!* (Paris: Pensée universelle, 1973).

8. There is no need to go all the way to Egypt to amuse ourselves with the "pearls" of sexism; our neighbor, Belgium, suffices. "The posts of inspection for the Office of Milk are reserved to candidates of the masculine sex ... The basis for excluding feminine candidates for inspector of food products is that these agents are sometimes exposed to difficult situations, verbal taunts, and even threats and physical blows" [*sic*], as stated in the labor law. By the same token, inspectors of agricultural services must be men, because they have to run through the fields in all seasons and help with the functioning of agricultural machines" [*sic*], and the designers of the Commission of Monuments and Sites, because they "have to visit towers and structures that are difficult to access." Concerning customs officials: "There is no question of the admission of women, as these diverse functions don't lend themselves to *the use of female personnel*." (See *Sexuality and Morals Today*, no. 45, Brussels.) What happened to the charter, signed by fifty-two nations, forbidding the refusal of a post or a profession to someone on the basis of race, religion, *or sex*?

9. Frantz Fanon, *A Dying Colonialism*, 1959.

10. Sheila Rowbotham, *Women, Resistance and Revolution* (London: Verso, 2013 [1972]), 229.

11. Rowbotham, *Women, Resistance and Revolution*, 230.

12. Rowbotham, *Women, Resistance and Revolution*, 231.

13. Rowbotham, *Women, Resistance and Revolution*, 233.

14. [The macho man and South American women] Collection Femme (Denoël-Gonthier, 1972).

15. We can't leave the topic of Brazilian women without treating the abominations of torture inflicted on the revolutionary militants of this country, with a particular sexual bent, that is used only for them or for very young boys arrested by the butchers. (There is even a special term for this occasion, a special term in the police jargon that designates a sort of disgusting "show," a spectacular follow-up to sexual abuse: *la curra*!)

   Maria Barcellos (a medical student) was arrested on November 21, 1969, in São Paulo. They stripped her and punched her for six hours, "they made her watch the most monstrous obscenities, gestures accompanying the words," they forced Chaël, one of her tortured companions, to "fuck her all over her body," they pushed her husband, Antonio Roberto, on top of her, nude body against nude body, after having crushed one of his testicles; "still not satisfied, they pushed her against the wall and, with a billy club on her genital organs, they simulated the act of *buen pene* (good pain), as they put it in their language of torturers," then, "in front of soldiers cramming in the windows and doors," they pummeled her with blows, slapping her breasts around, threw buckets of water on her, and then applied electric shock.

   Mara Alvarenga, an artisan, thirty-four years old, arrested in Porto Alegre on July 1, 1970, "karate kicks, strangulation, and moral tortures of a sexual nature." In prison, she met Emily Vareira, having been paralyzed by blows and electric shocks to her hands, and a noblewoman, Efigenia de Oliveira, hospitalized for two months after electric shocks to her vagina.

   Sonia Regina Yessin Ramos, a law student, arrested April 21, 1970, in Barrio de Mesquita. Tortured during her imprisonment (electric baths, among other things) until January 1971, when they released her.

   Immaculata de Oliveira, twenty-four, secretary in the Union of Metalworkers, from April to September 1969, electric shocks and blows all over her body, forced to watch sexual torture of young men (for example, her friend José Adao, sodomized with a broom handle) and women: Delçi Gonsalves and Gilse Maria "forced to parade nude in front of countless soldiers," then tortured.

   Carmela Pezzuti, forty-four years old, civil servant, arrested April 30, 1970, received the usual treatment, blows, electric shocks, etc., and said that "Sonia Lacerda Macedo and Vania Abrantes were tortured in an indescribable way." And her friend Dulce: "tied up at the ankles and the wrists, completely nude, they put a crocodile on her."

   These are only some examples taken from the brochure published in Brussels, *The Brazil Files*, by the International Association of Democratic

Lawyers. All these accounts of torture came from prisoners chosen among the seventy exiles in Chile in January 1971, accounts gathered by Anina de Carvalho, lawyer at the Court of São Paulo (whom we can easily recognize in the role of the leftist parliamentarian in the film *State of Siege*, condemning the School for Torture in fascist Latin America, with its transmission of techniques from state to state.)

16. Translator's note: Front de libération nationale (National Liberation Front). The principal group, founded in 1954, fighting for independence of Algeria from France.

17. Translator's note: Union des femmes françaises (Union of French Women).

18. Claudie Broyelle, *La moitié du ciel: Le mouvement de libération des femmes en Chine* [Half the sky] (Femmes, 1972).

19. Translation: "Movement for the liberation of women in China." This subtitle seems to presuppose a sort of Chinese MLF—that is, a kind of protest movement and a struggle, or at least demands or claims made, even in polite fashion, as in Boumédiène's Algeria. The book's contents reveal that it is no more than a different status for women, set and organized by the revolutionary male power.

20. We notice that the hetero-cop structure is not absent from such remarks. Just as in the American-Western bloc, "sexual liberation" boils down most often to these relations, and to the right to pleasure in the marriage; for a very small bourgeois minority, love in a group. Beyond that, for these brave pioneers, "perversion" begins. In Han Suyin's language, immense territories of sexuality, including those of bisexuality, although having become commonplace, are not even considered to exist.

For a Planetary Feminist Manifesto (Continued)

1. Germaine Greer, *The Female Eunuch* (MacGibbon & Kee, 1970), 338–9.

2. Her article in the November/December 1966 issue of *New Left Review*, "Women: The Longest Revolution," that had a lot of impact, "endeavors to integrate feminism into the proletarian revolution knowing all the while that nothing, either in political groups or existing socialist regimes, indicates that such a contract would be respected" (Greer, 335–9). And, in fact, "The oppression of women is the result of thousands of years; capitalism inherited it rather than having produced it," says Lonzi in *Let's Spit on Hegel*.

3. See Philippe Nahoun, *Allemagne anti-autoritaire* [Antiauthoritarian Germany], Collection Changer le monde (1971).

4. See my contribution, *Histoire et actualité du féminisme* [Feminism, its history and current state]. The other three cornerstones are *A Room of One's Own* by Virginia Woolf, *The Second Sex* by Simone de Beauvoir, and *Sexual Politics* by Kate Millett.

5. Norman Mailer, "The Acolyte," in *The Prisoner of Sex* (Little, Brown, 1971), 53.

6. Greer, *The Female Eunuch*, 334.

7. Betty Friedan, *Les femmes à la recherche d'une quatrième dimension* [Women in search of the fourth dimension], Collection Femmes (Denoël-Gonthier, 1969).

8. Beverly Jones and Judith Brown, *Toward a Female Liberation Movement* (Boston: New England Free Press, 1968).

9. Greer, *The Female Eunuch*, 343.

10. *Let's Spit on Hegel*, in the same vein, speaks of the "hidden face" of the earth: the feminine sex.

11. Jones and Brown, *Toward a Female Liberation Movement*, 32.

12. A poster was put up in the fine arts school after the morning visit of young fascists wearing helmets and armed with iron bars, making the rounds of the universities in November 1971, which read: "Fascists, the FHAR is waiting for you." Translator's note: FHAR is "Front homosexuel d'action révolutionnaire," the Homosexual Front for Revolutionary Action.

13. Pati Trolander, "Crotch Clawers," *Off Our Backs* 1, no. 13 (November 8, 1970): 10, quoted in Mailer, "The Acolyte," 41–2.

14. *Actuel*, no. 4 (January 1971).

15. *Actuel*, no. 4.

16. "Me, the Bitch." Caroline Hennessey, *I, B.I.T.C.H.* (New York: Lancer, 1970), 180. The book appeared in French in 1971. (Paris: Denoël).

17. Richard Neely, *Le tourmenteur* (Gallimard, 1971). Originally published in English as *The Walter Syndrome* (New York: McCall Publishing, 1970).

18. This is an article by Gershon Legman translated by *Les Temps Modernes* in 1950: "Avatars de la garce" ("Avatars or transformations of the bitch"). The author, who was studying this hatred between the sexes in black American literature, noted the following: "The absence of literary qualities matters not the least in the world in this case. Books that sell 2 million copies would be important even if they were written in uneducated slang and printed without punctuation." And Legman, with the excessive importance of the "bitch," expressed that "woman's resentment of the American male was bordering

on neuroses." Studying this phenomenon of hatred between the sexes after him, I have concluded:

"The highly published scribblers named Ben Ames Williams, Henning Mankell, Dashiell Hammett, Matthew Head, etc., describe a universe dripping with blood, hallucinating and mortally naive, where eroticism is obsessive, not by its presence, but by implication ... Official decency codes repress it to the luminous borders of the specter without ever allowing it to leap into broad daylight." *Le complexe de Diane* [The Diane complex], (Paris: Julliard, 1951), 265.

I then sought the causes for women to be discontented in the country considered a "matriarchy" and found that in 1945, a feminine convention grouping together women from all over the world in Paris heard the declaration of the US delegates: they explained the impossibility of equal salaries and described the sometimes scandalous gap between men's and women's wages. "That means that when they quote the slogan 'America, a feminist country,' it is the condition for the upper class that is presented, not that of the innumerable working-class members" (*Le complexe de Diane*).

19. Atkinson defines women's love elsewhere: "a victim's reaction to rape."

20. See *La victoire de la femme* [Woman's victory], "Panoramas of History," Pont Royal editions. Perhaps poor Bremer did not deserve this falsely laudatory comparison.

21. Only 30,000 spots for 80,000 children. There exist still, in Sweden, gender-based inequities in salary and a certain amount of unemployment among women.

22. And now, the most recent publications from the UN, while they were preparing the theme for "1975, year of the woman," show the state of decisions made in three European countries to extend education on household upkeep to both sexes: Sweden, Norway, and Poland.

23. Translator's note: The French expression is "Mon ventre est à moi." (Literally, "my belly belongs to me.")

24. These small groups functioned without knowing about the others, in the same radical perspective of a total reworking of society. The groups joined together much later, between April and October 1970.

25. It would be interesting to study the word "sauvage" used so often since that time: "sauvage" strike, "sauvage" childcare center, "sauvage" psychoanalysis, and the abrupt return to Rousseauism in university circles; that French rationalism mocked for two centuries, "the myth of the good savage," seems

to be back in style, thanks to the dispute about the civilized by the civilized themselves. The word "sauvage" is taking over bit by bit from the saying of the '60s: "in anger/rage."

But for the leftist resistance opposed to the MLF even before its birth, see in the appendix: "Le macho-gauchisme c'est encore du machisme." (Translation: "Macho-leftist thought is still machismo.") Translator's note: I have chosen to keep the word "sauvage" from the original in this note for the cultural context of the word and for the reference to Rousseau's concept of "le bon sauvage." "Sauvage" is the cognate of "savage," of course, but it also means *wild, untamed, primitive, uncivilized* (so all the nuances are important for d'Eaubonne's discussion).

In the translation, however, I have chosen to give an approximate equivalent (usually pop-up or impromptu) to avoid interrupting the flow of the text.

26. Translator's note: *Hara-Kiri* was a weekly satiric publication, a precursor to the present-day *Charlie Hebdo*.

27. Similar fun and humor in songs: "We'll put on mechanics' caps. / We'll go to China on the Trans-Siberian train. / We'll sit out in the sun, we'll throw him in the train. / And, in the end, we don't give a damn, everything we do is good."

28. Translator's note: A prison for women from 1930 to 1974, when it was demolished.

29. Translator's note: Front homosexuel d'action révolutionnaire (Homosexual Revolutionary Action Front).

30. Where, in 1953, Father Xavier Tilliette pronounced these prophetic words: "Homosexuals and emancipated women stand together."

31. Translator's note: *Minute* is an extreme right-wing weekly publication that still exists today.

32. Translator's note: "Faiseurs d'anges" (angel makers) was the pejorative term for those performing abortions and those having one.

33. The same as before Nazism (and often still with it), psychoanalysts talked only about "neurotic disobedience" and never "neurotic obedience," just as these Sunday moralists and lonely hearts advisers, who were in a superior position up until these last few decades, never imagined this "abandonment of the defense" (or the morality) that is implied by the self-destructive resistance of "all the instincts" (meaning, first of all, the sex drive).

34. Translator's note: At the Maison de la Mutualité (a large auditorium in Paris), at the conference organized with the right-to-life movement.

35. Translator's note: This translation by Jake Grassi.
36. Évelyne Sullerot, in *Woman, Society, and Change*, denounced the persistent refusal of international employers to accept this reform, even after the signature of this convention; she showed by which sudden mechanism of retribution on the basis of "points" that were merely arbitrary criteria, this very system of employers shied away from their promises. Women's salaries everywhere are considered ancillary; the difference is undoubtedly the most scandalous in France, the committee for adjustment of salaries in May 1968 having discovered, during its inquiry into the issue, a mass of female workers making significantly less than minimum wage for the same work as men, and in work conditions that are often much harder.
37. Yves de Saint-Agnès, *Eros international: Scandinavie* (Paris: Balland, 1971).
38. Saint-Agnès, *Eros international*. Translator's note: "MLH" means Movement for the Liberation of Men.

For a Planetary Feminist Manifesto (End)

1. FHAR: Homosexual Front for Revolutionary Action; IHR: International Revolutionary Homosexual; MLH: Movement for the Liberation of Men, a group supporting the MLF.
2. Germaine Greer, *The Female Eunuch* (MacGibbon & Kee, 1970), 243.
3. Translator's note: MODEF is a political party called Mouvement de défense des exploitants familiaux (Movement for the Defense of Family Farming).
4. *Histoire et actualité du féminisme* [Feminism, its history and current state] (Alain Moreau, 1972).
5. Virginia Woolf, *A Room of One's Own* (London: Hogarth Press, 1929).
6. Suzanne Lilar with Alfred Gilbert-Dreyfus, *Le malentendu du deuxième sexe* [The misunderstanding of the second sex] (Presse Universitaire de France, 1970).
7. With a few nuances, obviously, due above all to the level of culture and the economic level.

Departure for a Long March

1. Vivian Gornick, Preface to the *SCUM Manifesto* (London: Olympia Press, 1971), xxix.
2. *Nouvelle Revue Française*, Gallimard, 1971.

3. Simone de Beauvoir reminds us, in the interview cited earlier, of the Soviet woman who appears in *Cancer Ward* by Alexander Solzhenitsyn: a great medical doctor, also constrained to household work that exhausts her; a particular and paradoxical aspect of women in the socialist regime.

4. See Germaine Greer, *The Female Eunuch* (MacGibbon & Kee, 1970), 339.

5. We can, in this perspective, reconsider the marked difference between the treatment that male homosexuality and lesbianism received in all periods of history. The reason comes from this secular economic nonproductivity by women (the very one Hesiod reproached them for); it's this inertia in the directly productive circuit that saved her from the open persecution that always struck Eros in the minority expression for men). Just as, in all times, she was permitted to make of her body an instrument of economic return, an object to sell, whereas man, the male, had the right only to sell his arms or his brain. If he sells his body, he is abhorred by all morals, no matter what sex his "client" is; in antiquity, the Greek states that were the most favorable to homosexuality punished by death the man who prostituted himself. It is because, in all civilizations based on productivity, the man must *produce* to justify his life; he who works sells an activity, he who prostitutes himself sells a function. The woman, reduced to being an animal of function and not of activity, owes society a production, that of her body; that's why the system in power is infinitely more severe regarding abortion than for lesbianism or feminine prostitution. We see by that the "totalitarianism" of a demand like that of free disposition of one's body.

6. It goes without saying that we are using the words "masculine" and "feminine" outside all metaphysical uses. It is a question only of two cultural poles, arbitrarily chosen, of the universalism up to now incarnated by man alone, even if one admits, as we do, that in each woman at the outset, through her femininity (and not her feminitude), there is a predisposition toward the feminine, a possible predominance of it, along with her part of masculinity; just as, in the man, there is a predisposition toward the masculine and possible predominance of it, along with his part of femininity.

New Perspectives

1. *Le Grand Soir*, a pro-situationist paper, copied by *Le Fléau Social*, May 1973. Translator's note: The work has not appeared in English. Its title translates as "The social plague."

2. The anti-psychiatric movement has engendered an "International Association of Loony Lunatics," which contests "normality" even more radically than do the movements for the liberation of homosexuals. Translator's note: The original text reads "Internationale des Fous Furieux." I have chosen to translate "fous furieux" as "loony lunatics" to approximate the strength of the alliteration. In doing so, I may have obscured the fury implicit in "furieux"—a concept that is particularly important in this context.

3. See *Halte à la croissance?* (Paris: Fayard, 1972). Translator's note: The work appeared first in English as Donella H. Meadows, Dennis L. Meadows, Jørgen Randers, and William W. Behrens Ill, *The Limits to Growth: A Report for the Club of Rome's Project on the Predicament of Mankind* (London: Earth Island, 1972).

4. Translator's note: "underground" is in English and italicized in the original text.

Ecology and Feminism

1. Translator's note: Pierre Samuel, *Ecologie: Détente ou cycle infernal* (Paris: Union Générale de I'Edition 10/18, 1973).

2. Actually, the figures claimed to be exaggerations have since been greatly surpassed.

3. Irène Chédeaux, *Anti-clichés sur l'Amérique* [Anti-clichés about America] (Paris: Robert Laffont, 1971). The general proportion of these figures has risen 2 to 6 percent in noxious substances.

4. Jean-François Revel, *Without Marx or Jesus: The New American Revolution Has Begun* (Garden City, NY: Doubleday, 1971).

5. Cyril Kornbluth and Frederik Pohl, *The Space Merchants* (New York: Ballantine Books, 1953). (Translator's note: The book first appeared as a serial entitled *Gravy Planet* in the June 1952 issue of *Galaxy Science Fiction*.) Well before the question of pollution and of the destruction of the environment, this novel predicted a devastating future where oak wood has become such a precious material that rings are made from it, where the privileged class is composed of publicity technicians and the immense and impoverished mass is composed of "consumers," and where the struggle to protect nature is the clandestine domain of "conservers," who are treated ... like communists.

6. *Actuel*, October 1971. The figures quoted have since increased sharply.

7. Édouard Bonnefous, *L'homme ou la nature* (Paris: Hachette, 1970). Trans. "Man or nature."

8. Currently, agriculture has lightheartedly joined forces with industrial polluters. During the summer of 1973, one of my female friends contracted a fungal infection and bronchial poisoning while working on an apple plantation near Montpellier. The farmer sprayed the trees with a mixture of *three* violently toxic products designed to avoid black spots on the fruit. On top of that, he painted the apples with a layer of wax the night before taking them to the markets. This example is far from an isolated event.

9. Translator's note: *Pravda la Survireuse* was a comic strip by Guy Peellaert published in *Hara-Kiri*, the precursor to *Charlie Hebdo*. It was published from January to December 1967.

10. She predicted 6 billion inhabitants by the year 2000. Elizabeth Draper, *Birth Control in the Modern World: The Role of the Individual in Population Control* (London: Allen and Unwin, 1965).

11. The right's answer to the classical argument: overpopulation is a "developing world" problem.

12. Simone de Beauvoir, *The Second Sex* (New York: Vintage Books, 1974).

13. See my contribution to the subject in *Histoire et actualité du féminisme* [Feminism, its history and current state] (Paris: Alain Moreau, 1972).

14. See the film by the same title: *Little Murders*, Alan Arkin, 1971.

15. "Pourquoi nous avortons" [Why we abort], *Tout*, no. 12 (April 23, 1971): 4. Issue banned as an affront to morality.

16. *Actuel*, no. 4 (January 1971).

17. *Guérir*, August 1971. Translator's note: The title of the publication means "to heal."

18. See August Bebel, *Woman in the Past, Present and Future* (San Francisco: G. B. Benham, 1897), and Wolfgang Lederer, *Fear of Women* (New York: Harcourt Brace Jovanovich, 1968).

19. See *Partisans, Libération des femmes: année zero* [Liberation of women: year zero] (Paris: Maspero, 1970).

20. Translator's note: Jean Royer, secretary of commerce and crafts, April 5, 1973–February 27, 1974; Jean Foyer, secretary of public health, July 6, 1972–March 28, 1973.

21. Pierre Gordon, *L'initiation sexuelle et l'évolution religieuse* [Sexual initiation and religious evolution] (Paris: Presse Universitaire de France, 1945); and my work *Histoire et actualité du féminisme* [Feminism, its history and current state].

22. The Feminist Front, spurred on by an ecofeminist, wrote to all the representatives from Paris to Parliament to demand an investigation into the financing of this manipulative operation that, many affirm, comes from these dairy product advertisements.

23. An assertion that will make my Marxist friends indignant. But, if women of the proletariat have something to gain from the "victory of the proletariat," it would only be crumbs of the power supposedly acquired by male proletarians. In the meantime, women of the bourgeoisie would lose these same crumbs (or even large parts) to which their men gave them access. Never will power as such be given to women. At any rate, it is not even desirable, as the only significant revolution is one that abolishes even the notion of power, and the proletarian state at the same time as sexism.

24. Charles Nuetzel, ed., *If This Goes On* (Bevery Hills, CA: Book Company of America, 1965).

25. It is significant that, at the present time, the collective unconscious is accepting more and more the idea of a necessary apocalypse and is consoling itself with theories about "afterward," instead of thinking of avoiding it. As Victor Hugo said, "Catastrophes have a somber way of arranging things."

26. Translator's note: The film was directed by Jacques Doillon, 1972.

27. See Gilles Deleuze and Félix Guattari, *Anti-Oedipus: Capitalism and Schizophrenia* (New York: Viking Press, 1977), and especially Serge Moscovici, *Society against Nature: The Emergence of Human Societies* (New Jersey: Humanities Press, 1976). Both support at different levels *Let's Spit on Hegel*, which I have discussed at length in an earlier chapter.

28. A community established two years ago in the Cévennes has accomplished this same miracle—trout have come back to the streams, butterflies to the meadows: things that had not been seen in that area for fifteen years. "Nature has prepared the seeds, and all man has to do is join in," the founder of this community told me. Join in to love it and not to exploit it.

29. Lenin described the incapacity of the proletariat to go beyond the level of trade unionist. That was correct during his time, but he made the mistake of not realizing that it was a question of the historical stage of capitalism that did not create conditions favorable to a revolutionary "spontaneity," given the economy of shortage, and above all, he made the mistake of wanting to "give an ahistorical and eternal value to this contingent reality." See *La bande à Baader: Ou, la violence révolutionnaire* [Baader's band or revolutionary violence] (Paris: Champ Libre, 1972), 25. The author of this text refers to "Lenin's lack of comprehension of the dialectic between *production*

relations and *distribution* relations." It may not be out of place to establish a parallel between this limitation evinced by Lenin and the one he shows regarding the place of the sexual question in the revolutionary analysis. A correct dialectic that differentiates "production" (procreation) from "distribution" (eros) is also missing there.

Appendices

1. The system guarantees in this world that a greater possibility of freedom, for a woman, is attached to a loss of social prestige, discernible above all in the lower classes.
2. About fifteen years ago, a woman whose national identity card caused her some trouble (because she had three names: her husband's, her own because she had just gotten divorced, and a pseudonym) had to find a sympathetic police chief to write "divorced" on her identity card. Even when she asked, the civil state official refused to "harm" her by revealing this shameful secret.
3. Xavière is the pseudonym for Xavière Lafont.
4. Émile Marenssin, *La bande à Baader* (Éditions Champ Libre, 1972).
5. Françoise d'Eaubonne, *Y a-t-il encore des hommes?* [Are there any men left?] (Flammarion, 1965).
6. Emphasis mine. The text says: "Women *fascinated* by an idealized image of virility and its privileges."

Bibliography

This bibliography consists of the works in d'Eaubonne's original bibliography as well as works cited within her text.

Books

Ballorain, Rolande. *Le nouveau féminisme américain* [The new American feminism]. Denoël-Gonthier, 1972.

Barde, Jean-Pierre, and Christian Garnier. *L'Environnement sans frontières* [Environment without borders]. Seghers, 1971.

Beauvoir, Simone de. *The Second Sex*. Knopf, 1953.

Bonnefous, Edouard. *L'homme ou la nature* [Man or nature]. Hachette, 1970.

Broyelle, Claudie. *La moitié du ciel: Le movement de libération des femmes aujourd'hui en Chine* [Half the sky: The women's liberation movement in China today]. Denoël-Gonthier, 1973.

Dorst, Jean. *La nature dé-naturée: Pour une écologie politique* [Nature perverted: For political ecology]. Le Seuil, 1965.

Draper, Elizabeth. *Birth Control in the Modern World: The Role of the Individual in Population Control*. Allen and Unwin, 1965.

Fanti, Silvio. *Against Marriage*. Philosophical Library, 1978.

FHAR. *Rapport contre la normalité: Le front homosexuel d'action révolutionnaire rassemble les pièces de son dossier d'accusation* [Report against normalcy: The homosexual front of revolutionary action gathers together its indictment files]. GayKitschKamp, 2013.

FHAR. *Rapport contre la normalité* [Report against normalcy]. Champ Libre, collection Symptôme 3, 1971.

Firestone, Shulamith. *The Dialectic of Sex: The Case for Feminist Revolution*. William Morrow and Company, 1970.

Freud, Sigmund. *Civilization and Its Discontents*. Norton, 1930.

Friedan, Betty. *The Feminine Mystique*. Norton, 1963.

Fromm, Erich. *The Crisis of Psychoanalysis*. Holt, Rinehart and Winston, 1970.

Gauthier, Xavière. *Surréalisme et sexualité* [Surrealism and sexuality]. Gallimard, 1971.

Gordon, Pierre. *L'initiation sexuelle et l'évolution religieuse* [Sexual initiation and religious evolution]. Presse Universitaire de France, 1945.

Gornick, Vivian. Preface to Valerie Solanas, *SCUM Manifesto*. Olympia Press, 1971.

Greer, Germaine. *The Female Eunuch*. Harper, 1970.

Guinchard, Marie-Thérèse. *Le macho et les Sud-Américaines* [The macho man and South American women]. Denoël-Gonthier, 1972.

Hall, Edward. *The Hidden Dimension*. Doubleday, 1966.

Hennessey, Caroline. *I, BITCH, Have Had It*. Lancer, 1970.

Horney, Karen. *Our Inner Conflicts*. Norton, 1945.

Kollontaï, Alexandra. "New Woman," in *The New Morality and the Working Class*. Translated by Salvator Attansio. Herder and Herder, 1971. (Original text in Russian published in 1918.)

Kornbluth, Cyril, and Frederik Pohl. *The Space Merchants*. Ballantine Books, 1953.

Lafont, Xavière. *La punition* [The punishment]. La Table Ronde, 1973.

Lonzi, Carla. *Let's Spit on Hegel*. Broche, 1970.

Mailer, Norman. *The Prisoner of Sex*. Little, Brown, 1971.

Marcuse, Herbert. *Eros and Civilization*. Beacon Press, 1955.

Marcuse, Herbert. *An Essay on Liberation*. Beacon Press, 1971.

Meadows, Donella H., Dennis L. Meadows, Jorgen Randers, and William W. Behrens III. *The Limits to Growth: A Report for the Club of Rome's Project on the Predicament of Mankind*. Earth Island, 1972.

Memmi, Albert. *Portrait of a Jew*. Orion Press, 1962.

Millett, Kate. *Sexual Politics*. Doubleday, 1970.

Morgan, Robin, ed. *Sisterhood Is Powerful: An Anthology of Writings from the Women's Liberation Movement*. Random House, 1970.

Nahoun, Philippe. *Allemagne anti-autoritaire* [Anti-authoritarian Germany]. Collection Changer le monde. Edition du cercle et Editions de la Tête des Feuilles, 1971.

Nuetzel, Charles, ed. *After ... the Atomic War*. Marabout, 1970.

Reiche, Reimut. *Class Struggle and Sexuality*. Verso, 1970.

Revel, Jean-François. *Without Marx or Jesus: The New American Revolution Has Begun*. Doubleday, 1971.

Rocheblave-Spenlé, Anne. *Les rôles masculins et féminins* [Masculine and feminine roles]. PUF, 1964.

Saint-Agnès, Yves de. *Eros international: Scandinavie*. Balland, 1971.

Samuel, Pierre. *Ecologie: Détente ou cycle infernal* [Ecology: Détente or vicious cycle]. 10/18, 1973.

Sartin, Pierrette. *La femme libérée?* [Liberated woman?]. Stock, 1968.

Solanas, Valerie. *SCUM Manifesto*. Olympia, 1968.

Sullerot, Évelyne. *La femme dans le monde moderne*. Hachette: 1970.

Translated by Margaret Scotford Archer as *Woman, Society and Change*, MacGraw-Hill, 1971.

Tiger, Lionel. *Men in Groups*. Nelson, 1969.

Vernier, Jacques. *La bataille de l'environnement* [The battle of the environment]. Laffont, 1971.

Ware, Celestine. *Woman Power: The Movement for Women's Liberation*. Tower Publications, 1970.

Wittman, Carl. *Gay Manifesto*. 1970.

Woolf, Virginia. *A Room of One's Own*. Harcourt, 1929.

Periodicals

Actuel. Numbers 4 (January 1971), 12 (September 1971), and 13 (October 1971).

Apprentu sulla rivoluzione morale [In preparation for a moral revolution]. Amsterdam.

Bulletin X.Y.Z., Conscientious Objectors. Liège, 1970–71.

Elle. December 1970 and November 1971.

Fuori! Numbers 0, 1, 2, 3. Milan, 1972.

L'Idiot Liberté. June 1971.

Le livre blanc de l'avortement [The white book on abortion]. 1971.

Partisans, Libération des femmes: année zero [Liberation of women: year zero]. Numbers 54–55. 1970.

New York Times. August 31, 1970.

Le torchon brûle. Numbers 1 and 2 (1971) and numbers 3 and 4 (1972).

Tout! Number 12, 1971.

Other Works by the Author

Le complexe de Diane [The Diane complex]. Julliard, 1951.

Y a-t-il encore des hommes? [Are there any men left?]. Flammarion, 1965.

De Marcuse, de Freud et du puritanisme révolutionnaire [On Marcuse, Freud, and revolutionary puritanism]. Arcadie, 1969.

Eros minoritaire [Minority Eros]. Andre Balland, 1970.

Histoire et actualité du feminism [Feminism, its history and current state]. Alain Moreau, 1972.

Glossary of Names

Adorno, Theodor W. (1903–1969) German philosopher and sociologist.

Allen, Chude Pamela. (b. 1943) American civil rights activist and founder of New York Radical Women.

Allende, Salvador. (1908–1973) Former president of Chile; a socialist who succeeded Eduardo Frei Montalva.

Andersson, Bibi. (1935–2019) Swedish actress.

Andromeda. (n.d.) The mythological daughter of Cepheus and Cassiopeia.

Aquinas, Saint Thomas. (1225–1274) Italian philosopher and Catholic priest.

Armand, Inessa. (1874–1920) French-Russian communist leader in Bolshevik Russia.

Atheneum (n.d.) Greek writer from the third century.

Atkinson, Ti-Grace. (b. 1938) American feminist and author.

Audouard, Olympe. (1832–1890) French feminist and author of *Guerre aux hommes*.

Balzac, Honoré de. (1799–1850) French novelist and playwright.

Banotti, Elvira. (1933–2014) Italian journalist and writer.

Barneville, Marie-Catherine Le Jumel de. (1651–1705) Countess of Aulnoy, she was a French writer known for her fairy tales.

Batlle y Ordóñez, José. (1856–1929) Known as Don Pepe, he served two terms as the president of Uruguay.

Baudelaire, Charles. (1821–1867) French poet and author of *Les fleurs du mal*.

Beaumarchais, Pierre-Augustin Caron de. (1732–1799) French polymath and revolutionary.

Beauvoir, Simone de. (1908–1986) French writer, philosopher, and political activist.

Bebel, August. (1840–1913) German socialist politician.

Ben Bella, Ahmed. (1916–2012) Algerian politician and soldier who held the first presidency of Algeria.

Benston, Margaret. (1937–1991) Chemistry professor who authored *For a Political Economy of the Liberation of Women*.

Bertrand, Mireille. (b. 1941) Member and officeholder of the French Communist Party.

Bertuccelli, Jean-Louis. (1942–2014) French filmmaker.

Bonnefous, Édouard. (1907–2007) French politician and advocate of greater European integration.

Booth, Heather. (b. 1945) American civil rights activist and feminist.

Bordeaux, Henry. (1870–1963) French writer and lawyer.

Boumédiène, Houari. (1932–1978) Former chairman of the Revolutionary Council of Algeria.

Bradley, Marion Zimmer. (1930–1999) American fantasy and science-fiction writer.

Bremer, Fredrika. (1801–1865) Swedish feminist and author of *Hertha*.

Brion, Hélène. (1882–1962) French socialist teacher arrested for spreading pacifist propaganda.

Brontë, Emily. (1818–1848) English novelist known for her only work, *Wuthering Heights* (1847).

Brown, Judith. (n.d.) American feminist and coauthor of *Toward a Female Liberation Movement* (1967).

Broyelle, Claudie. (n.d.) Author of *La moitié du ciel*, a book about women's liberation in China.

Calhoun, John B. (1917–1995) American ethologist known for his behavioral research.

Cassandra. (n.d.) In Greek mythology, she was a Trojan priestess of Apollo.

Castro, Fidel. (1926–2016) Cuban revolutionary and former Cuban prime minister and president.

Cau, Jean. (1925–1993) French writer and journalist.

Céline, Louis-Ferdinand. (1894–1961) The pen name of Louis Ferdinand Auguste Destouches, a French novelist.

Césaire, Aimé. (1913–2008) Martinican politician and poet with an influence on Francophone literature.

Chauchard, Paul. (1912–2003) French physician.

Chédaux, Irène. (n.d.) French author of *Anticlichés sur l'Amerique*.

Chénier, André. (1762–1794) A French poet associated with the victims of the French Revolution.

Chevalier, Marie-Claire. (1921–2011) The young woman accused at the Bobigny trial.

Choisy, François-Timoléon de. (1644–1724) French abbé known for cross-dressing.

Chopin, Frédéric. (1810–1849) Polish composer and virtuoso pianist.

Chrysostome, Saint John. (n.d.–407 AD) Early church father and archbishop of Constantinople.

Clavel, Maurice. (1920–1979) French writer and journalist.

Comte, Auguste. (1798–1857) French philosopher known for formulating positivism.

Corneille, Pierre. (1606–1684) One of three great French dramatists.

Curie, Marie. (1867–1934) French chemist and physicist who researched radioactivity.

Damas, Saint Jean de. (675–749 AD) John of Damascus, a Christian monk and apologist.

Debré, Michel. (1912–1996) Former prime minister of France.

Deng Xiaoping. (1904–1997) Chinese statesman and Mao theorist.

Desbordes-Valmore, Marceline. (1786–1859) Nineteenth-century French poet and novelist.

Deschamps, Fanny. (1920–2000) French writer.

Diba, Farah. (b. 1938) Former queen and shahbanu of Iran.

D'Iris, Jehanne. (n.d.) Greek mythological rainbow goddess.

Draper, Elizabeth. (1744–1778) English author known for her letters from India and her observations on historical demography in *Birth Control in the Modern World*.

Dubos, René. (1901–1982) French American microbiologist and Pulitzer Prize winner for general nonfiction.

Einstein, Albert. (1879–1955) German theoretical physicist.

Engels, Friedrich. (1820–1895) German philosopher and political theorist.

Fajon, Étienne. (1906–1991) Member of the French Communist Party and advocate of the French labor movement.

Fanon, Frantz. (1925–1961) French–West Indian psychiatrist.

Fenger Møller, Grete. (b. 1941) Danish feminist and politician.

Firestone, Shulamith. (1945–2012) Canadian American feminist and author of *The Dialectic of Sex: The Case for Feminist Revolution* (1970).

Fourier, Joseph. (1768–1830) French mathematician.

Freeman, Joreen. (b. 1945) American feminist and political scientist.

Frei Montalva, Eduardo. (1911–1982) Former president of Chile.

Freud, Sigmund. (1856–1939) Austrian neurologist who founded psychoanalysis.

Fréville, Jean. (1895–1971) French author.

Friedan, Betty. (1921–2006) American author of *The Feminine Mystique* (1963), which sparked the second wave of feminism in America.

Gaddafi, Muammar. (1942–2011) Libyan revolutionary and politician.

Garraud, René. (1849–1930) French jurist and professor of law.

Gatti, Armand. (1924–2017) French playwright, poet, and World War II resistance fighter.

Gaulle, Charles de. (1890–1970) French army officer who fought against Nazi Germany in World War II and proceeded to become the president of France.

Gauthier, Xavière. (b. 1942) French author of *Surréalisme et sexualité.*

Gébé. (1929–2004) Pen name for Georges Blondeaux, a French cartoonist.

Germain, Sophie. (1776–1831) French mathematician and philosopher.

Ginsberg, Allen. (1926–1997) American poet.

Godard, Jean-Luc. (b. 1930) A French-Swiss filmmaker.

Gorguloff, Paul. (1895–1932) Russian émigré who assassinated Paul Doumer, the president of France.

Gougaud, Henri. (b. 1936) French writer and poet.

Gracchi brothers. Tiberius Gracchus (n.d.–133 BC) and Gaius Gracchus (154 BC–121 BC) both served as tribunes of the plebs between 133 and 121 BC.

Greer, Germaine. (b. 1939) Australian writer and intellectual; author of *The Female Eunuch.*

Grégoire, Ménie. (1919–2014) French journalist and writer known for a radio talk show, *Hello, Ménie*, from 1967 to 1982.

Groddeck, Georg. (1866–1934) German physician and author of *Au fond de l'homme, cela*.

Guevara, Che. (1928–1967) Argentine Marxist and guerrilla leader in the Cuban Revolution.

Hecquet, Stephen. (1919–1960) French writer.

Hesiod. (750–650 BC) Ancient Greek poet.

Himes, Norman. (1899–1949) American sociologist known for his work on the history of contraception.

Hypatia. (360 AD–415 AD) Hellenistic philosopher and astronomer who invented the aerometer.

Istrati, Panait. (1884–1935) First Romanian novelist to portray homosexual character in his work and author of *Domnit̨za de Snagov* (1926).

Jones, Beverly. (1936–2017) American feminist and coauthor of *Toward a Female Liberation Movement* (1968).

Kennedy Onassis, Jacqueline. (1929–1994) American socialite and former first lady of the United States.

Kollontai, Alexandra. (1872–1952) Russian revolutionary and Marxist.

Kornbluth, Cyril M. (1923–1958) American science-fiction writer.

Krahl, Hans-Jürgen. (1943–1970) German politician.

Kruchow, Edele. (1915–1989) Danish politician and president of the National Council of Danish Women.

Labé, Louise. (n.d.–1566) French feminist Renaissance poet from a wealthy family.

Laclos, Pierre Choderlos de. (1741–1803) French novelist and army general.

Laertes. (n.d.) From Greek mythology, the son of the king of Ithaca and Chalcomedusa.

Lafont, Xavière. (b. 1941) French writer and author of *La punition* (1962).

Lamare, Noël. (n.d.) A doctor with the Paris hospitals who is quoted frequently by d'Eaubonne.

Larguía, Isabel. (1932–n.d.) Argentinian feminist theorist.

Lartéguy, Jean. (1920–2011) French writer and former soldier.

La Vergne, Marie-Madeleine Pioche de. (1634–1693) Countess of La Fayette, she was a French writer known for her historical novels.

Lazo, Carmen Aída. (b. 1976) Salvadoran economist elected as one of nine female representatives in the former chamber.

Lederer, Wolfgang. (1919–2015) Austrian American psychiatrist and author of *The Fear of Women* (1968).

Lejeune, Jérôme. (1926–1994) French pediatrician and geneticist.

Lely, Gilbert. (1904–1985) French poet.

Lenin, Vladimir. (1870–1924) First head of government of Bolshevik Russia.

Leyhausen, Paul. (1916–1998) German ethnologist.

Liberalis, Antonius. (ca. 200 AD) Ancient Greek grammarian who authored *The Metamorphoses*.

Lombroso, Cesare. (1835–1909) Italian criminologist and physician.

Lonzi, Carla. (1931–82) Italian art critic and feminist.

Lorenz, Konrad. (1903–89) Austrian zoologist and ethologist.

Magnus, Albertus. (n.d.–1820) Saint Albert the Great of Cologne for whom the Place Maubert in Paris was named.

Mailer, Norman. (1923–2007) American novelist and journalist, author of *The Naked and the Dead* (1948).

Malthus, Thomas Robert. (1766–1834) English scholar and economist; author of *The Principle of Population* (1798).

March Torres, Aleida. (b. 1936) Known as Lydia, Che Guevara's second wife.

Marcuse, Herbert. (1898–1979) German American philosopher and political theorist.

Marenssin, Émile. (n.d.) Author of *La bande à Baader*.

Marx, Karl. (1818–1883) German philosopher and political theorist; author of *The Communist Manifesto* (1848).

Mbuyi, Joseph. (1929–1961) Congolese politician.

Meinhof, Ulrike Marie. (1934–1976) German journalist and founder of the Red Army Faction in West Germany.

Memmi, Albert. (1920–2020) Jewish-French writer and essayist.

Millett, Kate. (1934–2017) American feminist writer; author of *Sexual Politics* (1970).

Mitchell, Juliet. (b. 1940) British psychoanalyst and feminist.

Montaigne, Michel de. (1533–1592) Philosopher from the French Renaissance.

Morandi, Anna. (1714–1774) Professor in Bologna in the seventeenth century, who discovered the exact insertion of the ocular muscle.

Morin, Edgar. (b. 1921) French philosopher and sociologist.

Moscovici, Serge. (1925–2014) French social psychologist and author of *La société contre nature* (1972).

Musset, Alfred de. (1810–1857) French dramatist and poet known for his autobiographical novel *La Confession d'un enfant du siècle* (*The Confession of a Child of the Century*, 1836).

Nasser, Gamal Abdel. (1918–1970) Former president of Egypt who died in office.

Nietzsche, Friedrich. (1844–1900) German philosopher who had a profound influence on Western thought; author of *The Birth of Tragedy* (1872).

Nixon, Richard. (1913–1994) Former president of the United States who faced the impeachment process and resigned.

Nozières, Violette. (1915–1966) French woman who murdered her father after being sexually abused by him.

Pascal, Blaise. (1623–1662) French mathematician and Catholic theologian.

Pétain, Philippe. (1856–1951) Chief of state of the "French State," the collaborationist government ruling the part of France not occupied by the Nazi forces from 1940 to 1944.

Poquelin, Jean-Baptiste. (1622–1673) Also known as Molière, a French playwright, actor, and poet.

Proudhon, Pierre-Joseph. (1809–1865) French socialist and politician known for coining the term "anarchist."

Rabelais, François. (n.d.–1553) French Renaissance writer.

Racine, Jean. (1639–1699) French playwright known for his tragedies.

Reed, Evelyn. (n.d.) A member of the Socialist Workers' Party who tried to show the socialists that struggle for women was a part of the class struggle.

Reich, Wilhelm. (1897–1957) Austrian doctor and psychoanalyst.

Reiche, Reimut. (b. 1941) German sociologist and psychoanalyst.

Restif de la Bretonne, Nicolas. (1734–1806) French novelist, author of *Le pied de Fanchette* (*Fanchette's Pretty Little Foot*, 1769); *Le paysan perverti* [The perverted peasant], 1775; *Ingenue Saxancour*, 1785; and *Anti-Justine*, 1793.

Revel, Jean-François. (1924–2006) French journalist and philosopher.

Rousseau, Jean-Jacques. (1712–1778) Genevan Enlightenment philosopher.

Rowbotham, Sheila. (b. 1943) British historian and feminist; author of *Women's Liberation and the New Politics* (1969).

Sade, Marquis de. (1740–1814) French philosopher and politician known for his texts depicting deviant sexual behavior and degradation of women.

Saint Augustine. (354–430 AD) Augustine of Hippo, theologian and bishop in Numidia.

Saint Antonius. (251–356 AD) Anthony the Great, a Christian monk from Egypt.

Saint Monique. (331–387 AD) Mother of Augustine of Hippo.

Saint Paul. (n.d.–ca. 64 AD) Paul the Apostle, an early Christian apostle.

Samuel, Pierre. (n.d.) Author of *Écologie: détente ou cycle infernal* (1973).

Sand, George. (1804–1876) Pen name for Amantine Aurore Lucile Dupin, a female French novelist.

Sander, Helke. (b. 1937) German feminist filmmaker.

Santolalla, Irene Silva de. (1902–1992) Peruvian politician and first female senator.

Sappho. (n.d.) Greek poet from Lesbos.

Sartin, Pierrette. (1911–2007) French poet.

Sartre, Jean-Paul. (1905–1980) French playwright and philosopher known for his influence on existentialism and phenomenology.

Schelsky, Helmut. (1912–1984) Most influential post–World War II German sociologist.

Schmidt, Vera. (1889–1937) Russian educationist and revolutionary psychoanalyst of the 1920s.

Schopenhauer, Arthur. (1788–1860) German philosopher.

Schwarzer, Alice. (b. 1942) German journalist and feminist.

Ségur, Sophie de. (1799–1874) Countess of Ségur, she was a French writer originally from Russia.

Sévigné, Marquise de. (1626–1696) Marie de Rabutin-Chantal, known as Marquise de Sévigné or Madame de Sévigné. French aristocrat known for her letters, most of which were addressed to her daughter.

Seyrig, Delphine. (1932–1990) Lebanese-French actress and filmmaker.

Shelley, Martha. (b. 1943) American writer and feminist.

Sixtus V, Pope. (1521–1590) Served as the bishop of Rome from 1585 to his death.

Smal, Guy-André. (n.d.) Specialist in physical therapy.

Solanas, Valerie. (1936–1988) American radical feminist, author of the *SCUM Manifesto* (1967).

Spengler, Oswald. (1880–1936) German historian and philosopher.

Stekel, Wilhelm. (1868–1940) Austrian physician.

Sternberg, Jacques. (1923–2006) French science-fiction writer.

Stroessner, Alfredo. (1912–2006) Former dictator of Paraguay.

Sullerot, Évelyne. (1924–2017) French feminist author.

Sutherland Martínez, Elizabeth. (b. 1925) American Chicana feminist, author of *The Youngest Revolution* (1969).

Suyin, Han. (1916–2012) Eurasian physician from China.

Tertullian. (AD 160–n.d.) Early Christian author from Carthage.

Thant, U. (1909–1974) Former Burmese diplomat and secretary-general of the United Nations.

Thomas, Carol. (b. 1933) Feminist activist who was arrested for her participation in the Women's Liberation Movement.

Tiger, Lionel. (b. 1937) Canadian anthropologist.

Tillion, Germaine. (1907–2008) French ethnologist who worked extensively in Algeria.

Tisserant, Eugène. (1884–1972) French prelate and cardinal in the Catholic Church who advocated domesticity for women.

Turner, Daniel. (1667–1741) English physician.

Vermeersch, Jeannette. (1910–2001) French politician who advocated for social reform rather than access to contraception.

Vigny, Alfred de. (1797–1863) French Romantic poet.

Voltaire. (1694–1778) French Enlightenment philosopher.

Ware, Cellestine. (b. 1970) Feminist author of *Woman Power: The Movement for Women's Liberation* (1970).

Warhol, Andy. (1928–1987) American artist and filmmaker.

Weisstein, Naomi. (1939–2015) American cognitive psychologist.

Woolf, Virginia. (1882–1941) English author and one of the most innovative twentieth-century writers; author of *Mrs. Dalloway* (1929).

Yevtushenko, Yevgeny. (1932–2017) Soviet poet and essayist.

Zetkin, Clara. (1857–1933) German Marxist activist and advocate for women's rights.

Glossary of Terms

Aerometer. A tool used to measure density of gases in the air.

Aktionsrat für die Befreiung der Frauen. Action Committee for the Liberation of Women was a West Berlin feminist group.

Anathema. Something or someone who is shunned.

Anatomy. The study of the structure of organisms.

Biology. The study of living things.

Bobigny trial. A court case in which a young woman in Bobigny was accused of murder for having an abortion. The case sparked huge protests across France and served as the catalyst for the president, Valéry Giscard d'Estaing, to appoint Simone Veil as secretary of health to propose a law legalizing abortion.

Bolshevik Russia. Bolshevik-led Russia worked toward the goal of the world's first socialist state.

Capitalism. A theory of social and economic practices that advocate private ownership of capital and resources.

Cassandra. A rhetorical tool used to indicate something that is accurate but commonly dismissed.

Catholicism. A branch of Christianity that follows the practices of the Roman Catholic Church.

Coitus interruptus. Known commonly as the withdrawal method, this is a dated form of contraception in which the male ejaculates outside of and away from the vagina.

Colgate-Palmolive boycott. NOW (see below) sponsored a boycott of Colgate-Palmolive products to bring attention to the company's history of discrimination.

Colonialism. The practice of occupying and taking control of other countries to exploit them economically.

Declaration of the Rights of Man. A human rights document dating to the French Revolution.

Demography. The study of changing human population dynamics.

Detroit riots. A series of destructive and violent riots in Detroit in 1967 regarding race relations into which the National Guard was brought.

Dolle Mina. A Dutch feminist group based in Holland that would follow girls who were alone in the streets and beat up attackers.

Ecology. The study of spatial and temporal patterns of ecosystems.

Ecology Action. A movement emphasizing individual action founded by young engineers in Berkeley, California, in 1967.

Effigy. A representation or sculpture of a person, typically someone disliked.

Epistolary. Relating to letter-writing.

Equality. Having access to equal rights and opportunities.

Eros. A concept in Greek philosophy revolving around passionate love.

Ethnology. The academic study of the characteristics of different people and what relates them.

Ethology. The academic study of animal behavior.

Feminism. The advocacy of equality between the sexes, rooted in the fight for women's rights.

Feminitude. The term d'Eaubonne uses to refer to the legal, social, and psychological exclusion of women. (See Mary Daly, *Gyn-Ecology: The Meta Ethics of Radical Feminism* [Beacon Press, 1978], 53.)

FHAR. Homosexual Front for Revolutionary Action in France.

FUORI. Revolutionary homosexuality group based in Rome.

Frankfurter Weiberrat. A women's group formed during the West German student movement of the 1960s.

French Revolution. Period of revolt from 1789 to 1799 in France, from which many of the fundamental ideas of Western democracy evolved.

Futurologists. People who specialize in exploring possibilities about the future.

Gaucho. A skilled horseman from South America.

Homosexual. A person who is sexually attracted to the same gender.

Humanism. A system of thought centered on human existence rather than the divine.

L'Humanité. A daily newspaper with links to the French Communist Party.

Hydra. A many-headed serpent from Greek mythology.

L'INSEE. Institut national de la statistique et des études économiques (National Institute of Statistics and Economic Studies).

Islam. An Abrahamic religion based in monotheism and the belief that Muhammad is a messenger of God.

Issy-les-Moulineaux. A commune in the southwestern suburbs of Paris; the site of the raping of two women during an invasion on July 14, 1972.

Jew. An adherent of Judaism.

Judaism. A religion originating in Mesopotamia that expresses a covenant between God and the people of Israel.

Machismo. An aggressive sense of masculinity.

Malediction. A condition or curse.

Malthusianism. Relating to Thomas Robert Malthus's ideas about population and carrying capacity.

Maoism. A variation of Marxist and Leninist ideals created for socialist reform in preindustrial China.

Masochism. The derivation of pleasure from pain.

Menopause. The decline of reproductive hormones in a woman's reproductive system.

Metaphysics. Abstract theory of the underlying foundation of a subject.

Minos and Pasiphae. A story from Greek mythology detailing the events that led to the conception of the Minotaur.

Misogyny. Prejudice or disdain toward women.

MLF. Mouvement de Libération des Femmes is a French feminist movement that advocates for women's rights.

Monosexuality. Sexual attraction to one gender.

Monotheism. The belief in one god.

NOW. The National Organization of Women.

Occident. The Western world.

Phallocratism. A societal system dominated by men.

Phallus. A depiction of the penis as bearer of power.

Philosophy. The study of general questions surrounding existence and reality.

Précieuses. A French literary style that came about in the seventeenth century, inspired by conversations at literary and artistic salons and written usually by women.

Proletariat. A term used to represent the working or lower class.

Protestantism. A branch of Christianity that follows the practices of the Protestant churches.

Quinine. An anti-parasite drug used to treat malaria, sometimes consumed as a contraceptive before modern birth control.

Red China. Communist-controlled China.

SCUM Manifesto. A book by Valerie Solanas, published in 1967, that argues that men have ruined civilization and should be punished by castration.

Sexism. Prejudice or discrimination based on a person's sex or gender, especially against women.

Sierra Club. A grassroots environmental association in the United States.

Sine qua non. Latin for something that is essential.

Socialism. A theory of social and economic practices that advocate community ownership of capital and resources.

La société contre nature. A book by Serge Moscovici in which he investigates nature and the relationships among it, humans, and society.

Summa cum laude. Latin for "with the highest honors."

Sword of Damocles. An allusion to the omnipresent peril facing people in power. Derived from Damocles, a courtier in the court of fourth-century BC ruler Dionysius II of Syracuse.

Treaty of Rome. Signed in 1957, this treaty created the European Economic Community and attempted to implement equal wages.

Vagina. The tube connecting the cervix and external genitals in female reproductive systems.

WITCH. Women's International Terrorist Conspiracy from Hell.

Index

About the Author

Françoise d'Eaubonne (1920–2005) was a leading French feminist who is credited with coining the term "ecofeminism" in 1974. A former member of the French Communist Party, she cofounded the Front homosexuel d'action révolutionnaire in 1971 and created the Ecology-Feminism Center in Paris in 1972. D'Eaubonne was the author of more than fifty works, including novels, poetry, and essays. Her historical novel *Comme un vol de gerfauts* (1947) was translated into English as *A Flight of Falcons*. Extracts from *Feminism or Death* appeared in English in the anthology *New French Feminisms* in 1981, and an earlier translation of "The Time for Ecofeminism" appeared in Carolyn Merchant's *Ecology: Key Concepts in Critical Theory* in 1994.

Contributors

Carolyn Merchant is professor emerita of environmental history, philosophy, and ethics at the University of California, Berkeley. She is the author of *The Death of Nature: Women, Ecology, and the Scientific Revolution* (1980, 3rd ed. 2020), which has shaped the fields of the history of science, women's studies, and environmental history, along with nine other books, three edited books, and numerous research articles.

Myriam Bahaffou is a scholar-activist; her main field of research is animal ethics, in a decolonial ecofeminist perspective. In France, she tries to renew the vision of the ecofeminist movement, insisting on its radicality and showing the originality of its narrations.

Julie Gorecki is an ecofeminist scholar, writer, and activist. She works on new ecological feminisms by reexamining the systemic links between capitalism, gender, marginalized peoples, and the environment. At the center of her work is the transnational women and feminists for climate justice movement, which she is also a part of.

Translator and Editor

Ruth Hottell holds a PhD in French from the University of Illinois. Having published numerous articles on French literature, cultural studies, and film, she also coauthored three books on Francophone women filmmakers. Now professor emerita of French at the University of Toledo, she was recently named to the Order of Academic Palms by the French government.

Translator

Emma Ramadan is a literary translator based in Providence, Rhode Island, where she also co-owns Riffraff Bookstore and Bar. She has been awarded an NEA translation fellowship, a Fulbright, and the 2018 Albertine Prize for her work.